Complexity and the Experience of Managing in Public Sector Organizations

The perspective of complex responsive processes draws on analogies from the complexity sciences, bringing in the essential characteristics of human agents, understood to emerge in social processes of communicative interaction and power relating. The result is a way of thinking about life in organizations that focuses attention on how organizational members cope with the unknown as they perpetually create organizational futures together.

Providing a natural successor to the editors' earlier series *Complexity and Emergence in Organizations*, this series, *Complexity as the Experience of Organizing*, aims to develop this work further by taking very seriously the *experience* of organizational practitioners, and showing how adopting the perspective of complex responsive processes yields deeper insight into practice and so develops that practice.

In this book, all of the contributors work as managers in public sector organizations. They provide narrative accounts of their actual work, addressing questions such as:

- How do public sector organizations differ in the way they need to be managed and organized?
- How do specific pressures such as governance and accountability affect the way managers need to work?
- What insights can complex responsiveness theories offer us as an alternative to traditional systems perspectives?

In considering such questions in terms of their daily experience, the contributors explore how the perspective of complex responsive processes assists them to make sense of their experience and so to develop their practice. *Complexity and the Experience of Managing in Public Sector*

Organizations offers a different method for making sense of experience in a rapidly changing world by using reflective accounts of ordinary, everyday life in organizations rather than idealized accounts. The editors' commentary introduces and contextualizes these experiences as well as drawing out key themes for further research.

Complexity and the Experience of Managing in Public Sector Organizations will be of value to readers from among those academics and business school students and practitioners who are looking for reflective accounts of real life experiences of *managing* in public sector organizations, rather than further prescriptions of what life in organizations ought to be like.

Ralph Stacey is Director of the Complexity and Management Centre at the Business School of the University of Hertfordshire and Director of the Doctor of Management programme run by the Centre. He is one of the editors of the *Complexity and Emergence in Organizations* series, and the editor of five books in this series.

Professor **Douglas Griffin** is Associate Director of the Complexity and Management Centre at the Business School of the University of Hertfordshire and a supervisor on the Doctor of Management programme run by the Centre. He is also an independent consultant. He is one of the editors of the *Complexity and Emergence in Organizations* series, and the editor of three books in this series.

Complexity and the Experience of Managing in Public Sector Organizations

Edited by
Ralph Stacey and Douglas Griffin

Routledge
Taylor & Francis Group

LONDON AND NEW YORK

First published 2006
by Routledge
2 Park Square, Milton Park, Abingdon, Oxon OX14 4RN

Simultaneously published in the USA and Canada
by Routledge
270 Madison Ave, New York, NY 10016

Routledge is an imprint of the Taylor & Francis Group

© 2006 Ralph Stacey and Douglas Griffin

Typeset in Times New Roman by
Keystroke, Jacaranda Lodge, Wolverhampton
Printed and bound in Great Britain
by TJ International Ltd, Padstow, Cornwall

British Library Cataloguing in Publication Data
A catalogue record for this book is available from the British Library

Library of Congress Cataloging in Publication Data
A catalog record for this book has been requested

ISBN 0–415–36731–X (hbk)
ISBN 0–415–36732–8 (pbk)

Contents

Contributors

Séamus Cannon is Director of an Education Centre in Ireland. He graduated as Doctor of Management at the University of Hertfordshire in 2005.

Douglas Griffin is an independent consultant, visiting Professor at the Business School of the University of Hertfordshire, and Associate Director of the Complexity and Management Centre.

Penelope Lacey is a manager of Podiatry Services at an NHS Trust in the UK. She participated in the Master/Doctor of Management programme and was awarded the degree of Master of Arts by research.

Karen Norman was Director of Nursing and Co-Head of Clinical Governance at an NHS Healthcare Trust in the UK and has recently taken up the post of Director of Nursing and Patient Services of the Gibraltar Health Authority. She graduated as Doctor of Management at the University of Hertfordshire in 2005.

Nicholas Sarra works as a consultant adult psychotherapist in the NHS in the UK. He specializes in organizational consultancy and development for public sector services. He graduated as Doctor of Management at the University of Hertfordshire in 2005.

Ralph Stacey is Professor of Management at the Business School of the University of Hertfordshire, and Director of its Complexity and Management Centre. He is also a member of the Institute of Group Analysis.

Richard Williams was formerly CEO of a large further education college and is currently CEO of a charity working with young people and adults across the UK. He graduated as Doctor of Management at the University of Hertfordshire in 2005.

Series preface
Complexity as the Experience of Organizing

Edited by Ralph Stacey, Douglas Griffin and Patricia Shaw

Complexity as the Experience of Organizing is a sequel to the highly successful series *Complexity and Emergence in Organizations* also edited by the editors of this series. The first series has attracted international attention for its development of the theory of complex responsive processes and its implications for those working in organizations. The perspective of complex responsive processes draws on analogies from the complexity sciences, bringing in the essential characteristics of human agents, namely consciousness and self-consciousness, understood to emerge in social processes of communicative interaction, power relating and evaluative choice. The result is a way of thinking about life in organizations that focuses attention on how organizational members cope with the unknown as they perpetually create organizational futures together. This second series aims to develop that work by taking seriously the experience of organizational practitioners, showing how taking the perspective of complex responsive processes yields deeper insight into practice and so develops that practice.

Contributors to the volumes in the series work as leaders, consultants or managers in organizations. The contributors provide narrative accounts of their actual work, addressing questions such as: What does it mean, in ordinary everyday terms, to lead a large organization? How do leaders learn to lead? What does it mean, in ordinary everyday terms, to consult to managers in an organization? How does the work of the consultant assist managers when the uncertainty is so great that they do not yet know what they are doing? What does executive coaching achieve? What happens in global change programs such as installing competencies, managing diversity and assuring quality? Why do organizations get stuck in repetitive patterns of behavior? What kinds of change can be facilitated? In considering such questions in terms of their daily experience, the contributors explore how the perspective of complex responsive processes assists them in making sense of their experience and so develops their practice.

The books in the series are addressed to organizational practitioners and academics who are looking for a different way of making sense of their own experience in a rapidly changing world. The books will attract readers seeking reflective accounts of ordinary everyday life in organizations rather than idealized accounts or further idealized prescriptions.

Other volumes in the series:
A Complexity Perspective on Researching Organizations
Taking experience seriously
Edited by Ralph Stacey and Douglas Griffin

Complexity and the Experience of Leading Organizations
Edited by Douglas Griffin and Ralph Stacey

Experiencing Emergence in Organizations
Local interaction and the emergence of global pattern
Edited by Ralph Stacey

Experiencing Risk, Spontaneity and Improvisation in Organizational Change
Working live
Edited by Patricia Shaw and Ralph Stacey

1 Introduction

Ralph Stacey and Douglas Griffin

- The perspective of complex responsive processes
- The properties of complex responsive processes of relating
- The consequences of taking a complex responsive processes perspective
- The chapters in this book

Over the period 2000 to 2002, a number of us at the Complexity and Management Centre at the Business School of the University of Hertfordshire published a series of books called *Complexity and Emergence in Organizations* (Stacey *et al.*, 2000; Fonseca, 2001; Stacey, 2001; Streatfield, 2001; Griffin, 2002; Shaw, 2002). These books developed a perspective according to which organizations are understood to be ongoing, iterated processes of cooperative and competitive relating between people. We argued that organizations are not systems but rather the ongoing patterning of interactions between people. Patterns of human interaction produce further patterns of interaction, not some *thing* outside of the interaction. We called this perspective *complex responsive processes of relating*.

Since 2000, some of the authors in the series, together with other Complexity and Management Centre colleagues in association with the Institute of Group Analysis, have been conducting a research programme on organizational change leading to the degrees of Master of Arts by research or Doctor of Management. This is necessarily a part-time programme because the core of the research method (see another volume in this series: Stacey and Griffin, 2005) involves students taking their own experience seriously. If patterns of human interaction produce nothing but further patterns of human interaction, in the creation of which we are all participating, then there is no *detached* way of understanding organizations from the position of the objective observer. Instead, organizations have to be understood in terms of one's own personal experience of participating with others in the co-creation of the patterns of interaction that are the organization. The students' research is therefore their narration of current events in which they are *involved* together with their reflections on themes of particular importance emerging in the stories of their own experience of participation with others. The research stance is thus one of detached involvement.

The purpose of this volume is to bring together the work of a number of programme participants who have been concerned with the experience of working in public sector health and educational organizations which now have to operate in a performance management regime established by central government. Over the past two decades there has been a major change in the mode of public sector governance in most countries in Europe and North America. There has been a significant move away from a decentralized, collegial form of governing health and educational institutions to a highly managerial, centralized one. This centralization involves central government taking a much more intrusive role in setting targets and requiring monitoring procedures to be followed. Within the institutions themselves there is a further centralization in which managers at the top of the hierarchy have much more say over what groups of professionals within the organization do. The figuration of power relations has thus shifted from one in which the ratio of power was tilted towards groups of professional health and education workers who had considerable autonomy in governing themselves to one in which the power ratio is tilted towards senior managers and central government. This power figuration is underpinned by an ideology of marketization and managerialism which emphasizes control, compliance, uniformity, efficiency and improvement. Such an ideology contrasts sharply with the ideology underlying the old mode of public sector governance, which was characterized by professional freedom and vocational motivation. In the United Kingdom, and probably elsewhere, the new mode of governance requires the expenditure of large sums of money on monitoring. Despite the enormous cost, however, it is far from clear that the new mode of governance is delivering the efficiency, uniformity of service and improvement it promises. This volume is concerned with why this is happening. It focuses on the way of thinking that underlies the move to marketization and managerialism, and explores its consequences in the experience of those working in the health and education sectors in the United Kingdom and Ireland.

The questions of central concern in this volume are as follows. Has the dramatic change in the model of governance delivered what those imposing it promised? Does it actually improve efficiently and quality? What are the emotional consequences for the people who work in health and educational institutions? Academic research and a steady stream of newspaper articles over the past few years make it clear that the move as a whole has not been a clear success. Yet despite the antagonism of so many in health and education, there is little sign of a wholesale move to some other form of governance. How is it that so many in the health and education sectors feel powerless to argue against the model imposed upon them, despite their intense feelings of alienation? Why is it so difficult to argue against the new model? What is the thinking underlying it? These are central questions which are addressed by the contributors in the form of their personal experiences of working at various levels in both health and education. Chapter 2 will argue that a fundamental problem with public sector governance today has to do with the way of thinking which it reflects. This is a way of thinking in which an organization is thought of as a 'thing', as a system, which can be designed to deliver what its designers choose. This volume, and others in the series, questions this way of thinking and takes a perspective in which organizations are complex responsive processes of relating between people.

Two other volumes in this series are relevant to the questions posed above. The volume *Experiencing Emergence in Organizations: Local interaction and the emergence of global pattern* is concerned with the manner in which people take up global policies in their ordinary, everyday local interactions with each other. Richard Williams (author of Chapter 3 in this volume) describes how the cult values to do with performance and targets are taken up in the local interaction between college CEOs and those charged with implementing government policies. In particular he identifies the anxieties aroused by the threats to identity which these policies give rise to. The volume *Complexity and the Experience of Leading Organizations* presents a complex responsive processes perspective on leadership. Richard Williams describes the impact of the current mode of public sector governance on the relationship between himself and his managers.

The following section gives a necessarily brief indication of what the theory of complex responsive processes has to say about organizations – a much fuller development is given in the first series of books referred to above, and Chapter 2 (this volume) also presents some aspects of the theory relevant to the central questions in this volume. Subsequently, this chapter gives a brief indication of what each of the ensuing chapters will cover. We will also be introducing each chapter with an editorial comment. We turn now to a brief review of the theory of complex responsive processes.

The perspective of complex responsive processes

From the perspective of complex responsive processes, organizations are thought of as patterns of interaction between people that are iterated as the present. Instead of abstracting from the experience of human bodily interaction, which is what we do when we posit that individuals create a system in their interaction, the perspective of complex responsive processes stays with the experience of interaction which produces nothing but further interaction. In other words, one moves from thinking in terms of a spatial metaphor, as one does when one thinks that individuals interact to produce a system outside them at a higher level, to a temporal processes way of thinking, where the temporal processes are those of human relating. Organizations are then understood as processes of human relating, as the simultaneously cooperative–consensual and conflictual–competitive relating between people in which everything organizational happens. It is through these ordinary, everyday processes of relating that people in organizations cope with the complexity and uncertainty of organizational life. As they do so, they perpetually construct their future together as the present.

Complex responsive processes of relating may be understood as acts of communication, relations of power, and the interplay between people's choices arising in acts of evaluation.

Acts of communication

It is because human agents are conscious and self-conscious that they are able to cooperate and reach consensus, while at the same time conflicting and competing with each other in the highly sophisticated ways in which they do. Drawing on the work of the American pragmatist George Herbert Mead (1934), one can understand consciousness (that is, mind) as arising in the communicative interaction between human bodies. Humans have evolved central nervous systems such that when one gestures to another, particularly in the form of vocal gesture or language, one evokes in one's own body responses to one's gesture that are similar to those evoked in other bodies. In other words, in their acting, humans take the attitude, the tendency to act, of the other, and it is because they have this capacity that humans can know what they are doing. It immediately follows that consciousness (knowing, mind) is a social process in which meaning emerges in the social act of gesture–response, where the gesture can never be separated from the response. Meaning does not lie in the gesture, the word, alone but in the gesture taken together with the response to it as one social act.

Furthermore, in communicating with each other as the basis of everything they do, people do not simply take the attitude of the specific others with whom they are relating. Humans have the capacity for generalizing so that when they act they always take up the attitude of what Mead called the generalized other. In other words, they always take the attitude, the tendency to act, of the group or society in relation to their actions – they are concerned about what others might think of what they do or say. This is often unconscious and it is, of course, a powerful form of social control. According to Mead, self-consciousness is also a social process involving the capacity humans have to take themselves as an object of subjective reflection. This is a *social* process because the subject, 'I', can only ever contemplate itself as an object, 'me', which is one's perception of the attitude of society towards oneself. The 'I' is the often spontaneous and imaginative response of the socially formed individual to the 'me' as the gestures of society to oneself. Self is this emergent 'I–me' dialectic so that each self is socially formed, while at the same time interacting selves are forming the social. The social may be understood as a social object. A social object is not an object in the normal sense of a thing that exists in nature but is a tendency on the part of large numbers of people to act in a similar manner in similar situations. The social object is a generalization that exists only when it is made particular in the ordinary local interaction between people. Communication, then, is not simply the sending of a signal to be received by another, but rather complex social (that is, responsive) processes of self-formation in which meaning and the society-wide pattern of the social object emerge.

Relations of power

Drawing on the work of Elias ([1939] 2000), one understands how the processes of communicative interacting constitute relations of power. For Elias, power is not something anyone possesses but is rather a characteristic of all human relating. In order to form, and stay in, a relationship with someone else, one cannot do whatever one wants. As soon as we enter into relationships we constrain and are constrained by others and, of course, we also enable and are enabled by others. Power is this enabling–constraining relationship where the power balance is tilted in favour of some and against others depending on the relative need they have for each other. Elias showed how such power relationships form figurations, or groupings, in which some are included and others are excluded, and where the power balance is tilted in favour of some groupings and against others. These groupings establish powerful feelings of belonging which constitute each individual's 'we' identity. These 'we' identities, derived from the groups we belong to, are inseparable from each of our 'I' identities. As with Mead, then, we can see that processes of human relating form and are formed by individual and collective identities, which inevitably reflect complex patterns of power relating.

Choices arising in acts of evaluation

In their communicative interacting and power relating, humans are always making choices between one action and another (Stacey, 2005). The choices may be made on the basis of conscious desires and intentions, or unconscious desires and choices; for example, those that are habitual, impulsive, obsessive, compulsive, compelling or inspiring. In other words, human action is always evaluative, sometimes consciously and at other times unconsciously. The criteria for evaluating these choices are values and norms, together constituting ideology. We are thus using ideology in the sense of Elias (1970), who held that we always act according to some ideology, and negating one ideology immediately gives rise to another. Here ideology arises in the experience of bodies interacting with each other rather than as some 'whole' abstracted from experience with the potential for this to give rise to 'false' consciousness where people are alienated from their direct experience.

Norms (morals, the right, the 'ought') are evaluative criteria taking the form of obligatory restrictions which have emerged as generalizations and become habitual in a history of social interaction. We are all socialized to take up the norms of the particular groups and the society to which we belong, and this restricts what we can do as we particularize the generalized norms in our moment-by-moment specific action situations. Elias' work shows in detail how norms constitute major aspects of the personality structures, or identities, of interdependent people.

Values (ethics, the 'good') are individually felt voluntary compulsions to choose one desire, action or norm rather than another. Values arise in social processes of self-formation (Joas, 2000) – they are fundamental aspects of self, giving meaning to life, opening up opportunities for action. They arise in intense interactive experiences which are seized by the imagination and idealized as some whole to which people then feel strongly committed. Mead (1938) describes these as cult values which need to be functionalized in particular contingent situations, and this inevitably involves conflict.

Together, the voluntary compulsion of value and the obligatory restriction of norms constitute *ideology*. Ideology is the basis on which people choose desires and actions, and it unconsciously sustains power relations by making a particular figuration of power feel natural. We can see, then, that complex responsive processes of human relating form and are formed by values, norms and ideologies as integral aspects of self/identity formation in its simultaneously individual and collective form.

In describing the fundamental aspects of the complex responsive processes of human relating, we have referred on a number of occasions to *patterns* of communicative interaction, *figurations* of power relations, and *generalizations/idealizations* that are *particularized/functionalized* in specific situations. These patterns, figurations, generalizations/ idealizations and particularizations/functionalizations may all be understood as themes, taking both propositional and narrative forms, which emerge and re-emerge in the iteration, in each succeeding present, of the interactive processes of communication, power and evaluation. These themes organize the experience of being together and they can be understood, in Mead's terms, as social objects and the imagined wholes of cult values which are taken up by people in their local interaction with each other in specific situations of ordinary, everyday life.

The properties of complex responsive processes of relating

By analogy with complex adaptive systems (Goodwin, 1994; Kauffman, 1995; see also Waldorp, 1992), the thematic patterning of interaction is understood to be:

- *Complex*. Complexity here refers to a particular dynamic or movement in time that is paradoxically stable and unstable, predictable and unpredictable, known and unknown, certain and uncertain, all at the same time. Complexity and uncertainty are both often used to refer to the situation or environment in which humans must act and this is distinguished from simple or certain environments. Prescriptions for effective action are then related to, held to be contingent upon, the type of environment. However, from the complex responsive processes perspective it is human relating itself which is complex and uncertain in the sense described above. Healthy, creative, ordinarily effective human interaction is then always complex, no matter what the situation. Patterns of human relating that lose this complexity become highly repetitive and rapidly inappropriate for dealing with the fluidity of ordinary, everyday life, taking the form of neurotic and psychotic disorders, bizarre group processes and fascist power structures.

- *Self-organizing and emergent.* Self-organizing means that agents interact with each other on the basis of their own local organizing principles, and it is in such local interaction that widespread coherence emerges without any programme, plan or blueprint for that widespread pattern itself. In complex responsive processes terms, then, it is in the myriad local interactions between people that the widespread generalizations such as social objects and cult values emerge. These are particularized in the local interaction between people.
- *Evolving.* The generalizations of social object and cult value are particularized in specific situations, and this inevitably involves choices as to how to particularize them in that specific situation, which inevitably means some form of conflict. The generalizations will never be particularized in exactly the same way, and the nonlinear nature of human interaction means that these small differences could be amplified into completely different generalizations. In this way, social objects and cult values evolve.

The consequences of taking a complex responsive processes perspective

We are suggesting, then, that we think about organizations in a way that is close to our ordinary, everyday life in them. We understand organizations to be the widespread patterns of interaction between people, the widespread narrative and propositional themes, which emerge in the myriad local interactions between people, both those between members of an organization and those between them and other people. Thinking in this way has two important consequences.

First, no one can step outside of their interaction with others. In mainstream thinking, an organization is thought of as a system at a level above the individuals who form it. It is recognized that this organizational system is affected by patterns of power and economic relations in the wider society and these are normally thought of as forces, over and above the organization and its individual members, which shape local forms of experience. Individuals and the social are posited at different levels, and causal powers are ascribed to that social level. In the kind of process terms we are trying to use, there are no forces over and above individuals. All we have are vast numbers of continually iterated interactions between human bodies, and these are local in the sense that each of us can interact with only a limited number of others. It is in the vast number of local (in this specific technical sense) interactions that widespread, global patterns of power and economic relations emerge. The widespread patterns emerge as repetition and potential transformation at the same time. We can then see highly repetitive patterns iterated over long time periods. The general comments we make about such patterns refer to what is emerging rather than to any force over and above those in whose interaction it is emerging. In their local interaction, people will always be particularizing, taking up in their local interactions these generalizations, and they may not be aware that they are doing so. No one can step outside of interaction to design that interaction.

Second, then, there is no overall programme, design, blueprint or plan for the organization as a 'whole'. Designs, programmes, blueprints and plans exist only insofar as people are taking them up in their local interactions. Any statements that the most powerful make about organizational designs, visions and values are understood as gestures calling forth responses from many, many people in their local interactions. The most powerful can choose their own gestures but will be unable to choose the responses of others, so their gestures will frequently produce surprising outcomes.

If one thinks of organizations as widespread narrative patterns emerging in local interaction, then how are we to think about public sector governance? This is the question explored in Chapter 2.

The chapters in this book

Chapter 2, by Ralph Stacey, explores the way of thinking underlying today's dominant mode of public sector governance, identifying it as a rather crude form of first-order cybernetic systems thinking. The chapter also covers the ideology underlying current public sector governance, identifying it as the cult of performance which replaces purpose. It has the hallmarks of the cult, namely presentation of a hopelessly idealized future and heavy demands for conformity. The approach is characterized by the instrumental use of naming and shaming people and institutions to enforce compliance, aided by a form of emotional blackmail as people are exhorted not to let their colleagues down. Stacey then goes into how the cult of performance is actually operationalized in ways that involve the manipulation of figures and the distortion of clinical decisions to ensure the appearance of meeting targets. The result is a culture of deceit and spin in which appearance/presentation/spin replaces substance and people become alienated from their experience. Instead of leading to authentic quality, the whole approach amounts to a system of counterfeit quality. Stacey then moves on to ask whether the model of governance actually works, reaching the conclusion that while there may have been pockets of improvement there is very little evidence indeed for overall improvement. In the face of this conclusion it becomes important to ask why it is so hard to argue against this mode of governance. The first reason is that doing so leads to challenging the dominant ideology and so risking exclusion. The second reason is that the underlying way of thinking is so taken for granted, and an alternative way of thinking is not immediately apparent, that there seems to be no way out. After all, who can be against improvement and efficiency? He then goes on to argue for a move away from system thinking to the perspective of complex responsive processes. If an organization comprises patterns of relations between people but policy makers think organizations are systems, then what will happen as they enforce their policies? From the complex responsive processes perspective, such policies are simply gestures, the articulation of cult values, or social objects which have to be operationalized. What matters is how people operationalize the policies. The remaining chapters in this volume give an insight into the operationalizing of policies.

In Chapter 3, Richard Williams, who at the time of writing this chapter was Principal and CEO of the Westminster Kingsway College of Further Education in the UK, contrasts the official approach to developing leaders for the public sector in special leadership colleges with his own day-to-day experience of his work as leader of his college. He argues that the official approach amounts to a leadership mythology based upon a reified and sanitized representation of organizational change and the roles of staff occupying senior positions. Organizational leadership in the public sector takes place in a context of intense scrutiny and pressure to deliver performance targets. In responding to this pressure, those in leadership positions focus on the management of information required to supply evidence of the achievement of national performance indicators. Pressures to increase performance at lower rates of unit cost are sustained by the intervention of regulatory, audit and inspection agencies. These regimes apply right across the public sector, and the impact on individuals leading organizations under this pressure sometimes surfaces in the national media as scandals concerning the manipulation of data and the emergence of sudden and catastrophic financial failures. 'Leadership', as a process enacted by individuals in the public sector, is situated in this narrative context. These processes engender great waves of anxiety, feelings of loss and threats to identity of those caught up in them. They also engender potent insider/outsider feelings, since all these processes entail the identification of winners (those promoted, whose status and salaries are enhanced, who are retained, moved to 'better', 'safer', more secure jobs) and losers (e.g. those demoted, made redundant, sidelined). Williams describes his lived experience of occupying a leadership role by reflecting on the detail of his interactions with his chairman which reveal issues of power, norms and values.

Chapter 4 is by Nicholas Sarra, who works as a psychotherapist and organizational consultant for an NHS Trust in the UK. In this highly imaginative study he explores the meaning of the metaphor which people in his organization sometimes use when they talk about the senior executive corridor. Having once called it the 'golden mile', they now refer to it as the 'green mile', which they associate with Stephen King's book and a consequent film about death row. In the story, the green mile is the walk to the electric chair. The condemned men wait their time in cells on either side of this forbidding passage. From this, Sarra suggests that working within senior management was perceived as a high-risk occupation in which emotional pain, self-sacrifice and feelings of humiliation were to be expected. The way of talking about the corridor may also reflect the ironic use of humour both as a means of catharsis and as a way of coping with perceived power relations through the use of mockery. This was a climate in which targets and perceived performance to attain those targets were the only legitimate discourse. Through this process managers were held individually accountable for a linear progression in organizational outcomes which they often struggled with, or found impossible or pointless to achieve. The cultural climate tended to predicate feelings of exclusion, isolation and dissonance in sense making as organizational realities became unduly weighted and constructed in top-down ways. National policy with its emphasis on the top-down modernization of the health service was therefore inevitably leading to a pressure for correct appearances in line with that policy. This pressure created a split between the required external appearances and the complex experiences of day-to-day service provision. Thus a dissonance between private experience and corporate appearance arose which increasingly threatened to undermine the ontological security of health service workers. Such dynamics threaten to alienate health service workers. They give rise to metaphors such as the 'green mile' whereby people express, in sardonic form, feelings of acute insecurity, powerlessness and alienation from the given organizational norms.

Chapter 5 is by Karen Norman, who, at the time of writing, was Director of Nursing at a National Health University Trust in the UK. In the NHS, key accreditation bodies such as the Healthcare Commission (formerly the Commission for Health Care Audit and Inspection), Clinical Negligence Schemes for Trusts (CNST), and Risk Pooling Scheme for Trusts (RSPT) all require NHS Trusts to have a clinical risk management strategy and processes to ensure that it is implemented. Norman explores how this global risk management policy is functionalized in practice. She uses narratives from her own practice to explore serious clinical incidents (SCIs) which have occurred in the NHS. One narrative includes a child dying due to a mistaken injection into his spine. Another explores a serious near miss involving a patient who had an inaccurate blood sugar reading by staff who were following an outdated practice that an alert from the Medical Devices Agency had identified several months previously. She explores why it is that global policies seem unable to prevent these problems.

Chapter 6 is by Penelope Lacey, manager of a podiatry service at an NHS Trust. The Podiatry Service receives a large proportion of the complaints made by patients to her organization and it is her job to deal with them. Her organization nurtures a 'no-blame culture', which is referred to in two major documents from the Department of Health, *An Organization with a Memory* (2000) and *Building a Safer NHS for Patients* (2001). Within this philosophy, complaints are 'welcomed' as a way of registering feedback from direct patient–service contact and a means of 'learning lessons' from poor practice. The 'no-blame' culture was developed in the early 1990s following investigations into major incidents or serious near misses in nuclear and aviation industries. The underlying concept was that if blame was removed, employees would not cover up small accidental errors. In the long term this should lead to a reduction in the risk of major catastrophes. However, 'no blame' as a conceptual label did not translate well in practice in the NHS because of the procedural frameworks, which focused on 'locating' blame as a way of explaining what had gone wrong. Furthermore, the Board of the Trust takes a fairly punitive stance if a particular service receives too many complaints. The Board takes the view that something has to be done to resolve this; someone must be to blame for these complaints. Thus despite the no-blame rhetoric, it seems as though there does in fact exist a powerful blame culture. The belief behind this seems to be that once the offending person or thing has been located, further mishaps will not occur. Lacey explores in some detail how one particular complaint was dealt with and how this reflects on national policies.

Chapter 7 is by Séamus Cannon, Director of an Education Centre in Ireland. He describes his response to the requirement placed upon him by those inspecting his Centre to have a strategic plan. In asking for the strategic plan, the inspectors were doing what had been requested of them by their immediate superiors, who were in turn responding to theirs, and so on, until we reach the people within the DES who were responsible for the requirement. Control is at the heart of strategic choice theory and this, he concludes, was the intention behind the DES strategy and the review by the inspectors. But what does it mean to be 'in control'? The senior managers within the DES are seeking to exercise control in order to create a state of equilibrium, of stability in the education system. But can control be exercised to this degree? Does his lack of a plan mean that his organization is an aberration? He admits that a continuous state of 'not knowing' and not being 'in control' is characteristic of his life as a manager. He does not think that this is unusual, and if this is the case what use is the plan? The essential management capacity is the courage to participate in the construction of meaning in spite of not being 'in control'. For management here, read senior staff in the DES as well as local staff in the Education Centre. In describing how his organization actually works, Cannon attempts to identify other ways of looking at himself in his work 'from the inside', as it were, and not from the detached and 'objective' viewpoint of an external observer. He argues that human relating is a complex and responsive process; that human interaction in organizational life requires the constant exercise of a practical judgement that goes far beyond the illusory lure of predictability contained in mainstream theory. To proceed in this way is to discard notions of being 'in control' in favour of thinking of oneself as being in a paradoxical state of 'in control' and not 'in control' at the same time. It is in this state of constant flux that new meaning, the constant construction of organizations into the future, takes place.

References

Elias, N. ([1939] 2000) *The Civilizing Process*, Oxford: Blackwell.

Elias, N. (1970) *What is Sociology?*, Oxford: Blackwell.

Elias, N. (1987) *Involvement and Detachment*, Oxford: Blackwell.

Fonseca, J. (2001) *Complexity and Innovation in Organizations*, London: Routledge.

Goodwin, B. (1994) *How the Leopard Changed its Spots*, London: Weidenfeld & Nicolson.

Griffin, D. (2002) *The Emergence of Leadership: Linking Self-organization and Ethics*, London: Routledge.

Joas, H. (2000) *The Genesis of Values*, Cambridge: Polity Press.

Kauffman, S. A. (1995) *At Home in the Universe*, New York: Oxford University Press.

Mead, G. H. (1934) *Mind, Self and Society*, Chicago, IL: University of Chicago Press.

Mead, G. H. (1938) *The Philosophy of the Act*, Chicago, IL: University of Chicago Press.

Shaw, P. (2002) *Changing Conversations in Organizations: A complexity approach to change*, London: Routledge.

Stacey, R. (2001) *Complex Responsive Processes in Organizations: Learning and knowledge creation*, London: Routledge.

Stacey, R. (2005) 'Values, spirituality and organizations: a complex responsive processes perspective', in D. Griffin and R. Stacey (eds) *Complexity and the Experience of Leading Organizations*, London: Routledge.

Stacey, R. and Griffin, D. (eds) (2005) *A Complexity Perspective on Researching Organizations: Taking experience seriously*, London: Routledge.

Stacey, R., Griffin, D. and Shaw, P. (2000) *Complexity and Management: Fad or radical challenge to systems thinking?*, London: Routledge.

Streatfield, P. (2001) *The Paradox of Control in Organizations*, London: Routledge.

Waldorp, M. M. (1992) *Complexity: The Emerging Science at the Edge of Chaos*, Englewood Cliffs, NJ: Simon & Schuster.

2 Ways of thinking about public sector governance

Ralph Stacey

- **The consequences of performance management in the health sector**
- **The consequences of performance management in higher education**
- **Dominant ideologies and ways of thinking about public sector governance**
- **Taking it for granted that organizations are systems**
- **The theory of complex responsive processes**
- **The implications for public sector governance of the theory of complex responsive processes**
- **Conclusion**

Over the past two decades there has been a growing orthodoxy in many countries on the form that public sector governance should take. This chapter explores the ideology and the way of thinking which this orthodoxy reflects, taking as particular examples the health and education sectors in the United Kingdom, although the same points apply to other public sector activities and other countries as well.

For two decades now, the trend in the United Kingdom has been a movement away from a model of governance for public sector health and education which had persisted for more than half a century. This model exhibited a number of key features. First, it was highly decentralized. Somewhat independent institutions delivered health and education services and their line of accountability was to local bodies such as special statutory local area authorities or local government. These were basically funding bodies, and the relatively independent institutions were accountable to them for the way in which they spent the funds allocated to them according to standard formulae. The delivering institutions were also accountable to validating bodies for what they did. Professional bodies, generally of very long standing, represented professional standards and had certain disciplinary powers, often legitimized by statute. Professional regulation was thus, to a significant extent, a voluntary, self-governing affair. The role of central government was primarily one of allocating funds to the local funding agencies and also of nationally coordinating the activities of those bodies, as well as legitimizing the professional bodies. Central government had a policy role in allocating resources and establishing responsibility for the adequate provision of health and education. The central government also had a fiduciary role in ensuring transparent accountability for the expenditure of public funds.

Within this decentralized, rather loosely controlled framework, health and education services were delivered by institutions which were internally governed in a highly collegial manner. Professional groupings within any institution tended to govern themselves through collegial, and often very rivalrous, negotiation. Central management in these institutions was rather weak and often had great difficulty exercising any form of detailed control over the professional groups. In other words, public sector governance was characterized by a particular figuration of power relations in which individual professional practitioners, and professional groups, had considerable freedom to make decisions about what they did, and how they did it, in the specific situations in which they operated. In the health sector, clinical decisions were made by professionals in particular situations – in effect they were making allocation decisions about how the scarce health resource should be distributed in specific cases. The result was a considerable variation in health care across the country. The same applied to educational institutions. That power figuration was sustained by an ideology of vocation and professional freedom.

The form of governance described above was not without its problems. For example, it was difficult to remove professionals who were clearly not performing, and periodically scandals concerning medical and educational errors hit the headlines. Not surprisingly, then, this model came under considerable attack about two decades ago, particularly in the United Kingdom under the Thatcher government. The powerful professional bodies, such as the British Medical Council, were said to be outdated 'old boys' clubs' incapable of policing their professional groups reliably. It was said that standards were too often low, even declining, and general government policies were not effective in rectifying this. Educational institutions were criticized for not matching their offerings to the needs of industry and the economy. The whole public sector was held to be inefficient, irresponsible, non-accountable for quality delivery and far from innovative. Unfavourable comparisons were made with the private sector, which was held up as an indubitably successful alternative to an approach to governance in the public sector seen as a left-over from the Victorian era.

Policy makers responded by making attempts to mimic markets in the public sector, and managerialism, the private sector theory of management, was imported and increasingly imposed by central government on the whole of the public sector. It was taken for granted that the supposed success of the private sector was caused by the method of governance practised in commercial and industrial organizations in a market setting. This was thought to involve the setting of targets, the formulation and implementation of plans, the monitoring of achievement, or lack of it, of the targets and the punishment of those who failed to achieve targets by the forces of the market. The taken-for-granted efficiency of the market mechanism was reflected in the rhetoric of marketization – patients and students should be regarded as consumers of health care and education, which meant that they should have more choice, and funds should follow demand. The public sector was supposed to work as a market. In fact, however, this has proved to be impossible, and behind the rhetoric of the market there has emerged its opposite, namely heavy regulation directly from the central government. It is the ministers and their policy advisers who set the rapidly multiplying targets for health and education, and it is a proliferating number of central government bodies that monitor performance against the centrally set targets. The aim is to standardize health care and education across the country. To increase transparency, league tables are published showing how well or how badly institutions are doing in meeting their targets. Those who do not meet the targets, who do not comply, are publicly named and shamed, and if this does not work the CEOs and senior managers of offending institutions are removed.

Thus what we now have is a highly centralized form of governance, involving detailed intervention from the centre – cabinet ministers may intervene in detailed local situations. The performance management regime, with its targets, plans and league tables, has resulted in a major increase in the number of public bodies whose role it is to scrutinize what the delivering institutions are doing – the Modernization Agency, the Quality Assurance Agency, the Clinical Health Inspection Agency, to name but a few. Naturally, this has led to a dramatic increase in the number of people employed to manage and conduct the scrutinizing activities, and a corresponding increase in numbers of managers and staff in the delivering institutions themselves whose role it is to manage the demands of the scrutinizing bodies. The result is a major change in the power figuration, such that power is heavily tilted to the scrutinizing bodies of central government and away from the delivering institutions. Within those institutions themselves there has been a corresponding shift in the power figuration, with the power relations now tilted firmly towards the top of the hierarchy of managers and away from the professionals who actually deliver the service. The collegial form of public sector governance has all but vanished, or perhaps more accurately is still practised to some extent in the shadow of the legitimate monitoring procedures. However, the particular form of power figuration which has emerged is sustained by a very different ideology to that which prevailed before. This is an ideology of efficiency, measurable quality and improvement. It is an ideology of managerial control to produce uniformity of service. It is an ideology of the market.

In this chapter, I explore the consequences of this change in corporate governance and ask whether the new model of governance actually works, reaching the conclusion that, while there may have been pockets of improvement, there is very little evidence of overall improvement. In the face of this conclusion it becomes important to ask why it is so hard to argue against this mode of governance. The first reason is that doing so amounts to challenging the dominant ideology and power figuration, so risking exclusion. The second reason is that the underlying way of thinking which supports the new model is so taken for granted, while an alternative way of thinking is not immediately apparent, that there seems to be no way out. After all, who can be against improvement and efficiency? This is why I think it is of central importance to reflect upon current taken-for-granted ways of thinking about the public sector and to explore the implications of alternatives.

This chapter, then, considers the way of thinking underlying today's public sector governance, identifying it as a rather crude form of first-order cybernetic systems thinking. It also covers the ideology underlying current public sector governance, pointing to the importance of marketization and managerialism in creating a cult of performance, which replaces purpose. It has the hallmarks of the cult, namely the presentation of a hopelessly idealized future and heavy demands for conformity. The approach is characterized by the instrumental use of naming and shaming people and institutions to enforce compliance, aided by a form of emotional blackmail as people are exhorted not to let their colleagues down. The chapter goes into how the cult of performance is actually operationalized in ways that involve the manipulation of figures and the distortion of clinical decisions to ensure the appearance of meeting targets. The result is a culture of deceit and spin in which appearance and presentation replace substance so that people become alienated from their experience. I argue that instead of leading to authentic quality, the whole approach amounts to a system of counterfeit quality.

I conclude by arguing for a move away from system thinking to the perspective of complex responsive processes where organizations are thought of not as things, but as patterns of relationships between people. If an organization comprises patterns of relations between people but policy makers think organizations are systems, then what will happen as they enforce their policies? From the complex responsive processes perspective, such policies are simply gestures, the articulation of cult values, or social objects which have to be operationalized. What matters is how people are operationalizing the policies. So how are they operationalising central government governance requirements and what are the consequences?

The consequences of performance management in the health sector

The first consequence of the current mode of public sector governance relates to the pattern of employment. For example, take the health sector. Figures published by the Department of Health in its document *Staff in the NHS 2003* show how various categories of staff in the Health Service have been changing. Total employment in the NHS has increased by some 185,000 since 1997 to reach approximately 1.3 million, an increase of about 14 per cent. Within this total, the number of qualified doctors (including general practitioners) has increased by some 15,000 to reach nearly 109,000, also an increase of nearly 14 per cent. Over the same period, the number of qualified nurses has increased by just over 17 per cent to reach a total of 364,692 in 2003. However, the total of managers and senior managers has increased by 45 per cent over the five-year period to reach 35,321, while the number of staff in central functions has increased by just over 24 per cent to reach 92,257 in 2003. Taking managers and central staff together, they now amount to 127,578, an increase of 34 per cent since 1997. Managers and central staff now significantly outnumber qualified doctors, having increased by some 29,000 between 1997 and 2003 compared to the increase of 15,000 over the same period in the number of doctors. The comparison is even more striking if one takes only doctors working in hospitals. There were 77,210 in 2003, up by only 2,527 since 1997. Furthermore, this pattern of increase over the past five years continues the trend which had been evident through the 1990s. This continuing growth in numbers of managerial and administrative staff no doubt reflects the growing apparatus for the monitoring and control of the NHS, indicating just how substantial the cost of this form of public sector governance is.

However, supporters of the new mode of governance argue that it has led to significantly improved performance in the NHS and so is worth the enormous cost. For example, on 21 June 2003 *The Sunday Times* (pp. 12–13) referred to a report by the NHS chief executive claiming that there had been a big increase in the number of patients treated, real progress in improving quality and significantly reduced waiting times for treatment. However, other sources told a different story. The same newspaper report referred to research by the King's Fund showing that the number of scheduled operations and consultant appointments had fallen. John Appleby, chief economist of this prestigious health research organization, was reported as saying: 'Looking at the data, there is no discernible connection between the amount of money going into the NHS and the number of patients treated' (p. 12).

The article went on to state:

> In many cases, targets are claimed to have been met when they are consistently missed. Last week's Health Service Journal produced research showing that apparent progress towards the key target for accident and emergency patients is unreliable. The government's NHS Plan set a target for 90% of patients waiting less than four hours in casualty departments by the end of March 2003. To meet this target, hospitals distorted their activities during the last week in March when waiting times were being checked. Doctors were asked to work double shifts and routine operations were cancelled. The ploy worked and hospitals achieved an average figure of 92.7% seen within four hours. Now, however, things are back to normal.

The article then quotes opinion polls showing that most people do not believe that the NHS is improving, although only a month later, on 30 July, *The Times* quoted an opinion poll in which the great majority of people were satisfied with the NHS. However, the same article reported that the number of beds in hospitals was falling, repeated again, a year later, in an *Evening Standard* report of 10 August 2004, and that centralized appointments systems were not working as well as the more decentralized systems they replaced.

On 29 July 2003, the *Evening Standard* referred to a report by an all-party Public Administration Select Committee of Parliament which had found that doctors had met targets to cut waiting times for new ophthalmic patients by cancelling thousands of follow-up appointments. In some cases this had led to blindness. The following day, *The Times* (p. 9) described research published in the *British Journal of Cancer* which showed that after targets for breast screening were introduced in 1999, the proportion of women who saw a consultant within two weeks rose from 66 per cent to 75 per cent. However, the proportion who received treatment within five weeks of this first appointment fell from 84 per cent to 80 per cent. The conclusion drawn was that arbitrary targets simply pushed patients from one waiting list to another. Over the past year or so there have been many other reports on rising readmission rates, the falsification of data, and the use of fine definitional differences to operate from two waiting lists, only one of which is officially published.

I would argue that what these newspaper reports indicate is how it is only possible for medical professionals and their managers to survive in the new cult of performance (Williams, 2005) by practising some form of deceit, or, to put it more mildly, playing games. Furthermore, one does not have to rely on newspaper reports in the United Kingdom to reach this conclusion. Researchers in Canada have found that managers and other professionals in public sector organizations develop techniques to corrupt the implementation of centralized control techniques (Lozeau *et al.*, 2002). They argue that applying techniques of control drawn from a theoretical framework which is not compatible with the actual work environment inevitably leads to the corruption of those techniques in order to resist organizational change, with unexpected consequences. The original intention of the techniques is lost in the political gaming between institutional professionals and government administrators:

> plans are serving as a tool in negotiations with the institutional
> environment represented mainly by the government . . . rather than
> serving as an instrument of change the technique is co-opted
> (corrupted).
>
> (Lozeau *et al.*, 2002, p. 547)

The researchers argue that this 'failure' is not due to management but to the techniques themselves. Because of the incompatibility between the theory and the actual setting it seeks to understand, norms represented by the techniques contradict the practice of the organizations and the result is hypocrisy, which in turn breeds the destructive force of cynicism. This cynicism is exacerbated by the frequency with which the control techniques are changed. The researchers go on to point out that:

> Lower-level managers avoid overt opposition, going through the motions of conformity rather than risk sanctions. In the process the very idea of quality management has been perverted. However, considerable energy has been expended.
>
> (Lozeau *et al.*, 2002, p. 553)

There are parallel research findings in the United Kingdom which argue that formal attempts at bureaucratic reform in the NHS have had little impact. According to Fitzgerald and Ferlie (2000, p. 726):

> One impact of externally driven change is to feel disempowered or 'driven' in a particular direction. . . . In the case of the quasi-market, for example, the drivers are central Government and both managers and professionals alike experience the impact. Within this context, some professionals perceive that their position and freedoms have been eroded and frequently blame 'management' for these changes.

In the USA, despite its very different way of structuring health care, similar conclusions are being reached by researchers. In 1999, the Institute of Medicine published a report entitled *To Err is Human*. This revealed that tens of thousands of Americans were dying each year due to medical mistakes and poor performance. This is widely thought to reflect a systems failure rather than individual culpability. In discussing this issue, Macklis (2001, p. 71) points out how there is virtually no indication that American health care has become safer despite large-scale programmes for improvement. The responses to this failure typically continue to be a call to analyse and publish 'best practice'. He argues:

> Although newly organized medical error reduction initiatives now abound, a close inspection of what is actually being accomplished through these initiatives may unfortunately lead one to believe that many of these 'quality' efforts are geared more toward a socially and legally defensible public relations stance rather than an actual attempt to produce lasting improvement in medical outcomes.

He draws attention to the few authoritative reports which document large-scale patient safety interventions, and suggests that:

> The application of human factors research . . . would suggest that sociocultural factors and task specific 'change management principles' may provide hints on the reason that global 'best practice' mandates and top-down reengineering are rarely successful.

He recommends that health care initiatives should be local rather than global. They should be internally driven by members of task groups who have standing and credibility. 'Best practice' in one local situation may not be 'best practice' in another. He reports on a number of local change initiatives in which he has been involved to back his argument. Lozeau, Langley and Denis, the Canadian researchers referred to above (2002, p. 560), conclude their research in a similar way:

> if one understands how and why techniques are socially constructed in the course of ongoing interactions, herein lies a way to rethink management intervention that reaches beyond the impasse.

It is the shift in thinking which these and other authors are calling for that I wish to explore later in the chapter. Prior to that, however, I take a brief look at what has been happening in the education sector.

The consequences of performance management in higher education

Quality assurance in education closely follows models of quality management in manufacturing and commercial operations. A system is designed in which teachers are required to set overall objectives for any programme they deliver, translated into the learning outcomes to be achieved in each teaching session they take. Each session must then be designed in terms of content and delivery method so that it achieves the outcome, thus fulfilling the overall objectives of the programme and the contract with students as consumers of knowledge. Students can then know in advance what they are to learn, check that they have learned it, and sue the institution if they have not! An audit trail must be established enabling others to follow just what the intended objectives and outcomes were and how the events during the session and the material distributed to the students achieved the outcomes. This procedure entails keeping detailed records of course programmes, session by session, and copies of all materials distributed. In addition to the traditional coursework and examinations, also forming part of the audit trail, other monitoring devices are put in place. Teachers monitor each other's classroom performance. Course leaders require students to fill in questionnaires on how they found the course. Reports on how well each session achieved its outcome must be prepared, as well as reports on student progress. Finally, there is the periodic monitoring of departments delivering courses in which the paper audit trail is inspected. The government in the United Kingdom has set up a Quality Assurance Agency to manage this monitoring process for universities and rank them according to compliance. There are other monitoring bodies for other educational sectors. The cost in terms of money, and even more in terms of time throughout the educational sector, is enormous.

In my own experience, when teachers are compelled to adhere to the system outlined above, they find it impossible to do other than articulate very bland objectives and outcomes and do the paperwork required to create an audit trail that appears to comply with requirements. A great deal of effort is directed to this paper process, to the detriment of the main task, namely teaching. The major monitoring exercises turn out to be a charade, but one that generates a great deal of frustration and anxiety. None of it has much to do with authentic quality; that is, the quality of the learning experience. Instead, it is a massive system for producing counterfeit quality. Why do I make this claim of counterfeit quality? Well, in each educational institution there is usually a central staff which collects and inspects the required paperwork. If the paperwork does not comply with the regulations, it is corrected so that when the inspectors arrive it is all as it should be. However, what they are inspecting is not what was used with the students. When the inspectors arrive they do attend some teaching sessions and talk to some students, although most of the time is taken up with the 'paperwork'. The staff who are to be inspected put an unusual degree of effort into the sessions in which they will be inspected so that what the inspectors actually see is not what normally happens. The staff and selected students are all rehearsed in what to say and what not to say to the inspectors. The irony is that most of the inspectors are themselves teaching staff from other education institutions who conduct the same practices when they are on the receiving end of an inspection. The inspectors know all about the games we are playing and we know that they know and they know that we know that they know. From my own experience, quality assurance systems of this kind amount to game playing which is a massive waste of resource and, even more, a damaging source of frustration and anxiety that actually reduces the authentic quality of learning.

As in the health sector, then, many managers in educational institutions also adopt local tactics of resistance and corruption of techniques (Prichard and Willmott, 1997; Prichard, 2000; Barry *et al.*, 2001; Shelley, 2002). From his research on higher education institutions, Shelley (2002, p. 240) concludes:

> Thus there is evidence of instrumental behaviour by staff and managers as they actively habituate time and routines to make space for their own interests (as Burawoy, 1979; Thompson, 1989), whilst playing the game dictated by competitive performance and quality measures. Such strategies may undoubtedly enable individual staff to maintain a psychological well-being, and can be seen as a form of resistance or emancipation, as staff play games to find their own space and time within the constraints imposed. However, they may also be viewed as exploitation and, moreover, the impression gained here is that of a decreasing opportunity for this kind of independence, relative to marketised direct control and responsible autonomy imperatives.

On 10 August 2004, the *Evening Standard* carried a report on soaring stress levels experienced by public sector staff. The report referred to research by the Health and Safety Executive showing that four in ten teachers, more than three in ten nurses and one in nine care workers experience high levels of stress. Experts ascribe this to the emotional demands of the job and the higher likelihood of being attacked by the public. I would add that a significant factor in the growing emotional demands relates to the model of public sector governance, which is undermining any sense of vocation, and leading to depression and feelings of alienation from one's own experience. If public sector workers are feeling increasingly cynical, stressed, depressed and alienated, how can they deliver quality services? It becomes very important, I argue, to explore the taken-for-granted way of thinking that leads to the situation I have been describing.

Dominant ideologies and ways of thinking about public sector governance

Over the past two decades, public sector governance has become increasingly based on quasi-market mechanisms such as internal markets which separate public sector institutions into client and contractor organizations. These are regarded as business units which are required to formulate strategic plans, price their services, negotiate service level agreements and engage in competitive tendering (Ferner, 1988; Pendleton and Winterton, 1993; Fitzgerald *et al.*, 1996; Shelley, 2002). As part of this change, central government's role has become one of auditing outcomes. The consequence has been a major shift in power towards central government, reflected in the significantly increased centralization of the control of public sector organizations, which is covered over by a rhetoric of consumer choice and decentralization.

This shift in the nature and underlying ideology of public sector governance is very evident in the higher education sector. Whereas education may once have been thought of as of value for its own sake, it is now firmly linked to economic performance with a major emphasis on delivering the skills and competences required by industry and commerce. Knowledge is regarded as a key economic resource and it is the role of the education sector to deliver the vocational preparation for employment (Ainley, 1994; Parker and Jary, 1995). In this 'performative' culture, knowledge is a commodity which may be bought and sold while teachers become suppliers and students become customers. The meaning of quality changes, and great emphasis is placed on the measurement of outcomes, monitored through the Research Assessment Exercise (RAE) and the Quality Assurance Agency (QAA). All of this has been accompanied by a massive increase in student numbers and a significant decline in funding per student. Shelley (2002) argues that this has created a crisis in UK higher education.

Marketization and demands for increased performance in higher education have led to a move to managerialism (Hardy, 1991; Middlehurst and Elton, 1992; Prichard, 2000). Managerialism in the public sector mimics private sector forms of governance through formal budgetary and quality controls, quantitative targets and measurement, formal reporting procedures, centralized resource allocation, hierarchical forms of authority, and techniques for punishment and reward. League tables of relative performance are published and failing institutions and their managers are publicly named and shamed. Policy makers seem to believe that by operating this system they will be able to manage the quality of learning throughout the educational sector.

Marketization and managerialism have thus become the dominant ideologies of public sector governance and these ideologies make particular power figurations feel natural, indeed quite unquestionable. The figurations of power relations I refer to are those in which, nationally, the power ratio is tilted heavily towards central government and its agencies of surveillance, and away from delivering institutions. Within those institutions themselves the power ratio is heavily tilted towards the top of the management hierarchy and away from the professionals who deliver the service. I want to turn now to the taken-for-granted way of thinking that sustains these ideologies and the power relations they unconsciously maintain.

Taking it for granted that organizations are systems

Over at least the past century in the West, a particular way of thinking about the relationship between individuals and groups/organizations/ societies has become predominant. This dominant discourse reflects a spatial metaphor in which an individual mind is thought of as an internal world/mental models/maps, all consisting of representations of an external world of physical objects, other individuals and groups/ organizations/societies. Individual minds as internal worlds are separated from the external world by a boundary and, in their interactions with each other, individuals form groups/organizations/societies, thought of as higher-level phenomena following their own laws and acting back on individuals as causes of their behaviour. This represents a dualistic form of thinking in which individual minds are understood in terms of psychology while organizations/societies are understood in terms of sociology/organizational theory. Different laws and different forms of causality are thought to apply to these two different realms, although they are always connected – there is *both* the individual *and* the collective. What is then being taken for granted is that organizations actually exist as 'things' outside of individuals, and those 'things' are normally understood to be systems. Furthermore, it is also taken for granted that, as rational beings, individuals, standing outside the system, can take the position of objective observer of organizational/social systems. Just as natural scientists do with regard to physical objects, so social scientists can do with social phenomena. They can identify the regularities of organizational life, revealing the links between cause and effect in organizational change, and by using this knowledge they can design, or engineer, such social systems. In this way, rational individuals can improve and modernize organizational systems so as to achieve what those rational individuals have decided in advance to be efficiency and improvement.

It is instructive, I think, to explore the origins of this now taken-for-granted way of thinking. The German philosopher Immanuel Kant (1790) was the first to propose the notion of 'system' in the way it is now used. He argued that while Newton's mechanistic, reductionist way of thinking, reflecting an 'if–then' causality, provided very powerful explanations for inanimate matter, it was much less useful for understanding organisms in nature. He suggested that it would be useful to think of an organism as consisting of parts interacting, in a self-organizing manner, to produce the whole organism and themselves. An oak tree could thus be thought of as consisting of roots, trunk, branches, twigs and leaves all interacting to produce both themselves and the whole oak tree. He also suggested that such a system could be thought of in developmental terms, by which he meant that an oak tree starts life as an acorn and then goes through the development stages of sapling and young tree to the final state of mature oak. What this developmental process is doing is unfolding the final, mature form of the tree from what is already enfolded in the acorn. It is this formative process of unfolding the enfolded which may be thought of as the cause of the organism's development.

With regard to this systemic way of thinking, Kant presented two cautions. First, he argued that it could be useful to think of an organism 'as if' it was a system because we cannot know a phenomenon as it is in itself – we can only know our perceptions and formulate hypotheses. The notion of 'system' was no more than a hypothesis. Second, he held that one would never think of human action in terms of a 'system'. For Kant, humans were autonomous beings who, through their powers of reason, could choose their own objectives, in their own interests, and the actions required to achieve those objectives. This amounted to arguing that human action had a rational cause. However, if a human were to be thought of as a part of a system this would amount to a denial of human autonomy. This is because, in order to be relevant as part of a system, that part has to act to form the system. In other words, it has to act in the interest of the system and not in its own interest, for if it does, it is not relevant as a part. While I do not regard humans as autonomous individuals because, as I argue below, they are interdependent, I nevertheless think that Kant's point is of major importance. Even interdependent persons have some kind of choice, take some kind of spontaneous action, and to the extent that they do they cannot be thought of as parts of a system.

However, Kant's strictures were later disregarded on both points. Through the first half of the twentieth century, neurologists, biologists, engineers and many others were developing systemic ways of understanding natural phenomena (e.g. Goldstein, 1939; von Bertalanffy, 1968). Most of them seem to have ignored Kant's caution about claiming that such phenomena actually were systems – the 'as if' nature of the system hypothesis disappeared and it was taken for granted that nature actually consisted of systems. By the early 1950s, a number of very important publications had taken the concept of system over from the natural sciences to the social sciences (Ashby, 1945, 1952, 1956; Wiener, 1948; Beer, 1979, 1981). It was soon accepted that human minds were actually cognitive systems and that human groups, organizations and societies were also actually systems existing at a higher level than the individual systems. It began to be believed that individuals, as subsystems, interacted with each other to form groups as systems, which interacted to form higher-level systems called organizations, which in turn interacted to form even higher-level supra-systems called societies and so on. Furthermore, each level in this nested system of systems acted down on the lower level as cause. Thus we have come to think that rational individuals, governed by a rationalist causality, can objectively study higher-level systems called groups, organizations and societies and redesign or re-engineer such systems. In effect these rational designers are enfolding visions, targets and so on into the human system which will then, it is assumed, be unfolded by the formative operation of the systems; that is, by the interaction of the individuals (parts) constituting them.

One strand in this development of systems thinking was of particular importance, namely cybernetics. The theory of cybernetic systems was developed primarily by engineers – it is a theory of control, and in importing it into the social sciences we have imported the engineer's idea of control and applied it directly to human action without carefully paying attention to the fact that human beings are conscious, self-conscious agents with some degree of choice and spontaneity. Cybernetic systems are self-regulating systems, open to their environment and able to sustain an equilibrium state in response to environmental change. The central heating machine is often used as an exemplar. Basically, a central heating appliance consists of an energy-producing machine and a regulator. An agent external to the appliance, the occupant of a room, determines a desired level for the temperature of a room by setting a device in the regulator. The regulator then measures the actual room temperature and compares it with the target. If the actual is below the target, the regulator triggers the energy source and the room temperature rises. As soon as it exceeds the target, the regulator turns off the energy source. In this way, through damping down deviations from target, known technically as negative feedback, the appliance maintains the target room temperature in a self-regulating way requiring no further intervention on the part of the external agent. It is in this way that the system controls the environmental state selected by the external regulator.

This notion of a self-regulating system became more and more prominent in the literature on organizations and management and it found its way increasingly into the thinking of managers in commercial and industrial organizations everywhere. All planning and budgeting systems are cybernetic systems, as are all performance appraisal and quality assurance systems. They all involve external agents, managers and leaders, setting idealized states and monitoring procedures to identify the gap between actual and ideal, prompting action to close the gap. Quality assurance systems were particularly well developed by engineers for manufacturing processes and later taken up in most repetitive administrative procedures as well. The engineer's notion of control became the most visible form of control in private sector organizations in practice and occupied most of the space in the literature on management and organizations. This emphasis on control focused attention on procedures, bureaucracies and paper trails to such an extent that the fundamental importance of human interaction, trial and error, and the highly political ways in which private sector organizations in fact function tended to be obscured. We could say that the ordinary day-to-day, rather messy nature of managing in commercial organizations became invisible, cloaked by a myth of calculating rationality. Human beings became resources used by an 'it' called an organization. Human beings became a 'dimension' of this 'it'.

It was this myth of instrumental, calculating rationality, I would argue, that was taken up and propagated by politicians in the 1980s and ever since as *the* way to govern the public sector. A whole taken-for-granted way of thinking is represented in the target setting and monitoring procedures of performance. What seems beyond question in the rhetoric of improvement and modernization is its underlying way of thinking. This is to implicitly assume that public sector organizations, even those as large as the National Health Service, are actually cybernetic systems and can be operated as such. It seems we have come to think of public sector organizations as actually resembling large central heating appliances with all those persons operating in them actually being like little central heating appliances. I argue that a particularly naive form of systems thinking has become the fundamental notion underlying public sector governance today. Policy makers seem unaware of Kant's strictures.

First, the hypothetical notion of a system, the 'as if', seems to have been completely obliterated. Second, there seems to be little awareness of the problems inherent in applying a way of thinking to human action which is at odds with the potential for human choice, novelty and spontaneity and the need to continually respond to local contingencies. There seems to be little evidence of any impact on national policy and means of governance of the much more sophisticated second-order systems thinking. It is little wonder, therefore, that the consequences take the form described earlier in this chapter.

I am suggesting, then, that the basic approach to public sector governance, the monitoring procedures of target setting and monitoring, reflect a particularly simple form of systems thinking. Of course, not all systems thinking about human action is this naive. For example, the systems dynamics (Forrester, 1961; Senge, 1990) strand in systems thinking takes account of amplifying feedback in which small deviations can escalate out of control to produce unexpected and unintended outcomes. Here much greater account is taken of interconnection and how one action (say, requiring a reduction in waiting times) can trigger unexpected outcomes such as a rise in readmission times. Furthermore, second-order systems thinking – for example, soft systems (Checkland, 1981) and critical systems thinking (Jackson, 2000; Midgley, 2000) – does emphasize the 'as if', or hypothetical nature of the systems construct. It also takes account of human interaction in a far more sophisticated manner and calls for the exploratory use of different perspectives and different system models. In addition, there are various institutions in the NHS where people are using these more sophisticated forms of thinking in working out how to operate more effectively in the performance management regime. However, these more sophisticated forms of systems thinking are not reflected in the uniform imposition of centrally set targets and monitoring procedures.

However, as colleagues and I have argued elsewhere (Stacey *et al.*, 2000), all forms of systems thinking present a dual causality, where the origin of novelty lies not in the system but in the individuals external to it. All forms of systems thinking run into the difficulty of choice when people are thought of as parts of a system. All forms of systems thinking posit an external position outside the system from which it is to be understood and they do not deal with the problem of infinite regress which this brings. It is for these reasons that I am interested in trying to understand the consequences of current public sector governance policies from a temporal process perspective; that is, a complex responsive processes perspective. The book series *Complexity and Emergence in Organizations* (Stacey *et al.*, 2000; Fonseca, 2001; Stacey, 2001; Streatfield, 2001; Griffin, 2002; Shaw, 2002) provides a detailed development of the theory of complex responsive processes. Some aspects of this theory which are particularly relevant to the issue raised in this chapter are described in the following section.

The theory of complex responsive processes

The theory of complex responsive processes draws on analogies from the natural complexity sciences, which are concerned with phenomena characterized by nonlinear dynamics (some examples from the literature are Gleick, 1988; Prigogine and Stengers, 1984; Goodwin, 1994; Kauffman, 1995). One strand in the natural complexity sciences is concerned with complex adaptive systems (Goodwin, 1994; Kauffman, 1995). A complex adaptive system consists of very large numbers of interacting entities known as agents. In their interaction they adapt to each other, forming a system that adapts to its environment. Examples of phenomena whose behaviour is being modelled in this way are termites building large structures, ants signalling food locations, birds flocking and billions of neurons interacting in a brain to produce coherent patterns of thought and action. This agent-based approach is of particular interest to social scientists because human groups, organizations and societies may also be thought of as agents interacting with each other. Phenomena such as these are explored through computer simulations in which each individual agent is represented by a set of computer instructions, or rules, which specify how the agent is to interact with a limited number of other agents. Each agent then is a set of computer instructions to do with interaction. There is no program or blueprint for any overall, global pattern, only the programs which are the individual agents. Large numbers of agents are then left to interact with each other, and what the simulations demonstrate is that such iterated local interaction, called self-organization, produces an overall or global pattern despite there being no global design, plan or programme. Furthermore, these global patterns are paradoxically predictable and unpredictable at the same time, and when the agents differ from each other, both they and the global patterns emerging in their interactions evolve, so producing novelty (Allen, 1998).

However, in thinking about the implications of complex adaptive systems simulations for human action it is essential to take account of the nature of human agents. First, it is highly simplistic to think of humans as simple rule-following beings. Even if one were to say that our action takes the form of following rules, we would have to recognize that we need rules to interpret the rules and rules to interpret the interpretive rules, and so on to infinite regress. In our acting, we may take account of rules but may hardly be said to follow them blindly as do the digital agents in computer simulations. The essential and distinctive characteristic of human agents is that they are living bodies who are conscious and self-conscious beings capable of spontaneity, imagination, fantasy and creative action. Human agents are essentially reflexive and reflective. Furthermore, they are essentially social beings in a distinctive way in that they do not interact blindly according to mechanistic rules but engage in meaningful communicative interaction with each other. In addition, in interacting with each other, humans exercise at least some degree of choice as to how they will respond to the actions of others and this involves the use of some form of evaluative criteria. Furthermore, in their interdependence humans constrain and enable each other. Since power is such an enabling constraint, power is an irremovable aspect of all human relating. Patterns of power relations are always emerging in human interaction (Elias, 1939, 1970). In addition, human agents use simple and more and more complicated tools and technologies to accomplish what they choose to do. It is these embodied attributes of consciousness, self-consciousness, reflection and reflexivity, creativity, imagination and fantasy, communication, meaning, power, choice, evaluation, tool use and sociality that should be explicitly brought to any interpretation, as regards human beings, of the insights derived from complex adaptive system simulations.

George Herbert Mead's (1932, 1934, 1938) theories of conversation provide a powerful way of understanding the essential human characteristics mentioned in the last paragraph. He understands consciousness as arising in the communicative interaction between human bodies. Humans have evolved central nervous systems such that when one gestures to another, particularly in the form of vocal gesture or language, one evokes in one's own body responses to one's gesture that are similar to those evoked in other bodies. Mead refers to this as communication in the medium of significant symbols. In other words, in their acting, humans take the attitude, the tendency to act, of the other, and it is because they have this capacity to communicate in significant symbols that humans can know what they are doing. It immediately follows that consciousness (knowing, mind) is a social process in which meaning emerges in the social act of gesture–response, where the gesture can never be separated from the response. Meaning does not lie in the gesture, the word, alone but only in the gesture taken together with the response to it.

Furthermore, in communicating with each other, as the basis of everything they do, people do not simply take the attitude of the specific others with whom they are relating at any one time. Humans have the capacity for generalizing so that when they act they always take up the attitude of what Mead called the generalized other or the social object. In other words, they always take the attitude of the group or society to their actions – they are concerned about what others might think of what they do or say. This is often unconscious and it is, of course, a powerful form of social control. Furthermore, self-consciousness, taking oneself as an object to oneself, is also a social process because the subject, 'I', can only ever be an object to itself as 'me', and the 'me' is one's perception of the attitude of society towards oneself. Mead talked about a person taking the attitude of the group to himself, where that attitude is the 'me'. In the 'I–me' dialectic, then, we have a process in which the generalization of the 'me' is made particular in the response of the 'I' for a particular person at a particular time in a particular place. The 'I' is the often spontaneous and imaginative response of the socially formed individual to the 'me' as the gesture of society to oneself. Communication, then, is not simply the sending of a signal to be received by another, but rather complex social, that is, responsive, processes of self-formation in which meaning and society-wide patterns emerge.

In Mead's work we have a theory of consciousness and self-consciousness emerging in the social interaction between human bodies in the medium of significant symbols, and at the same time widespread social patterns also emerge, as they do for the complex adaptive system simulations described earlier. Human interaction forms and is formed by the social at the same time; local interaction forms and is formed by the global pattern at the same time.

Furthermore, communicative interaction between people in organizations frequently involves the use of highly sophisticated tools. Obvious examples are telephones, the Internet, email, documents of all kinds and the wider media of television and newspapers. Less obvious, perhaps, are management systems of information and control, including budgets, plans of all kinds, monitoring, evaluation and appraisal systems, databases and so on. National and international financial systems may also be thought of as tools in communicative interaction, so entering into the patterning of the themes of communicative interaction in organizations and other groups. When people interact with each other in their local situations they talk to each other in ways that have reference to these systems and procedural tools. In fact, these tools shape the themes of communicative interaction, both enabling and exercising powerful constraints on that communication. However, meaning does not lie in the tools but in the gestures–responses made with the tools.

Mead, then, was concerned with complex social acts in which many people are engaged in conversations through which they accomplish the tasks of fitting in and conflicting with each other to realize their objectives and purposes. People do not come to an interaction with each other afresh each time, because they are born into an already existing, socially evolved pattern and they continue to play their part in its further evolution. In order to accomplish complex social acts, people need to be able to take the attitude of all of those directly or indirectly engaged in the complex social act. In the evolution of society many generalizations, many social objects, emerge which are taken up, or particularized, in people's interactions with each other.

This is a point of major importance. Mead draws attention to paradoxical processes of generalization and particularization at the same time. Mental and social activities are processes of generalizing and particularizing at the same time. Individuals act in relation to that which is common to all of them (generalizing) but responded to somewhat differently by each of them in each current time period (particularizing). A social object is thus a kind of gesture together with tendencies to respond in particular ways. Social objects are common plans or patterns of action related to the existent future of the act. Social control is the bringing of the act of the individual into relation with the social object, and the contours of the object determine the organization of the act. Social control depends upon the degree to which the individual takes the attitude of the others; that is, takes the attitude which is the social object. All institutions are social objects and serve to control individuals who find them in their experience. It is important to notice how Mead used the term 'object' in a social sense as a 'tendency to act' rather than as a concept or a thing, which are meanings appropriate to physical objects. In a social setting, then, Mead used the term 'object' in tension with the usual understanding of object as a thing in nature. The pattern or tendency Mead calls an object is in a sense an object in that it is what we perceive in taking it up in our acting, but this is perception of our own acting, not a thing.

In another formulation of the interaction between the general and the particular, Mead draws a distinction between cult values and their functionalization. Cult values are idealizations that emerge in the evolution of a society. Mead said that they were the most precious part of our heritage, and examples of cult values are democracy, treating others with respect, regarding life as sacred, belief in being American or British and so on. Such cult values present people with the image of an idealized future shorn of all constraints. If such values are applied directly to action, without allowing for variations contingent on a specific situation, then those undertaking such action form a cult in which they exclude all who do not comply. In the usual course of events, however, this does not happen, since people act on current interpretations of cult values. For example, a cult value to do with the sacredness of life is not directly applied in some places, leading to conflict regarding, for example, abortion. Functionalization of cult values inevitably leads to conflict and the negotiation of compromises around such conflict. Functionalizing of values is the enactment of values in the ordinary, local interactions between people in the living present. In his notion of cult values, Mead points not only to the generalizing tendencies of interacting people but also to the idealizing tendencies characteristic of their interaction. Such idealizations may be good or bad depending upon who is doing the judging.

The implications for public sector governance of the theory of complex responsive processes

From the perspective of complex responsive processes outlined above, how would one think about government policy relating to the National Health Service in the UK? The NHS is thought of as a social object; that is, generalized tendencies to act in similar ways by large numbers of people in similar situations. On closer inspection, however, there is not one monolithic social object but many linked ones. Each hospital, for example, is to some extent a distinctive social object, as are groups of different kinds of medical practitioners and managers in that hospital. There are therefore many social objects, many generalized tendencies by large numbers of people to act in similar ways in similar situations. Furthermore, the medical profession, the NHS and the many different institutions and groupings it comprises are all idealized. Cult values, such as 'providing free health care', 'doing no harm', 'providing all with the highest standard of care' and 'providing the same standard of care in all geographical locations to all classes of person', are essential features of what the NHS means. 'Performance' and 'quality' are recent additions to these cult values. The generalizations and idealizations can all be recorded in written artefacts, sound recordings and films as propositions and/or narratives. These artefacts may take the form of policy documents, legal contracts, procedures, instructions from the Department of Health and so on. Such artefacts are then used as tools in the communicative interaction and power relating between members within the NHS, and between them and those concerned with its governance. However, the artefacts recording the generalizations and idealizations are just artefacts, not the generalizations and idealizations themselves. Whether recorded or not, the generalizations and idealizations only have any meaning in the local interactions of all involved in each specific situation – they are only to be found in the experience of local interaction.

Thus, for example, when groups of policy makers meet to decide what to do about the NHS, they are clearly interacting locally. What they will be reflecting upon and discussing are the generalizations and idealizations of the NHS or parts of it. They may issue a consultation document, a green paper, to large numbers of people for comment. This is then taken up for discussion in the professional bodies representing different groups in the NHS. Again the discussion is local interaction, as is the subsequent negotiation of changes in any of the policies. What they are discussing and negotiating in this local interaction is changes to the global, to the generalizations and idealizations. Eventually a white paper, or policy statement, is produced and instructions sent to, say, all the hospitals in the country setting out what new targets they must meet in order to demonstrate quality and performance and in what way they will be penalized if they do not comply. What I have been describing is processes of local interaction, local negotiation, in which emerge articulations of the general and the ideal as far as the NHS is concerned. The process is one in which people have been trying to design the general and the ideal, and in the way they currently do this in the UK they reflect a particular way of thinking about the NHS. In setting targets and establishing monitoring processes they display a way of thinking derived for cybernetics systems thinking. They are trying to design and install a self-regulating system.

However, the NHS is not a self-regulating system, but many local patterns of interaction in which the general is continually emerging as continuity and change as it is iterated from one present time to the next. What then becomes important is how people are taking up, in their local interactions, the generalizations and idealizations articulated in the artefacts of written instructions and procedures. The meaning cannot be located simply in the gesture which these artefacts represent but at the same time in the myriad responses this gesture calls forth. In a specific situation on a specific day, there may simply not be the physical capacity to achieve the targets set. In each specific situation there will always be conflicts about what the targets mean and how they are to be adhered to. The target might then become something that has to be avoided, manipulated, and even falsified. For example, a specific decision may be to meet, say, a target of reducing waiting lists, by sending people home too early after an operation, leading to a rise in readmissions. The cult value of 'equal treatment' has to be functionalized in a specific situation at a specific time, and may mean giving expensive medication to one person and not to another. The global generalization/cult value that the policy makers designed is thus being transformed in the local interaction so that it comes to mean something different – instead of uniform high performance it may come to mean 'cover-up' and 'deceit'.

As the unexpected emerges in many, many local interactions, the global pattern is transformed, and, of course, in their local interactions the policy makers are reflecting upon this. They may then conclude that the now burgeoning number of targets is proving too much of an embarrassment and should be scrapped. However, still thinking in system terms, they feel that they must design some other form of generalization to stay in control and secure adequate performance. The proposal now in the NHS is that 700 targets should be abandoned but only to be replaced with twenty-two qualitative standards. Once again, however, the meaning does not lie in the generalization alone but in its particularization in many local situations. It will be interesting to see what emerges from this new move.

This way of understanding focuses attention on the inevitably conflictual nature of particularizing the general and the idealized. If people simply apply some generalization or idealization in an absolutely rigid way there need be no conflict, but particularizing them in specific, unique situations means making choices. Since different individuals and different groupings of them will be making different interpretations of the situation, they will be pressing for different choices to be made. Which of those conflicting choices is actually made will be the result of negotiation and this immediately raises the matter of power. The particular choices made will reflect the figurations of power – the choices of individuals and groups will prevail when the power ratio is tilted in their favour.

Conclusion

I have been arguing that current modes of public sector governance reflect a taken-for-granted way of thinking in terms of systems, particularly a simplistic, naive form of cybernetic system. Instead of recognizing the hypothetical nature of the systems construct, policy making proceeds on the implicit assumption that public sector organizations are actually cybernetic systems. It is also implicitly assumed that people are parts of the systems and this ignores the human capacity, constrained by interdependence, to make some choices in how they act in local, contingent situations which are always throwing up unexpected developments requiring to be dealt with by people in conflictual negotiation with each other. The whole approach amounts to an attempt to design a system which will predictably produce a desired global pattern of activity. However, from the perspective of complex responsive processes, organizations are not actually existing things called systems but, rather, are ongoing, iterated patterns of relationships between people. Organizations are temporal processes of negotiating conflicts in ordinary, everyday local situations and it is in this responsive negotiating that people go on together. The global patterns we recognize as the health service or the educational service are continually emerging in these myriad local interactions. The policies negotiated by local groups in central government are then understood as articulations of the emerging global patterns, as generalizations and idealizations. The targets and surveillance procedures are understood as tools that people in other local negotiations are being required to use in their communicative interaction with each other. As generalizations and idealizations, these tools have to be made particular and functional, over and over again, in the particular contingent situations in which people find themselves. They cannot simply apply directly the generalized and idealized tools specified by groups of people at the centre of government.

If one takes this perspective, then the co-option and corruption of the tools and techniques, the game playing and deceit all become perfectly understandable. They are the manner in which people find it possible to give at least the appearance of compliance and yet go on together to do the work of health care and education. All of this happens because the policies, tools and techniques reflect a way of thinking about organizations that is inappropriate in that it completely covers over the ordinary, everyday contingencies which people must negotiate in order to carry on doing what they need to do. An enormously expensive mode of public sector governance produces not improvement, but the distortion of judgements in local situations and the requirement to expend huge amounts of emotional energy to get the work done while appearing to comply.

The question then becomes that of how we are to develop forms of public sector governance that do take account of the essentially local nature of human interaction, the essentially contingent and conflictual manner in which people are able to go on together to do their work. Instead of importing mechanistic notions of quality from manufacturing we need to be asking ourselves what quality actually means in the local situation in which health care and education are actually delivered.

References

Ainley, P. (1994) *Degrees of Difference: Higher Education in the 1990s*, London: Lawrence & Wishart.

Allen, P. M. (1998) 'Evolving complexity in social science', in G. Altman and W. A. Koch (eds) *Systems: New Paradigms for the Human Sciences*, New York: Walter de Gruyter.

Ashby, W. R. (1945) 'The effects of control on stability', *Nature*, 155: 242–243.

Ashby, W. R. (1952) *Design for a Brain*, New York: Wiley.

Ashby, W. R. (1956) *Introduction to Cybernetics*, New York: Wiley.

Barry, J., Chandler, J. and Clark, H. (2001) 'Between the ivory tower and the academic assembly line', *Journal of Management Studies*, 38, 1: 35–42.

Beer, S. (1979) *The Heart of the Enterprise*, Chichester: Wiley.

Beer, S. (1981) *The Brain of the Firm*, Chichester: Wiley.

Calnan, M. and Ferlie, E. (2003) 'Analysing process in healthcare: the methodological and theoretical challenges', *Policy and Politics*, 31, 2: 185–193.

Checkland, P. B. (1981) *Systems Thinking, Systems Practice*, Chichester: Wiley.

Currie, G. (1999) 'The influence of middle managers in the business planning process: a case study in the UK NHS', *British Journal of Management*, 10: 141–155.

Elias, N. (2000/1939) *The Civilizing Process*, Oxford: Blackwell.

Elias, N. (1978/1970) *What is Sociology?*, Oxford: Blackwell.

Ferlie, E., Fitzgerald, L. and Wood, M. (2000) 'Getting evidence into clinical practice: an organizational perspective', *Journal of Health Services and Policy*, 5, 2: 96–102, The Royal Society of Medicine Press.

Ferner, A. (1988) *Governments, Managers and Industrial Relations: Public Enterprise and their Political Environment*, Oxford: Blackwell.

Fitzgerald, I., Rainnie, A. and Stirling, J. (1996) 'Coming to terms with quality:

UNISON and the restructuring of local government', *Capital and Class*, 59: 103–134.

Fitzgerald, L. and Ferlie, E. (2000) 'Professionals: back to the future', *Human Relations*, 53, 3: 713–739.

Fitzgerald, L., Ferlie, E. and Hawkins, C. (2003) 'Innovation in healthcare: how does credible evidence influence professionals?', *Health and Social Care in the Community*, 11, 3: 219–228.

Fonseca, J. (2002) *Complexity and Innovation in Organizations*, London: Routledge.

Forrester, J. (1961) *Industrial Dynamics*, Cambridge, MA: MIT Press.

Gleick, J. (1988) *Chaos: The Making of a New Science*, London: William Heinemann.

Goldstein, K. (1939) *The Organism*, New York: American Book Co.

Goodwin, B. (1994) *How the Leopard Changed its Spots*, London: Weidenfeld & Nicolson.

Griffin, D. (2002) *The Emergence of Leadership: Linking self-organization and ethics*, London: Routledge.

Griffin, D. and Stacey, R. (eds) (2005) *Complexity and the Experience of Leading Organizations*, London: Routledge.

Hardy, C. (1991) 'Pluralism, power and collegiality in universities', *Financial Accountability and Management*, 7, 3: 127–142.

Jackson, M. C. (2000) *Systems Approaches to Management*, New York: Kluwer.

Kant, I. (1790/1987) *Critique of Judgment*, trans. W. S. Pluhar, Indianapolis, IN: Hackett.

Kast, P. and Rosenzweig, F. (1970) *Management and Organization*, New York: McGraw-Hill.

Kauffman, S. A. (1995) *At Home in the Universe*, New York: Oxford University Press.

Langley, A., Mintzberg, H., Pitcher, P., Posada, E. and Saint-Macary, J. (2001) 'Opening up decision making: the view from the black stool', *Organization Science*, 6, 3: 260–279.

Lozeau, D., Langley, A. and Denis, J. (2002) 'The corruption of managerial techniques by organizations', *Human Relations*, 55, 5: 537–564.

Macklis, R. D. (2001) 'Successful patient safety initiatives: driven from within', *Group Practice Journal*, November/December: 65–91.

Mead, G. H. (1932) *The Philosophy of the Present*, Chicago, IL: University of Chicago Press.

Mead, G. H. (1934) *Mind, Self and Society*, Chicago, IL: University of Chicago Press.

Mead, G. H. (1938) *The Philosophy of the Act*, Chicago, IL: University of Chicago Press.

Middlehurst, R. and Elton, L. (1992) 'Leadership and management in higher education', *Studies in Higher Education*, 17, 3: 251–264.

Midgley, G. (2000) *Systemic Intervention: Philosophy, Methodology, and Practice*, New York: Kluwer.

Parker, M. and Jary, D. (1995) 'The McUniversity: organization, management and academic subjectivity', *Organization*, 2, 2: 319–338.

Pendleton, A. and Winterton, J. (1993) *Public Enterprise in Transition: Industrial Relations in State and Privatised Corporations*, London: Routledge.

Prichard, C. (2000) *Making Managers in Universities and Colleges*, Buckingham: Open University Press.

Prichard, C. and Willmott, H. (1997) 'Just how managed is the McUniversity?', *Organization Studies*, 18, 2: 287–316.

Prigogine, I. and Stengers, I. (1984) *Order out of Chaos: Man's New Dialogue with Nature*, New York: Bantam Books.

Senge, P. M. (1990) *The Fifth Discipline: The Art and Practice of the Learning Organization*, New York: Doubleday.

Shaw, P. (2002) *Changing Conversations in Organizations: A complexity approach to change*, London: Routledge.

Shelley, S. (2002) 'Marketising control? A cross-occupational study of work in UK universities', University of Hertfordshire (unpublished thesis).

Stacey, R. (2001) *Complex Responsive Processes in Organizations: Learning and knowledge creation*, London: Routledge.

Stacey, R. (ed.) (2005) *Experiencing Emergence in Organizations: Local interaction and the emergence of global pattern*, London: Routledge.

Stacey, R., Griffin, D. and Shaw, P. (2000) *Complexity and Management: Fad or radical challenge to systems thinking?*, London: Routledge.

Streatfield, P. (2001) *The Paradox of Control in Organizations*, London: Routledge.

von Bertalanffy, L. (1968) *General Systems Theory: Foundations, Development, Applications*, New York: George Braziller.

Wiener, N. (1948) *Cybernetics: Or Control and Communication in the Animal and the Machine*, Cambridge, MA: MIT Press.

Williams, R. (2005) 'Leadership, power and problems of relating in processes of organizational change', in D. Griffin and R. Stacey (eds) *Complexity and the Experience of Leading Organizations*, London: Routledge.

Editors' introduction
to Chapter 3

In this chapter, Richard Williams, formerly Principal and CEO of a major further education college in the UK and now CEO of a large charitable organization, draws our attention to what it means to do leadership in today's education sector. He does this by presenting a narrative account of a short meeting with the Chairman of his Board of Governors. In doing this he makes us aware of the relational nature of leadership and how this immediately constrains what he can do as a leader. He is answerable in many ways to his Chairman, and both of them, as leaders, are constrained by their legal contracts and by the policies of the government regarding education. What he is emphasizing here is how leaders in the public sector, and in any organization for that matter, mediate policies that are not of their own devising and, indeed, may be contrary to their own values in many ways. He says that leaders are constrained to be local advocates of macro policies so that leadership involves a preoccupation with the administration of power and authority to create a framework of discipline within which others in the organization must work. This way of seeing leaders and leadership stands in stark contrast to the conventional way of writing, talking and teaching leadership. This dominant way presents an image of the leader as a lone individual who decides on visions and strategies, inspiring and enthusing others to share these with him or her. The result is a highly idealized view of leadership which Williams describes as a cult of leadership.

The chapter provides a review of the work being done by the Learning and Skills Research Centre to devise a national policy on developing leaders for the further and higher education sector. This work identifies different leadership typologies appropriate to different contexts and proceeds on the assumption that people can be trained at national leadership colleges to acquire the competencies required to practise leadership appropriate to context. Williams argues that these typologies are idealizations, and rest on an unexamined and rather dubious assumption that people can be trained to switch leadership styles according to the context within which they find themselves. Instead he suggests that the implicit motive of this approach is to train leaders who will act as the instruments of government policy, implementing the modern performance and surveillance regime.

From his own experience, Williams finds this cult of performance and surveillance highly problematic because of, among other reasons, the instrumental use that is made of public shaming to keep people in line. He shows, in his own experience, how entrenched public sector policy now is in the micro detail of everyday lived experience of leaders in educational institutions. These leaders now have personal accountability for the delivery of performance targets determined by the government, leading to a work ethic in which ontological security is contingent upon sustaining a performance of success. Williams describes the deep-seated ontological insecurity this has created in the educational sector and the almost intolerable stress that people in his position now experience. He also points to how people in his position, in the climate of fear created by the cult of performance, feel that they cannot contest what is happening without taking enormous risks in terms of their own position and the position of their organization. It is only when people retire or move to another career that they feel able to speak out about their experience.

In contrast to the idealized view of leadership found in the dominant discourse, Williams argues that leadership is about understanding the nature of participation in human processes of relating and therefore of ethics. For him leadership is not the attributes of an autonomous individual but a social and relational process which involves a great deal of vulnerability and emotion on the part of the leader, and the leader plays an important if unintentional part in the fantasy and emotional life of others in the organization. He describes modern public sector organizations as places of high anxiety and threats to identity.

For us, this chapter is important because it:

● Critiques the highly idealized views of leading and leadership to be found in mainstream discourse and explores instead, in some detail, the experience of ordinary, everyday leading and the role that idealizations of the leader and of leadership play in organizational life.

- Presents an alternative understanding of what 'practical' means in discussion about leadership. The normal expectation is that leadership training should provide people with 'tools' and 'techniques' which they can use in the practice of leading. The idealized nature of these 'tools' and 'techniques' is usually ignored. What Williams finds practical is the activity of reflecting seriously on one's own experience as a leader interacting with others.
- Makes us aware of the constraints on leaders and how they are pressured into mediating the wider requirements of government and society in their own organizations. It becomes clear how leaders in educational organizations are being used as instruments of the cult of performance and surveillance which now prevails in public sector policy.
- Describes the consequences for people of this performance and surveillance cult in terms of threats to identity, anxiety and ontological insecurity, pointing to how leaders in the sector are effectively silenced in a culture of fear.
- Underlines the dubious ethics of the instrumental public shaming upon which the performance cult depends.

Williams also explores his experience of leading in the public sector in other volumes in this series. He wrote a chapter called 'Leadership, power and problems of relating in processes of organizational change' in *Complexity and the Experience of Leading Organizations* (edited by D. Griffin and R. Stacey), and another chapter, 'Experiencing national education policies in local interaction', in *Experiencing Emergence in Organizations: Local interaction and the emergence of global pattern* (edited by R. Stacey).

3 The experience of leading public sector organizations in a performance management regime

Richard Williams

- The Leading Learning Project
- Complex responsive processes and the thinking of G. H. Mead
- A meeting
- Conflict, power, emergence
- Affectual responsiveness
- Seeing leadership differently

In January 2004 I resigned from my post as principal of a large inner city college of further education to take up a new post as CEO of a national charity working with young people across the UK. Coincident with my resignation I received a copy of the first report from the Learning and Skills Research Centre (LSRC) arising from a new national project that investigates 'effective leadership for improving performance in post-compulsory learning'. Living with the experience of resignation from one organization and career path and the thought of starting a new job at the head of a very different type of organization made me particularly alert to the questions, themes and issues raised in this report. Reading it triggered a series of personal reflections about my role, the personal and organizational meaning of this and the wider context in which I enact it.

The Leading Learning Project

Leading Learning: International Comparator Contexts (LSRC, 2004) is a significant report because of its provenance (sponsored by a major government department) and audience (the current leaders and senior managers of further and higher education in the UK). Copies of this document were sent to the principals/heads of every post-16 institution in the further and higher education sectors. It was sent also to ministers and senior policy-makers charged with tackling the leadership problem as they perceive it to exist across post-16 education. In the past ten years the post-16 learning and skills sector has moved progressively to the centre of government policy with regard to the drive for economic competitiveness and prosperity. Within a policy paradigm of a globalized knowledge economy, education and skills, and therefore the leadership of the key institutions charged with delivering the national education and skills agenda, are issues of front-line policy and political significance. The research questions of the report therefore reflect the policy debate taking place among ministers and senior policy-makers in relation to the nature of what is deemed to be effective leadership and how this can be nurtured within the wider public sector reform agenda.

The questions which those engaged in the Leading Learning Project are concerned with are set out in the following terms on the cover of their document: 'What is leadership, who makes it happen and how does it improve organizations?' The report therefore sets out to discover whether 'researchers and practitioners in other public services in the UK and abroad have found answers to these questions'. Interestingly, the principal conclusion of the report is that a great deal of further 'empirical' research is needed.

I reflect upon my particular interest in this report in the following terms. I have been in senior management roles in education now for much longer than I was ever a teacher. While I have worked in further education for twenty-five years, I have been in non-teaching management and leadership roles for eighteen of these. Now I approach the later stages of my career also working in a leadership capacity, albeit in a different organization and sector of employment. Throughout this period, I have engaged in a great deal of personal development activity as a participant in training and academic programmes of various sorts in an attempt to come to my own understanding of the questions posed by the LSRC researchers. I have never felt confident of my understanding of what 'leadership' in organizations actually *is*, or of my ability to explain or account for what I do in a leadership role that accords with the kind of well-ordered typologies so often presented by organizational theorists. Notwithstanding my efforts, I, like the researchers, have never been able to answer these questions in a way that has proved satisfying. At times, coming away from a particular encounter with a new set of ideas about leadership and management, I have found myself to be in the grip of what I thought would turn out to be this critical insight: I think of my enthusiasm for Senge's work (1990) on the learning organization as the most significant of such experiences. After a period of immersing myself in the ideas associated with *The Fifth Discipline*, I found that my everyday experiences of being with others at work would give rise to circumstances that contradicted the explanatory force of these insights. I could no longer make sense of what I believed my experiences to be in terms of the theoretical position with which I had aligned my then current thinking.

The terms of reference presented by the Leading Learning researchers are, I would argue, suggestive of a series of other unstated assumptions about causality that are a feature of the thinking which dominates present discourses about leadership and management. For example, effective leadership is said to *cause* improved performance. By implication, ineffective leadership is a barrier to improving performance. It is therefore implied that leadership constitutes a function in organizations, the parameters of which can be defined, trained for and directed at specific outcomes. Further, the idea of training for leadership (as represented, for example, in the further education national leadership college initiative launched in 2003) implies that it is possible to identify and develop a national cohort of leaders equipped with essential skills and knowledge whose behaviours at work will result in desirable organizational outcomes. Then the nirvana of continuous improvement will be realized; institutions will stop 'failing'; targets will be met; and policy objectives realized. Adversity would be explained by events occurring outside of human control: random, catastrophic events that no one could foretell or be held accountable for. The logic of the argument is in the idea that persons can be developed and then guided in peer and other support networks, whose behaviours at work will shape only the positive desirable outcomes of continuous improvement understood, of course, in terms of the performance management criteria against which such judgements are determined.

In their comprehensive review of the literature, the LSRC researchers identify six leadership typologies: transactional leadership; transformational leadership; servant leadership; empowerment, super-leadership and self-management leadership; synergistic leadership; and distributed leadership. Against each of these typologies they describe a series of behaviours that in some way exemplify the description. Transformational leadership, for example, entails engendering 'high levels of motivation and commitment among followers/members in order to achieve high performance'. This is in contrast to transactional leadership, where the focus is on 'leader–member relations' and 'situational contexts'. Super-leaders, however, act as

> teacher and coach rather than dictator and autocrat, therefore increasing employees' feelings of personal control and intrinsic motivation. Defined as 'someone who leads others to lead themselves', super-leadership is linked closely to self-management leadership and stresses the 'person-centred' aspects arising in situation theory.
>
> (LSRC, 2004, pp. 5–8)

In conclusion, the LSRC researchers identify two possible approaches to thinking about a leadership development strategy. The first follows the lines of a competency model in which lists of personal attributes and skills are identified and according to which individuals are then trained. The second approach acknowledges that the behaviour of those in leadership roles is 'contingent on the situations faced and also dependent and interdependent on the behaviour and response of others. In such situations, leadership should be regarded as a dynamic and living activity, an ongoing process of emergent interaction with emergent properties' (LSRC, 2004, p. 11). In recognition of this latter possibility, the researchers' recommendations are that programmes involving such activities as 360-degree feedback may be a more valid part of a larger process understood as a 'leadership development journey' than training focused upon notions of competency. But while they acknowledge the difficulties inherent in 'specifying' universally valid leadership typologies and suggest a need to view the behaviours of those in leadership roles against the particularities of their context, the researchers go on to offer a model setting out in four quadrants a Learning and Skills Research Centre Leadership Framework. This attempts to match the dimensions or possibilities for leadership behaviours according to contexts described as prescribed; collective; emergent; and individual (LSRC, 2004, pp. 10–16).

The researchers' task is to answer a question posed in three parts: What is leadership? What is effective leadership? How does effective leadership result in improved organizational performance? Working backwards, the crucial question is that of organizational performance. This is because the researchers are tasked with the problem of discovering and describing the kinds of behaviour on the part of individuals in designated responsibility positions that lead to organizational effectiveness. The question of what constitutes organizational effectiveness is not one that the researchers pay any attention to. Rather, they incorporate the generalized assumption that effectiveness is evidenced by continuous quality improvement. This too is self-referential in that both 'quality' and 'improvement' in public sector organizations are defined in terms of an organization's perceived ability to meet targets and service standards set by the policy agenda prevailing in government. Not only are the targets set in this way, so too are the definitions or measurements of effective performance. Thus for me, the underlying question being explored in this research, as in so many other publicly funded research projects of this type, is that of how behaviours which have a negative impact on the achievement of perceived system objectives can be identified and eliminated and, by contrast, how positive behaviours can be identified, modelled and inculcated. How, in effect, can a leadership ideal be realized?

The national leadership college initiative established in further education in 2003 is, I would argue, about just such a process of inculcation. Its establishment in post-16 education, as in the schools sector, is motivated by the belief that successful organizations result from the development and application of appropriate behaviours at every level of the organization. Distributed leadership models, as favoured in this current thinking, therefore demand comprehensive development programmes in which the training required of people heading institutions is cascaded or replicated down the line management structure. At root here is a belief, consecrated in the commitment of very large sums of public money, of a leadership ideal.

A powerfully linear notion of time and change is associated with this particular piece of LRSC research, as with most thinking about policy and issues of accountability in the public sector. At the macro-sociological level of governments and globalized corporations, Giddens has referred to such thought processes as thinking that attempts to 'colonize the future' (Giddens, 1991). Policy and business objectives are set against visions of the way in which they will be, at some point, understood as a future state. The operational task is then to move towards this colonized state, colonized because it is this sense of vision (manifesto pledges, organizational mission statements, business plans) that constitutes the good and in relation to which those in positions of power seek to order the world. The dominant leadership discourse shares exactly this perspective. Leaders have visions which they translate into goals and objectives. In the public sector context, of course, vision is increasingly that of a local interpretation of a national policy priority. Leaders imbued with supra-normal powers of communication motivate others to identify with these goals sufficiently to move an organization through time towards its predestined goal. Giddens situates much of what he describes as the anxiety of modernity in the process of pursuing the closure of the envisioned gap between experienced here-and-now reality and these fantasies of a colonized future. The idealization of leadership models linked to notions of continuous improvement is what I recognize in the preoccupations of LSRC researchers. It is also a pattern of thinking that provides the impulse to the increased use of supervision and surveillance technologies in organizational management, to know of and to be able to act, in order to limit the emergence of perverse, deviant and non-compliant behaviours and events that may distract from the realization of an envisaged goal state.

Complex responsive processes and the thinking of G. H. Mead

By contrast with this thinking, my argument is that the leadership role in organizations should be understood in a radically different way. I think that it is possible and meaningful to professional practice to do this in terms of the thinking associated with the idea of complex responsive processes (Stacey *et al.*, 2000; Stacey, 2001). This idea I take to refer to the way in which our experience (conscious and unconscious) as human beings emerges from the patterning of interaction occurring as we act with others socially together in a living present. This is a creative temporal process in which action in the present is stimulated by a sense of a future yet to come in the context of accounting for the past. The idea of a living present encapsulates this sense of perpetual temporal process: action occurring in a spatio-temporal locus oriented towards a future, influenced by and influencing accounts of the past, that in turn is realized in experience as an ongoing sense of the present. From such a perspective, human relating:

> is understood as communicative interaction in which power relations emerge. Individual minds/selves and social relationships, individual and collective identities, are all understood as aspects of the same phenomenon, namely, relating. There is no separation between individuals as one level and groups, organizations and societies as another level.
>
> (Stacey, 2001, p. 6)

To take such a perspective, it is essential in my view to stand back from the systems paradigm in which those in leadership and management roles are seen as agents situated in a part/whole relation to their organizations. Rather, I would argue that leaders and managers in organizations need to be understood as participants (albeit with a specific and qualitatively different kind of power weight from that of other participants) in an ongoing process of human relating. The conduct of leaders and managers is, as is that of others, enabled and constrained by the emergent qualities of the localized power relations that form their lived experience and in relation to which their own conduct is integral. Within this different way of thinking about leadership and management, I believe that it is therefore necessary to understand the importance of power, and power relating to processes of identity formation. I think too that the frailty of identity formation processes, the immanence of chaos in working lives and the struggle for personal survival in a living present are of fundamental significance to understanding the nature of leadership in organizations. For each of us, the development of a personal narrative account that makes sense to us of our presence in our ongoing relationships with others is fundamental to our life process. Irrespective of whether we work in the public or the private sector, most of us spend a large part of our lives doing this in the context of organizations (Czarniawska, 1998; Knights and Willmott, 1999). Understanding leadership, I would argue, is foremost a question of understanding the nature of our participation in human processes of relating and therefore of ethics. It is this argument that I want to develop in this chapter.

This argument, I believe, may be sustained without recourse to the kind of typological models of human relating and behaviour that typify so much modern management theory. Here I am referring to the tendency to construct diagrammatic representations of idealized behaviour modes as if these represented real individual strategic choices. The implication of such thinking is that leaders skilled enough for the task are free to select, using their reasoning powers, behaviour types (preferred leadership styles) according to their judgements regarding context. The LSRC research is based on such thinking, where it is implied that leaders can, by a process of rational choice, select behaviours to maximize their influence and so optimize their power weight relative to the perceived goals/needs of their organization. This thinking, I would argue, is symptomatic of the extent to which cybernetic assumptions have become entrenched in a dominant discourse which links the performative characteristics of organizations (for example, continuous quality improvement) directly with the application of models of leadership behaviour.

Here I want to introduce the thinking of G. H. Mead and specifically his conception of social objects (Mead, 2001, [1932] 2002). By social object Mead meant something that arises in perception and which is other than a physical object or an object purely of our imagination (so-called scientific objects). Social objects are the generalized patterns of gestures and responses emerging from human interaction. Social objects are, at the same time, our perceptions of action on the part of others and the feelings or tendencies to action that are aroused in us as we participate socially one with another. It is our ability to hold such objects in our reflexive awareness of our social environment that enables us to be actors within it, just as it is our perception of physical objects that enables and constrains our action in the physical world. Objects in perception are what Mead described as the 'stuff' of images and then ultimately, once signified in words and language use, the material through which we are able to communicate our sense of our experiences to others as significant symbols. Social objects, argued Mead, allow us to frame responses to our social context as we are able to both generalize and symbolize in language and word structures patterns of human interaction.

Understood in terms of Mead's philosophy, *leadership* refers to particular socialized tendencies for action, and as such is a type of social object that both enables and constrains ongoing patterns of human relating. It is specifically the social dimension of this process that I am interested in for the purposes of thinking about leadership. In the concept of social object, Mead, in my view, creates a powerful link between an account of how we experience the world phenomenologically and how, arising from the way in which we order this experience, we are able to act, where action is constrained by the emergence of particular mores of social conduct, and how, in turn, these are reflected in the language symbols we use to socialize our experience:

> Ideas are closely related to images. . . . Since the symbols with which we think are largely recognized as word images, ideas and images have a very close consanguinity. . . . Particularly do our habitual responses to familiar objects constitute for us the ideas of these objects. The definitions we give of them are the sure signs by which we can arouse identical or like attitudes in others. I am [interested] in the fact that as organized responses of the organism they enter into the experience we call conscious. That is, the organism responds to these organized attitudes in their relations to objects as it does to other parts of its world. And thus these become objects for the individual.
>
> (Mead, [1932] 2002, p. 97)

For Mead, institutions such as the church or a political party were good examples of what he meant by social object. For example, a church is a building. But the church is also more fundamentally a particular aspect of ongoing social processes of group formation in which human beings enact self-similar behaviours expressed in the form of roles that are taken up (priest, parishioner), and associated with which are other complex sets of behaviour involving attitudes, assumptions and rituals. Leadership, and particularly that reflected in the notion of a chief executive officer, is, I would argue, a social object in the Meadian sense of the term. Understood in these terms, *leadership* is clearly social and relational. As an object codified in language, leadership is constituted in the assumptions and values regarding the conduct of individuals occupying particular social roles. Leadership can therefore occur only relationally. As with Hegel's master/servant example, leaders can only enact leadership in the presence of followers. It is this process of mutuality, of recognition in the Hegelian sense, reproduced in human interaction, that enables leadership identities to emerge. Recognition is the normalizing aspect of conduct which in turn provides sufficient stability for identity to be felt and perceived across time and space.

Mead, however, also developed his thinking about the relationship existing between social objects and social values. Indeed, Mead argued that one of the functions of institutions was to preserve their identity via the preservation of the values with which they were associated in society. At times, as in the instance of the church, the values represent what Mead described as 'idealizations' of what the institution should be but which it does not in reality fully represent. Mead's attack on what he perceived to be the hypocrisy of the church should be understood in terms of this argument. Such values, Mead suggested, take the form of an allegiance to a cult: 'cult values'. Mead saw the preservation of cultishness as being contingent upon a particular psychology which he described as follows:

> The psychological technique of maintaining . . . a cult is the presentation by the imagination of a social situation free from the obstacles which forbid the institution being what it should be, and we organize social occasions which in every way favor such a frame of mind.
>
> (Mead, 1923, p. 240)

And:

> The emotional attitude in the cult of an institution flows from the very obstacles that defeat its proper functioning. We may become

profoundly interested in the reform of an institution for better service, but if we wish to appraise it emotionally, we envisage the wrongs, the vice, the ignorance, the selfishness which the ideal of the institution condemns, and which frustrate its operation.

(Mead, 1923, p. 241)

My argument is that the dominant discourse regarding leadership and the expectations of those deemed to occupy leadership roles in organizations may be understood in terms of Mead's observations concerning social objects and cult values. These attributions have a particular socio-cultural history that Douglas Griffin has described in his review of the emergence of our contemporary sense of leadership as a phenomenon, via Kant, of eighteenth-century philosophy. Griffin also describes this in terms of the development of systems thinking and its application to organizations. Leadership, therefore, involves taking up a role whose meaning exists in the practice of social relationships between people. It is only on this basis that leadership is functionalized in ongoing processes of human relating. As these relationships, patterns of mutual recognition, become reproduced in the turbulence of the wider social process, so too are the possibilities for individual behaviour enabled and constrained. As Griffin has observed:

All cult values, those esteemed by various groups in society as good or bad, as harmful or beneficial, are seen as grist to the mill of everyday social interaction in which they become functional values as the source of conflicts which both sustain identity and bring about change. Cult values are a vital part of the past and, as they are functionalized in the movement of the living present, social and personal identities are recreated and potentially transformed as people together construct their future.

(Griffin, 2002, p. 117)

Mead argued that there is no such thing as an absolute value. By contrast, leadership theorists, such as those engaged in the LSRC research programme, are participants in a process, the aim of which is both to define absolutely the meaning (value) of organizational leadership and to functionalize this meaning as a norm of professional conduct. This process is of itself an exemplification of processes of power relating within which one group seeks to legitimate its perception of the good as a norm of social conduct more generally. Since we recognize exceptional cases relative to norms, it is the normative conditions attaching to leadership roles which enable identities to be formed by those acting within such roles and those acting in relation to them. Since the issue of the determination of norms is clearly also an issue of power, conflict and authority, it also becomes one of ideology.

If these issues apply to the determination of the idea of what is leadership in organizations, the practice of leadership is itself also fundamentally about the administration of power and authority sufficient to sustain the stability in patterns of human relating for identity formation to occur. These power relations, I would argue, involve simultaneously the coincident actions of those in authority whose ongoing behaviours reproduce the mechanics of shame and threats to identity and those of their designated followers. Thus normative behaviours are also established by all of us in the context of the movement of these power relations as we take up the attitudes of what Mead described as the 'generalized other'. By this he meant the habits, routines and expectations that are associated with particular social roles and functions. This is the social process that Elias described as figuration (Elias, [1939] 2000), which he understood as the perpetual movement of relations between people as they enable and constrain each other. Management processes, I would argue, work in just this way across a continuum of compliance, the dimensions of which range between coercion and consent, to establish the roles in which individuals' identities at work are constructed and ordered according to the perceived primary tasks of the organization. It is therefore necessarily an aspect of the social object of leadership, as it is presently configured, that the supra-administration of the ordering of power across an organization be identified ultimately with the person deemed to represent the apex of the organizational hierarchy. Understood in terms of power relating, it is clear also that a process of leadership is a process of conflict. Since individual identity emerges in the movement of power relations occurring between bodies acting in the living present, identity itself is always in construction and always at the edge of chaos.

I would also argue that, in taking the social object of leader, one who occupies a perceived leadership role will also necessarily become an object in the affectual responses of those to whom they are directly and less directly related. Emotion, I would argue, is aroused in anticipation of, in the course of and in reflection of interactions between living human bodies. Processes of human interaction are both enabled and constrained in contexts of power relating. Power relating of itself implies differences and inequalities. At its most basic, the interchange of speech acts between individuals entails turn-taking. This requires knowledge and acceptance of rules, and a willingness to take and to let go of positions of pre-eminence in the movement of a relationship. In a more complex organizational setting, turn-taking includes notions of entitlement as to who is able to say what to whom, when and in what context. And as this process of interaction is amplified across the organizational context and intensified in its scale and detail, so then we are all caught up in patterns of behaviour whose themes and counter-themes challenge and create risk for our abilities to sustain our presence, recognition and identities in relation to and with each other. Modern organizations are places of high anxiety in which threats to identity are a norm of the processes of power relating that underwrite their apparent cohesion.

My narrative, presented in the following section, explores these themes. In it I attempt to shift the locus of my presence in the organization from one who in the dominant paradigm would be viewed as someone in high-level control to one who is clearly a participant. In the narrative I attempt to expose something of my own vulnerability to others as I, a participant actor, work also within the constraints of power and affect to sustain my own identity. I try also to illustrate in this narrative the significance of my presence for the identity of others with whom I am associated. I try to present a sense of how my gestures elicit responses from others which in turn transform the meaning of my actions in terms both of their social significance and of my own affectual responses. Finally, in my narrative account I attempt to exemplify the emergent nature of conflict and to point also to its destructive and creative possibilities in a way that would be consistent with Mead's concept of creativity.

A meeting

It is 7.30 a.m. on a Wednesday and I am sitting in the company of my chairman in an 'Italian' coffee shop in the middle of Covent Garden in central London. This is our now regular meeting place for our weekly one-to-one meeting. These meetings are always in the diary. If one of us cannot make it one week (for example, my chairman's job role can take him abroad quite often) then the agreement is that we cancel but turn up as arranged for the next one.

The practicalities of simply being in this coffee shop at 7.30 a.m. mean that I have to start my day at 5.30 a.m. in order to catch a train early enough to make sure that I am on time. Most weeks, my job involves me in an evening meeting of some sort. Often, these take place on a Wednesday. The ritual of my meeting with the chairman can therefore mean that I may leave home before 6.30 a.m. and not get back before 11 p.m. It is not uncommon for me to have more than one evening commitment of this sort a week. On occasions, when I am working with a particularly full diary of meetings and appointments, or managing some especially stressful project or other aspect of my job, this Wednesday morning meeting will have the effect of stretching my working week to the extent that by the weekend I have the sensation of jet-lag: a disorientation with respect to time and body function.

Suburban train services in London are notoriously unreliable, and sometimes my train will be late getting into Waterloo station. I remember on one occasion, during a particularly cold period in the winter, waiting for forty minutes for a train to arrive as a result of various delays and cancellations. Aware of my chairman sitting at our meeting place waiting for me, I called him on my mobile phone to apologize for being late. He did not answer and I was put through to his message service. I caught myself thinking how absurd it was to be standing completely alone, so early on a freezing cold winter's morning that was still pitch dark, apologizing for being late for a meeting. I was aware too of my mounting feelings of stress and anxiety at not being able to explain my lateness and the prospect of arriving so late that the meeting would be pointless. I was anxious too that my reason for lateness would not be understood and that my chairman might think, simply, that I had missed my alarm and slept in. I recall also having stood on the station in the grip of a rising feeling of panic at the idea of lateness, and wondering just how early I would have to get up and catch a train in order to fully hedge the risk of delay.

My chairman is a senior executive in a multinational energy company. He has worked for the same organization for over thirty years. He joined this company immediately after leaving university and, as his career has developed, he has risen to a role that makes him responsible for a number of the company's operations in Europe. I feel, however, that the ritual of our Wednesday morning meetings is part of a process in which we, rather pointlessly, enact stereotypical public/private sector differences. *Me*: feeling resentful at the idea of turning up for what in the winter is a crack-of-dawn encounter with the person to whom I am most directly accountable. *He*: adamant in his insistence that the demands of business upon business executives are such that a meeting of this kind and in this place is a reasonable everyday sort of occurrence. For these reasons, my attitude to these meetings is always ambivalent. I do value the opportunity that these meetings give for us to be together regularly on a private basis. At the same time, I feel the timing of the meetings, his insistence upon them happening, even if some weeks he gets up and leaves after thirty or forty minutes, are part of a ritualized display of petty authority. I know that I would not suggest such an arrangement myself. I am conscious too of my sense of feeling unable to challenge this ritual on a basis that would enable these meetings to happen with the same regularity but at a different time. In sensing that such questioning would be a confrontation, my feelings of petty tyranny are reinforced. I sense that my affectual response to this ritual has become one of tiredness. It is a routine that I know that I do not want to have to sustain into the indefinite future.

My relationship with this man is undoubtedly the most significant of my working life. When I was appointed to my first principal role eight years ago, he was vice-chairman of the board of governors. Apart from two years in that period he has been 'my chairman' ever since. This is a particular relationship of personal and professional intensity that I share with no one else. It is only when in a CEO role that it is possible to experience the particular qualities of such a relationship. Anyone other than the CEO will experience such a relationship secondhand. How he and I judge this relationship is therefore crucial to our ongoing ability to continue together, for the perceived integrity of key organizational management processes and for the wider reputation (internal and external) of the organization. The chairman sets my annual objectives on behalf of the board. He also conducts my appraisal and makes recommendations to the remuneration committee of the board with respect to my terms and conditions. The chairman is also my unofficial sounding-board and confidant in the way in which I am able to mediate or represent the views of senior managers to the board and/or my first line of defence and support when something 'difficult' has to be done or has gone wrong. I therefore have to be open with my chairman but not to the extent of revealing the full extent of my doubts, anxieties, the full detail of what is not 'going right' in the institution, such that he would lose confidence in his sense of my ability to be in control of my job and the institution.

What I say to the chairman is therefore always in some way based upon an assessment of the risk of what I am making available to him. As I write this, I realize that I am describing a process that is far less deliberative than it appears in text. I think of this awareness as the application of a process of self-restraint that operates mostly in an unconscious reflexive way as the chairman and I move through our conversations together. I am aware too that this is how people respond to me when they interact with me at work. Somehow being present in the face of authority constrains what it is that each of us feels we can say in a way that reflects our sense of risk. The disclosure to a present authority figure of what appear in the moment to be our innermost anxieties can in turn carry the implications of destructiveness of ourselves, our identities, in our relations with this other. My sense is that what any of us is willing to disclose to another is also in some way related to the degree of apparent distance that exists between us in terms of hierarchical order or position. As a CEO, I am conscious always of working with narratives that are very highly mediated by this sense of anxiety that is conveyed by the role and which, in this narrative, I am exploring in my relationship with my chairman.

The CEO–chair relationship is therefore paradoxically at the same time one of intimacy and distance. On balance, I have come to experience this relationship as being integral to the feeling of ultimate isolation that is so characteristic of being the head of an organization, and particularly one that is subject to great pressures for change, scrutiny and accountability. Caught in the middle between my senior team colleagues and the chairman, I will often find myself reviewing with them, in our context of confidence, aspects of my relationship with him that I and they may experience as being particularly difficult or problematic: for example, second-guessing his possible reaction to an event, proposal or issue. By contrast, I also find myself being open with him with regard to personal tensions, performance issues and anxieties within the senior team. The more I have worked with the dynamics of this relational process, the more I have come to understand it as essential to what holds us all together (he, the board of nineteen others, me, my team of four) in that these apparent betrayals of confidence – me talking with him about them, me talking with them about him and, at other times, they and he talking together about me – are what I would describe as essential contexts of discretion in which we are each co-creating a sense of identity and place in the unfolding life of this particular organization.

Today, much of our conversation has been taken up with a discussion of the recent events which led to the dismissal of a staff member for financial dishonesty. Prior to this meeting, I sent a report on the events in question to the chairman. Since I have to chair the appeal panels following instances of staff dismissal, I am not directly involved in first-line disciplinary hearings. I am also required to maintain an independence of view of these proceedings so as not to prejudice the outcome of a possible appeal process. In reality, the closeness with which I and my team work means that it is very unlikely that a process of this sort will be going on in the institution without my knowledge. I think this also exemplifies in some way the differences between the organizational processes that are acknowledged openly and the more covert processes through which power and authority are administered. On this particular occasion, however, the profile of this event within the organization means that I do know quite a lot about the background. My attitude to what has happened and to the dismissal of the staff member is tempered by the fact that while I believe him to have acted in a way that was technically dishonest, I also understand this to have occurred in a context where the conduct of his line managers and other weaknesses inherent in some key financial procedures invited his subsequent actions. Indeed, I understand his anger at his treatment, which he communicated to me and to certain other senior staff members with some force, to be also a reflection of his sense of entrapment by the organization. His argument was that he did what he did in order to get his job done, despite the best efforts of others. I know him to feel scapegoated and I know that I have some sympathy for his feelings. Equally, having attempted to explore this nuance in a senior team meeting, and on a previous occasion with the chairman, I am aware that to err too far on to his side would make me appear tolerant of financial dishonesty in the eyes of other senior staff, the chair and possibly also auditors and the regulatory body. I feel myself to be in conflict with the norms of behaviour expected of someone in my position. As I sense my awareness of this, I am also aware that I have been treading a very fine line in trying to encourage others involved in this case, including the chairman, to see the 'unacceptable' actions of an individual as having emerged from an organizational context rather than from individual pathology. I am aware that I am now pursuing this person's dismissal on the basis of expediency rather than with a genuine belief in, or commitment to, this course of action.

The financial regulations that form an important part of the accountability framework of public sector colleges require instances of fraud and/or serious malpractice to be reported to the regulatory body. This is justified on the basis of ensuring that the system learns from its mistakes. In pursuing this objective the regulators impose a requirement upon the regulated that they engage in a permanent process of self-scrutiny and exposure in order to assure probity and accountability for the application of public funds. In its widest sense, of course, such responsibilities both arouse and build upon the anxieties of individuals that are immanent in all

disclosure processes which are contingent upon the systematic imposition
(by submitting reports, inviting investigations from central audit teams, in
the negative judgements of auditor/investigators) of shame. Periodically,
the regulatory body will circulate good practice guides that draw attention
to weaknesses in the administration of colleges and other public sector
bodies. This reporting and investigation process seems also to me to
be part of a dynamic in which those charged with regulating the system
become ever more suspicious of, and interventionist in, the affairs of
those charged with delivering its services. Most situations one encounters
in this context require a judgement to be made by the CEO (as chief
accounting officer) as to the extent to which an instance of financial
misconduct has to be reported externally. The ability to make such a
judgement is of itself carefully calibrated to maximize the opportunity
for those in regulatory roles to have access to the knowledge that
something might be amiss. Thus the terms of the financial memorandum
between the regulatory body and the institution make it incumbent upon
the CEO, in the first instance, to report 'suspicions' of fraud or financial
irregularity to the local office of the regulatory body. The threshold of
'suspicion' is low. So too is the threshold at which formal notification
of financial irregularity is required to trigger an escalation of the reporting
requirement to the national office. Clearly, a failure of judgement with
respect to satisfying this reporting requirement has the potential to be
construed in a number of ways: complicity, ineptitude or lack of probity.
The capacity for public scandal in relation to any misappropriation
of funds in a public body is therefore considerable.

Knowing the chairman as I do, and have done over many years, I am
aware that he will approach this particular problem with an unqualified
commitment to demonstrating probity. There is unlikely to be the slightest
opportunity for what I think of as greyness in our approach. His instinct
will be to publicize as much of the detail of the case as possible to the full
board, following a thorough exposure of issues and debate within the
audit committee. Only if I am very lucky, or persuasive, will he agree to
holding off reporting all of the detail of the problems that have arisen
to the regulatory body.

As our conversation develops, I sense the tension between us on this
issue. I sense in particular the chairman's body language as he stiffens in
his seat slightly to signify that on this issue he will not be persuaded to
moderate, or to fudge, our intended course of action. I feel myself to be
pushed quite forcibly from the grey zone of the political fix (where after
many years I now feel to be the most comfortable and the most

productive) into the black-and-white zones of no compromise. As I start to argue for a more discrete, less public process of resolution and follow-up, I feel myself lacking in any confidence that my line of argument will result, if I push it, in other than a highly polarized argument from which I will have no option but to back down, given our relative and respective authorities. As I accede to the chairman's proposed 'no other option approach', my mind is already turning to just how I will implement the outcomes of our agreement following this discussion. Will I, yet again, find a way of satisfying the chairman's wishes and instructions and yet at the same time limit the knowledge of these issues and this conversation to those who, in my judgement, will know what to do with the information such that the task can go on of maintaining the front of an ever-improving, well-ordered organization which does not attract undue attention from the regulators or accumulate yet further negative points on the institutional ratings scale? Already, in the flow of this conversation, I am aware that my mind has turned to the issue of how I will go about executing this task.

Conflict, power, emergence

In the narrative of a single meeting with my chairman, I am trying to draw upon features of my everyday experience to explore how those in leadership and management roles actually come to frame their actions and what it is that they can be said to really do. In this way, I am contrasting my sense of lived experience with what I encounter as abstract descriptions of experiences of leadership in which they make strategic choices. Relative to my particular organizational context, my chairman and I occupy the two key positions of power. Viewed from the perspective of this dominant discourse concerning leadership in organizations, it might be argued that my chairman and I are uniquely placed both to choose our behaviour style and to determine a course of action. Yet when the distant gaze of abstract management theory is replaced by the intensity of a personal narrative account of lived experience, it is apparent that this is not what we are doing. When engaged in these conversations, we are not acting in a way that would indicate to a close observer an ability to determine a course of action or behaviour in any way that could be construed as simply rational or the result of strategic choice. Our actions in relation to each other, and to our wider context, are prescribed by a context of power relating that is both codified in the regulations that govern our formal relationship and arises simply from our being together as two human bodies. We struggle to make sense of the meaning of our context and association. Decisions that we make are more like hypotheses upon which we manage momentarily to agree and then seek to test in subsequent action. There is no certainty in any of our deliberations and no foreknowledge of outcomes. The tension that exists between us, which is paradoxically creative and inhibiting, appears to reside in the movement of our feeling states, the arousal of which appears in the patterning of the gestures and responses occurring between us, making it easy or difficult for us to reach agreement. We are engaged with a reality and creating our own reality at the same time.

Between the chairman and me there exists what is now a personal relationship of long standing. We have in some way learned how to be together in this relationship. We meet in a context where our affectual responses to each other are patterned over many years of rehearsal. We can anticipate each other's responses to issues, to our own moods, thinking and demeanour. However, at the same time we encounter each other afresh and with anxieties born of the paradox of knowing, and at the same time not knowing, what will emerge from our interactions. Our personal biographies are radically different. This applies both to our professional backgrounds and to our more personal family histories and routes to our current positions. Thus, in the background of our being together, there are aspects of our deep, private experience that we bring which colour our attitudes to authority, power, status and role. We have acknowledged this background from time to time in short snatches of narrative, personal biography, anecdote. Being together for so long has meant too that milestone events in our personal lives have occurred which we have acknowledged to each other: family illness, births, deaths and job changes. We know too something of each other's politics and therefore predisposition to acceptance of matters of policy. We have from time to time talked with each other about our motivations for doing the jobs (mine paid, his unpaid) that we do in relation to this organization.

Within the formality of our roles we are both conscious of the regulations that inform how we can be together. The roles of CEO and chairman of a further education corporation are set out in the statutory articles governing the conduct of the affairs of such a body. There are things that I am entitled to insist upon (rights and responsibilities) and over which I have authority that are not given to the chairman and vice versa. This circumstance also has a paradoxical effect on our relationship since for either party to insist upon their entitlement to action in accordance with the formal regulatory framework would be taken by the other as evidence of the breakdown of our ability to relate productively. Thus our being together is conducted on a basis in which we speak from behind the wall of these authorities without ever acknowledging them as a boundary.

Our interaction is also taking place within an infinitely multi-faceted context. There are the ongoing events that appear as milestones in the life of the institution and to which our attention is constantly being drawn. The attitudes of others (our assumptions and estimations of these) appear very concretely in our deliberations. If I/we agree to do A or B, what will persons or bodies X or Y say or do? We are highly sensitive to the affectual conditions of others close to us who are physically absent but, at the same time, highly present in these conversations. Will persons C or D be upset, offended, pleased, minded to recognize us differently, more positively, as a result of what we agree to say or do due to this interaction? We talk too about how to influence others; how to get our way; how to make our point; how to plan for the conduct of a meeting in which the outcomes that we desire occur. In summary, our conversation is an exchange of propositions, speculations, uncertainties and fantasies. Our actions are framed according to the extent to which we are able to feel confident of any of these as a basis of reality. And as we go on together, I, for my part, have no sense of whether my fantasies about the chairman's reasoning for us meeting in this way resonate in any way with his own conscious or unconscious motivations. I have no means of knowing whether what I experience as an imposition, an aspect of the irrationality of someone who cannot or will not compromise another set of commitments, is in fact a gesture of absolute altruistic generosity and fellowship. To explore the question would of itself take the relationship dangerously close to the edge of what we have negotiated as being common ground.

Further, when I reflect upon the outcome of these meetings (that is, what is different at 8.30 a.m. from what I believed to be the case at 7.30 a.m.), they are always unpredictable. Something occurs between us which is not as I could have fully anticipated when I and he walked through the door. I would say that these interactions, as all instances of human relating, are a process in which we co-create the sense of reality into which we act and, as we meet over and over again, each week we iterate this co-creative process. At times, when we have not been able to meet for one reason or another, I will experience a sense of loss or disjuncture. This I experience sometimes as a relief (a feeling of being let off from the ritual of this meeting) and at others as a source of anxiety (the loss of a triangulation point). When I think of my experiences of meeting and working with my chairman in this way, I recognize what it is that I spend most of my time doing. I think of this kind of interaction as being typical of how I experience what my life is as I enact my job. The form or pattern of relating obviously changes but not, I would say, in a dramatically significant way. Most of my time is taken up with meeting people on a one-on-one basis (members of my team, significant others involved with the administration of the further education sector, individual staff members). At other times I will sit in or chair meetings of small groups of staff. Less frequently I will interact with large numbers of people from inside or outside of the organization. Whatever the context, I think of the substance of what I experience in a leadership role as being the same. It is an experience of interaction with others within which the specificity of what emerges is not predictable and not within my control.

Here I want to return to the thinking of G. H. Mead. Embedded throughout the above narrative is Mead's concept of the social object. Indeed, without a sense of what Mead referred to in developing this concept, none of us would be able to make sense of the ways in which we categorize each other and the sets of behaviours in relation to which we recognize such categories. To describe myself as a leader, a principal, a CEO, and my chairman in similar terms, is to make use of a Meadian sense of the social object that makes sense of our places and roles in the vocabulary of organizational life. Put another way, as we hold a sense of these objects to ourselves of our positions relative to each other, we take up (again, in Mead's terms) a sense of what he described as the 'generalized other'. By 'generalized other' Mead referred formally to the 'organized social attitudes of the given social group (or of some one section thereof) to which he belongs' (Mead, 1934, p. 156). In Mead's terms, it is in our ability to take on this attitude that we are each able to adhere to a sense of 'me' as distinct from a sense of 'you': that is, of the other. For Mead, what he described as the I–me dialectic is the reflexive relationship of awareness of oneself in a social context that enables identities to be established and reproduced.

If I relate this Meadian conception to my interactions with my chairman, it is clear that neither of us has open to us the possibility of framing a course of action which is either wholly outside of the conventions of our role, or, more significantly, beyond what either of us would be willing to recognize as appropriate to the conduct of our roles. Further, what we will permit or allow of each other will of itself be a function of the qualitative characteristics of this recognition process. Here I am referring particularly to the degree of anxiety which each of us feels in relation to the extent to which we adhere rigidly to what we believe to be the socially contingent behaviours of the role. To exemplify this position, I would contrast the attitude of my current chairman on issues of probity to that of a previous chairman. In one instance, my relationship is with an individual of the left whose career path has been shaped in the context of a highly bureaucratized globalized corporation. In the other instance, my relationship was with an individual whose expectations of behaviour in public life were informed by a background of working in banking, as a director of a small company and with political belief in the tenets of Thatcherism. My experience of the opportunities for difference in the direction and quality of interaction has been that these lead to radically different experiences of being together and in turn of action. The issue is of the qualitative differences of behavior arising from the way in which the notion of role, or social object, or sense of the 'generalized other', was taken up in the lives of the individuals concerned. The qualitative differences that arise in the instances of these relationships are, I would argue, a result of a tension between the norms (of the generalized other) and the values of the actors. Most often in my relationship with my chairman, these distinctions emerge as a source of real interpersonal tension in contexts where I take a more expedient view of what would be the best thing to do in the moment from the one that he takes.

Affectual responsiveness

In my narrative, I describe a range of feelings I have about my job that are very present to my conscious sense of myself in role. I sense myself also as a roulette player, one who in this present context has managed to sustain the front of winning but who now finds the anxiety of this front too much to sustain. What I think of as the emotional dynamics of a leadership role have, in my experience of doing such a job, been a highly significant aspect of the work. Outside of the literature that focuses explicitly on psychodynamic perspectives of work, this aspect of the experience of leadership seems to me to be relatively underexplored. Yet at a time when a great deal of writing seems to recognize the high degree of fantasy that surrounds expectations of the CEO role, in the public sector at least, this thinking has not moved much beyond exhortations to discover one's emotional intelligence, the application of psychometric assessments to appointment processes, and the use of psychological typographies in team-building strategies. In some way,

I suspect that the resistance to thinking about the emotional dynamics of leadership roles, within the policy-forming domains in which studies such as the LSRC paper are located, is due to the possibility of compromising the ease with which it is assumed that blame, shame and accountability are played out.

What the LSRC researchers, and others engaged in similar research (Hay Group, 2002), are offering is a leadership mythology based upon a reified and sanitized representation of organizational change and the roles of staff occupying senior positions. Organizational leadership in the public sector takes place in a context of intense scrutiny and pressure to deliver organizational performance targets that are disaggregated from national outcome measures (Shore and Wright, 2000). In responding to this pressure, those in leadership positions focus on two key variables: the management of information, and the terms and conditions of employees. The focus on information is crucial to the supply of evidence of the achievement of performance indicators and so too of the institution's targets. The focus on terms and conditions of employment iterates as a response to pressures also to increase performance at lower rates of unit cost. In my own experience of working in institutions deemed to be 'failing', the intensity of the focus on such issues is in direct proportion to the degree of assumed 'failure'. Such pressures are sustained by the intervention of regulatory, audit and inspection agencies. These regimes apply right across the public sector, and the fracturing of individuals leading organizations under this pressure sometimes surfaces in the national media as scandals concerning the manipulation of data, the pursuit of speculative business ventures or the emergence of sudden and catastrophic financial failures.

'Leadership', as a process enacted by individuals in the public sector, is situated in this narrative context. It therefore entails the administration of the power centre that enables tighter control of the organizational processes. In my experience, this is the fastest way of demonstrating 'improvement' and it is also a whole organization issue that demands of every employee an acceptance of higher levels of personal control, scrutiny and conformity with standard operating procedures. Leadership is therefore, in part, also a process that entails the imposition of new work disciplines upon a group of employees, justified in terms of the importance of being judged effective. Most often, such changes are accompanied by other more radical attacks on traditional working practices that are deemed to be out of date or inefficient. This in turn has resulted in wholesale contractual change across the public sector: new terms and conditions of employment (flexible contracts), contracting out, restructuring, down-sizing service reorganization, merger and consolidation.

These processes I would argue engender great waves of anxiety, feelings of loss and threats to identity of those caught up in them. They also engender potent insider/outsider feelings, since all these processes entail the identification of winners (those promoted whose status and salaries are enhanced, retained, moved to 'better', 'safer', more secure jobs) and losers (those demoted, made redundant and sidelined). A leadership/CEO position is therefore one that necessarily carries also the potency of any mythical role that is associated with the appearance of absolute powers of creation and destruction.

When I became a college principal, I had in mind a role model from another era. For better or worse, college principals were not CEOs. In my view, the better ones were educationalists. The less able were, with varying degrees of competence, administrators who rose to the top of their profession as managerial amateurs. My fantasy about this pre-1988 way of doing things was that principals practised headship in much the same way that schools' headteachers did and often still do. They were academic or administration leaders of cost centres situated within a vast local authority spending account. They were not, as now, CEOs of complex social businesses operating within an environment in which the ability of government to lever its policy priorities was reflected in huge movements in the sensitivities attached to highly elaborate funding and resource allocation methodologies. My vision, then, at the start of my experience of this role, was to build (as I believed I had seen in the work of the principals who influenced my early thinking) a radical and innovative institution responsive to the educational issues emerging in the inner city.

While I believe that I have tried to sustain something of my early passion and sense of role, I have ceased to believe in the power of an individual to turn the course of events to his or her advantage sufficient to own the capacity to realize something understood as a vision. Increasingly, given the context in which I have chosen to work, I feel like a survivor in a generation of senior managers that has proved highly expendable in moments of adversity. My sense now is that having responded to countless new initiatives for the reform of post-16 education and having managed innumerable rationalization projects, restructuring and cost reduction programmes, my choice is simply to continue to enact a role in which I experience life-cycle repetition and a high degree of stuckness or to commit myself to an experience of the unknown and the radically different. After years of this conundrum, I now have the *feeling* of events having run their course, of fatigue, of having exhausted the possibilities for moving on with the people around me. I would say that from my experience we have become collectively stuck with patterns of relating in which each person can anticipate the actions of the other, where our strengths and weaknesses are accommodated, as too are our expectations formed. It is a sense of fatigue arising from being in one place or context for eight years carrying the appearance of being in control and acting that part when increasingly in the grip of an awareness that this is far from true that I find makes it now impossible for me to commit to sustaining the act that would be necessary to go on in the same place for another five years and five years after that. I am conscious that my own feelings of fatigue appear to typify those experienced by CEOs in large organization settings. It is both the fantasy of omnipotence (more in my experience in the regard of others than oneself) and emotional demands of self-managing high levels of personal anxiety that become intolerable (Haigh, 2004).

Seeing leadership differently

My view of what leaders *do* in organizations, and therefore what leadership *is*, is different from most of what I encounter in standard texts and research concerning good practice in the public sector.

First and foremost I would argue that leadership, at least in public sector settings, involves a preoccupation with the administration of power and authority. As such, leadership entails paying attention to the organizational processes that create a framework of discipline in relation to which others are encouraged to focus on primary organizational tasks. A sense of what constitutes legitimate and ethical primary tasks is often what informs disputes and debates that arise in the daily life of organizations. I am not, therefore, suggesting that effective leadership is the successful imposition of a blanket of conformity. I am suggesting, however, that leaders are the local advocates of macro policies and energizers of processes of control designed to ensure that others enact behaviours that are consistent and compliant with respect to the wider policy orientation of their service. This raises matters of ethics, particularly for leaders. Just what is it that we are advocating and energizing?

Those in leadership roles have the potential to enact authority in ways that mediate the wider context of power, authority and accountability for which they, at the head of an organization, are responsible. I tried to illustrate this point in my chapter in another volume of this series (Williams, 2005) where I described my own attempt to avoid demonizing rank-and-file staff members following a poor inspection outcome. I give a further illustration of this in the narrative above of the staff member at risk of dismissal. Leaders have this quite unique opportunity in the life of their organizations because their position makes them a gatekeeper for some aspects of the experience of others. In my experience, recognizing and trying to work with this aspect of a leadership role is a difficult and messy process. Leadership in the public sector is increasingly bound up with an expectation that individuals in such roles are *de facto* instrumental to the implementation of policy priorities. This I would argue is the thinking behind and justification for the huge resource commitment from central government to 'professionalizing' leadership across the public sector. Policy failure is increasingly associated with the failure of individuals in senior positions judged in terms of motivation and technical competence. To sustain the performance of a leadership role therefore entails also sustaining a commitment to enacting authority in a manner that is recognizably consistent with the implementation of policy imperatives. These policy imperatives are manifest in the myriad modernizing and reform initiatives that flow from ministers to agencies and into institutions. The presumption is therefore that those in leadership roles will administer (will operationalize) these initiatives.

Managerial behaviours are therefore crucial to enabling others whose identities are bound up with that of the organization to take up the more generalized themes of power prevalent in the wider community. Managerial anxiety therefore becomes deeply associated with a perceived need to be responsive to the political initiatives of others, such as government ministers, who appear to determine the framework of ultimate accountability within which local managers operate. In the public sector, initiatives are often short-term reflex responses to large-scale and complex policy aspirations on the part of government ministers. The anxiety of senior political figures to be seen to deliver is therefore taken up eventually in the priorities and behaviours of local managers. Leadership is deeply implicated in the reproduction of power relationships that threaten profoundly the ontological securities of other managers and front-line staff. The cult of public service reform therefore often entails the justification for an action (by an institution) being predicated on the delivery of benefits to society at large (the community or generalized other). The pursuit of this 'good', however, makes 'right' managerial processes in which the active shaming of subordinate others (expressed in performance targets, personal objectives, appraisal) is a normative condition of work.

Leaders therefore face daily ethical choices with regard to the extent to which, in their participation in the life of their organizations, they opt to cipher or to challenge such processes. To sustain the necessary performance one has to be the cipher of these larger, macro power relations. However, to survive the performance ethically, in a way which can be justified as entailing also an authentic recognition of the other, it is important at the same time to challenge the presumptions and the practices implicit in such performances. In working in recent years with a knowledge of this paradox, I would say that the experience can reasonably be described as a context of bounded uncertainty within which the ongoing sustainability of a role and a performance is continuously lived at the edge of chaos. Yet this is also an immensely creative context within which to work because the absence of certainty, security and a sense of belonging is of itself a source of inspiration in terms of exploring new ways to reach out and engage others in dialogue about how *it* and *we* might go on together.

What I have explored in this chapter is the way in which the themes of public sector policy are played out in the micro detail of everyday, routine working relationships. In ways that are still new to life in the public sector in the UK, personal accountability for the delivery of performance targets set by government has become entrenched in what I refer to as the micro detail of everyday lived experience. This, I think, posits a particular kind of work ethic: one in which ongoing ontological security is contingent upon one's ability to sustain a performance of success in a context which does not admit of the possibility of systemic policy failure but which localizes the causes of underachievement in the personal capabilities of individual unit managers. Individuals in senior management roles are in different ways implicated as agents of such processes of power and control and at the same time subject to the waves of ontological insecurity that such processes engender.

I also want to draw attention to the emergence of the issue of ontological insecurity as being at the centre of, or fundamental to, the essential character of working lives in public sector institutions. Here I think it is important to differentiate between the general feelings of anxiety that are common to all human beings engaged in uncertain organizing processes and a specific context of experience in which the provocation of deep feelings of ontological insecurity is an explicit action taken by those with power and designed to ensure conformity of behaviour on the part of those responsible to them. I associate this directly with the rise of a performative orientation to policy in relation to the management and delivery of public services.

This, I believe, is allied to a recurrence in recent political history of what Elias described as a 'centrifugal spurt' in the concentration of political power (Elias, [1939] 2000) leading to what we might call the 'courtly' nature of dominant political power relationships in the UK today, reminiscent of the time of absolute monarchs. This I see as deriving from a number of complex and interrelated factors: the phenomenon of the past twenty years of political parties forming governments with very large parliamentary majorities; the decentralization but increased regulation of public service delivery under the managerial aegis of unelected non-departmental government bodies (quangos); the emergence of a centre-right consensus which posits a post-industrial vision of the West as a knowledge producer in a globalized economy; the centrality in the ideology of the political centre-right of the idea of 'performance' and 'delivery'. The re-emergence of these 'courtly' political relationships has in the absence of other local centres of democratic opposition brought senior managers into direct face-to-face relationships with the administrators of central government policy. At a local and regional level such people are, I would argue, the new commissars of a particular kind of anti-democratic but devolved national government. To be brought into direct interaction with such people is to encounter a caste of political functionaries every one of whom is as caught up in processes of performative accountability as those in relation to whom and for whom they administrate. For those caught up in this process there is the sense of a compulsion to perform which drives and is driven by powerful feelings of ontological insecurity. It is this anxiety chain, or anxiety *figuration*, that is, I believe, the defining context of work in the public sector today.

Educational institutions (schools, colleges and universities) are all places in which those working within them have become implicated in the reproduction of relationships that functionalize knowledge, the idea of 'education' itself, and individuals (both teachers and students) as factors of production. Performative strategies in the field of education are therefore to be understood in terms of the cult values associated with the goals of economic competitiveness and the idea of an emergent knowledge economy. In a context of work (the public sector) framed by a tightly supervised performative culture in which the tendency is always to posit future states in terms of the failings of present and past, a positive sense of self for those in managerial roles is bound up with the realization of the fantasy future state. This is a bipolar condition where the options are starkly contrasted in terms of insider/outsider categories. It is each individual's struggle to hold face, to sustain one's reputation, to intuit the sensitivities of conveying the appearance of being on message, to appear always to be in control and to be an effective performer that emerges.

Another aspect of what I think of as *doing* leadership to which I want to draw attention relates to the question of the symbolism of power that leaders come to represent in the lives of others. It is impossible to progress into a CEO role for the first time and not experience the sensation of celebrity that such a position holds in the life of an organization. The attentiveness of everyone within an organization to what kind of person the CEO is, what he or she looks like, wears, eats, thinks, wants, can do, cannot do, is extraordinary in its degree. This obsession with the character of the leader is coupled with a tendency to see an organization in terms of the persona of the CEO: to locate the responsibility for the life, in its widest sense, of an organization with the individual. The identities of others become bound up with such symbolism. Leaders, whether they like it or not, assume roles of very central importance to the bigger picture in which each of us senses the location of our own individual lives.

From my own experience, I would argue that individuals in leadership roles cannot avoid becoming implicated in or bound up with the material that emerges from the symbolic potency of the role. In relation to this they do not have choices and they are not in control. Leadership can, however, entail a commitment to reworking the manner of one's own participation in the life of an organization. While such action will not diminish the significance of the actions of the leader in the lives of others, it can and will influence the dynamics that are associated with how people relate one to another. In taking such action, someone in a leadership role will become party to the emergence of new, transforming possibilities, which enable both themselves and others around them to see things differently. It is in the active participation in such sense-making processes on an organizational scale that each of our identities as social and organizational beings is elaborated. *Doing* leadership entails also paying attention on one's own account to the ethics of participation in the ongoing lives of others.

My narrative attempts to describe a personal study of the lived experience of occupying a leadership role. In the detail of my interactions with my chairman, in reflecting upon issues of power, norms and values I have tried to demonstrate that the real task of leadership occurs in such processes of interaction with others and in the degree to which our responsiveness to the other opens up new ways of acting and being together. I suggest that the relational process I try to exemplify in this instance of my interactions with my chairman is one that those in leadership roles replicate in similar but different ways in their interactions with others across the organizational context. I have also drawn attention to the intensity of the affectual dimension of the relationships with which those in leadership roles become engaged. Here I would argue that the particular intensity of these relationships is in some way to be accounted for by the fantasy that in our culture surrounds what is an iconographic fixation with the power of individuals to be responsible for others, for the control of the flow of events, and for the assurance of stability and continuity in individual lives. None of these attributes is remotely real. Sustaining the front of this role over a long period of time among a fairly stable community of the same individuals is therefore draining of the capacity for responsiveness.

My experience of leadership is not what I find described by researchers such as those engaged in the LSRC Leading Learning Project. I do not experience myself as an individual free to make strategic choices about my behaviour in relation to others. My local circumstance at work involves me in an ongoing struggle, working with a small group of others, to make sense of our place and context in order to frame agreements that enable us to act into a living present that we perceive to be pregnant with threat, insecurity and uncertainty. As we engage in this process together, we, in relation to each other and ourselves in relation to other staff members, experience intense movements in our affectual responses. These give coloration to our ongoing interactions, since in the social context of our being together the emerging themes and patterns of our responsiveness to each other become ordered in an ongoing process of power relating. The leadership position, I would argue, is a locus of power in this process. It is a reference point the particular qualities of which give stability to these emerging patterns of relating over time and across space. Leaders are participants in this process and leadership identities emerge too in the flux of the power-relating process. It is in the recognition of this fact, in noticing oneself as a participant and in being responsive to the immediate others who are the community to which Mead referred, that an ethics of leadership behaviour emerges.

In the above narrative I explored how the iteration of processes of power relating is bound up with ethics. It attempts to find a way of describing what leadership *is* and what those in leadership roles actually *do* without recourse to the idealizing language and typologies that characterize much of the 'expert' writing on this subject. This chapter, therefore, demonstrates that the actions of those in leadership roles emerge either as responses to an individual impulse to action informed by personal judgements about what is the right thing to do, or from complex conversational processes in which individuals, caught up in processes of power relating, struggle to negotiate a common sense of the good and the right that should inform the character of real-world action (Joas, 2000). In either event the manner of the resolution of a debate about the good and the right (that is, the tension between a sense of value and a sense of norm) and the action that emerges from this has profound implications for ethics and identity.

This narrative illustrates the sophistication of wider processes of social control that impel us towards normative behaviours (e.g. the social objects of regulatory bodies, rules articulated in legal statute) but also that individual responsiveness presents always the potential for nonconformity. The ethical struggle to pursue a course of action in the name of the good as against the name of the right can always go either way. It is the conditionality, the multiplicity of factors that might predispose an individual to act in a particular way, that each of us perceives as attaching to our uniquely personal sense of ontological security that in the moment will inform our action. Thresholds of fear and shame are clearly of vital importance here. An individual who, for whatever reason, has a high threshold of fear or of shame is more likely to act on the basis that their sense of the good also constitutes what is right. It is, I think, no accident that in the recent past in the public service context it is those who have just retired, or changed career or have been sacked who speak out in these terms. Other voices, those of individuals who need for whatever reason to go on and who sense the threat to identity of speaking out, are moderated by this sense of risk.

References

Allee, V. (2000) 'Knowledge networks and communities of practice', *OD Practitioner*, 32, 4: 22–35.

Czarniawska, B. (1998) *A Narrative Approach to Organization Studies*, London: Sage.

de Maré, P. (1975) 'The politics of large groups', in L. Kreeger (ed.) *The Large Group: Dynamics and Therapy*, London: Karnac.

de Maré, P., Piper, R. and Thompson. S. (1991) *Koinonia: From Hate, through Dialogue, to Culture in the Large Group*, London: Karnac.

Elias, N. ([1939] 2000) *The Civilizing Process*, Oxford: Blackwell.

Fromm, E. ([1942] 2002) *The Fear of Freedom*, London: Routledge.

Giddens, A. (1991) *Modernity and Self-identity: Self and Society in the Late Modern Age*, Cambridge: Polity Press.

Griffin, D. (2002) *The Emergence of Leadership: Linking self-organization and ethics*, London: Routledge.

Haigh, G. (2004) *Bad Company: The Strange Cult of the CEO*, London: Aurum.

Hay Group (2002) *Further Lessons of Leadership*, London: Hay Group Working Paper.

Hirschhorn, L. (1988) *The Workplace Within: Psychodynamics of Organizational Life*, Cambridge, MA: MIT Press.

Joas, H. (2000) *The Genesis of Values*, Cambridge: Polity Press.

Knights, D. and Willmott, H. (1999) *Management Lives: Power and Identity in Work Organizations*, London: Sage.

Lawrence, W. G. (2000) *Tongued with Fire: Groups in Experience*, London: Karnac.

Learning and Skills Research Centre (LSRC) (2004) *Leading Learning Project, International Comparator Contexts*, London: Learning and Skills Research Centre.

Lesser, E. L. and Storck, J. (2001) 'Communities of practice and organizational performance', *IBM Knowledge Management*, 40, 4: 831–841.

Mead, G. H. (1923) 'The scientific method and the moral sciences', *International Journal of Ethics*, 23: 229–247.

Mead, G. H. (1934) *Mind, Self and Society*, Chicago, IL: University of Chicago Press.

Mead, G. H. (2001) *Essays in Social Psychology*, ed. M. J. Deegan, London: Transaction Publishers.

Mead, G. H. ([1932] 2002) *The Philosophy of the Present*, New York: Prometheus Books.

Senge, P. M. (1990) *The Fifth Discipline: The Art and Practice of the Learning Organization*, New York: Doubleday.

Shore, C. and Wright, S. (2000) 'Coercive accountability: the rise of audit culture in higher education', in M. Strathern (ed.) *Audit Cultures: Anthropological Studies in Accountability, Ethics and the Academy*, London: Routledge.

Stacey, R. (2001) *Complex Responsive Processes in Organizations: Learning and knowledge creation*, London: Routledge.

Stacey, R. (2003) *Complexity and Group Processes: A radically social understanding of individuals*, London: Routledge.

Stacey, R., Griffin, D. and Shaw, P. (2000) *Complexity and Management: Fad or radical challenge to systems thinking?*, London: Routledge.

Turquet, P. (1975) 'Threats to identity in the large group', in L. Kreeger (ed.) *The Large Group: Dynamics and Therapy*, London: Karnac.

Williams, R. (2005) 'Leadership, power and problems of relating in processes of organizational change', in D. Griffin and R. Stacey (eds) *Complexity and the Experience of Leading Organizations*, London : Routledge.

Editors' introduction
to Chapter 4

In Chapter 3, Richard Williams describes from his experience in the education sector how the government's performance management regime is sustained by threatening the ontological security of those working in the sector. CEOs live under the ever-present threat of removal from their jobs if their organizations do not achieve the blanket targets set by the government for all educational establishments, irrespective of context. Other members of these organizations are subject to similar fears and all dread the judgement that their institution is failing. He also points to the instrumental use of shame to underpin the performance management regime. The climate of fear and anxiety has the effect of silencing all objections to the regime and people feel that they have no alternative but to conform. There is only one legitimate discourse and that is the discourse of performance. In this chapter, Nicholas Sarra explores a very similar situation in the health sector, describing how people who are publicly silenced nevertheless find a way to express their feelings about what is happening to them. Since expression is denied in the legitimate, public arena, people find a voice in what might be called the shadow arenas of gossip, humour and irony.

Sarra notices how people talk about the corridor occupied by his organization's top executives. Many refer to the corridor as 'the green mile' with direct reference to the film of that name. This film is about the inmates of a prison who are awaiting execution and 'the green mile' is their name for the corridor leading to the electric chair. Sarra explores with members of the organization what meaning this rather shocking symbolism has for them and what it is about their work that leads them to feel this way. In using this symbol, people are expressing how fearful they feel about working in an environment that is experienced by many as destructive. It appears to them that the performance management regime insists on individual responsibility and harsh punishment. People feel that individuals are held accountable and sacrificed, irrespective of context, for events over which they have no control. In talking to people about the green mile, it becomes clear that many feel overwhelmed but, at the same time, that this must be concealed if they are to survive.

Discussion about the green mile brings to the fore a process in which the top-down imposition of 'modernization' creates a split between private experience and required external appearances. It becomes necessary to put considerable emotional energy into appearance management, and a number of people talked about the profoundly disturbing experience of having their identity overtly managed by those higher up in the hierarchy, who in turn were having similar experiences. It is only the appearance of competent professional performance which is valid.

This study of the symbolism of a corridor powerfully brings out the emotional consequences of a dominant discourse in which performance is evaluated primarily in terms of the achievement of centrally planned targets. This involves the experience of a shift in the task of the organization from the provision of health care to one of justifying the organization's performance to inspecting agencies whose tools of coercion include shame and humiliation.

4 The emotional experience of performance management in the health sector: the corridor

Nicholas Sarra

The ways in which people talk about, and form, the spaces in which they work communicate attitudes towards organizational power relations. Within the National Health Service (NHS) in the United Kingdom, these power relations are strongly influenced by national policy. By studying local interaction in the context in which it occurs, we can gain insights into the ways in which policy forms interaction at a local level. I argue that by studying such phenomena, we make available opportunities for sense making and reflection. These qualities may in turn develop greater responsiveness between people, helping them to bear the inevitable anxieties of working in a complex environment and of finding ways of going on together. This represents a different approach to organizational development to those generally in vogue in the NHS, underpinned by government policy and the NHS plan. The NHS tends to favour a macro approach and packages from the Modernization Agency with templates which can be rolled out nationally. Such organizational development packages pay little attention to the importance of working to develop the quality of local interaction. They often make the assumption that individuals can be taught to behave in particular ways in a predictable manner and acquire specific traits which are presumed to constitute qualities such as leadership. I argue that such claims hold little validity in the complex relational matrix of organizational life where individuals and the choices they can make are continually formed through the enabling constraints of the organizational environment and those interacting within it.

Working within ongoing processes of interaction necessitates paying attention to the so-called shadow processes of organizational life such as what people gossip about, the stories they tell each other, and the way people present themselves to others. These activities are often not remarked upon in mainstream organizational development literature, as if they were not worthy of serious consideration. I argue that this should be a crucial area of concern in organizational development since desired outcomes are profoundly influenced by these processes. The work of Goffman, Elias, Bakhtin, Giddens and Mead, among others, offers insights into such processes and will be taken up in this chapter.

This chapter focuses on the senior management corridor, in an NHS Trust, known locally as 'the green mile'. I discuss the meaning of this metaphor for the participants and its meaning in broader terms as a response to government policy. I then use Laing's concept of ontological security to explore issues about, and threats to, identity for health service professionals. This leads into a discussion on the very physical experience of working in and around the corridor and the emotional impact on participants. I will be exploring how participants view the corridor and their own experiences of interaction upon it. How do people make sense of what occurs there? What feelings do they have in relation to it and to each other? How do people present themselves in such an environment? What functions if any does the corridor serve and to what ends? These data will be supplemented by *ad hoc* conversations and experiences related to the subject.

Geographical considerations

The senior management corridor is, properly speaking, an enclosed section of an extended configuration of passages. It is to be found on the first floor of a large building constructed in the style of Victorian Gothic and formerly a psychiatric hospital, known locally as Buncross House.

Although this function is still retained, it is far less so than previously, many of the patients and their services currently being catered for in community settings. There is therefore something anachronistic and semi-deserted about the atmosphere of the building. It is as if its population and activities do not quite fill the architectural spaces.

On the first floor of this building, a corridor runs some two hundred and fifty yards along its length and the senior management team resides in an enclosed section of this corridor. For ease of reference, I have divided the corridor into zones as follows:

- Zone one: An area used by clinicians and their secretaries, including a small library. This zone is referred to by some as 'the back of beyond' or by phrases such as 'I've no idea what goes on down there'.
- Zone two: A mixed area of administrators, clinicians and managers, including the reception area. This is referred to occasionally as 'the gulag'.
- Zone three: The senior management corridor. This is referred to as 'the green mile'. I have subdivided this area into sub-zones a, b and c.
- Zone four: An area used by consultant psychiatrists and their secretaries, known as 'the consultants' corridor'.

The physical décor of these zones can be strikingly different. Zones one and two are similar and present a deeply institutional image of health care that has changed little over the past sixty years. There are a few poorly selected cheap prints, dwarfed both by their sparsity and by the height of the corridors. Someone has put up some curtains of an incongruous design but these serve only to amplify the institutional effect. The most noticeable artefacts are fire safety equipment, exposed wiring on the ceiling and signs which announce the anticipated destinations of participants, such as meeting places and toilets. The whole is set off by lino flooring of an indeterminate colour and harsh neon lighting. Zone three (the green mile), by contrast, is a study in corporate anonymity. There is little here to suggest what the task of the organization might be or that we are in a hospital. Behind the closed doors people could just as plausibly be selling insurance as managing a health care organization. Gone are the harsh neon and lino and the lofty, chilly spaces. These are replaced by lowered ceilings, diffused lighting and a green carpet, much remarked upon in this study. Zone 4 differs in that it bears traces of the participants who inhabit it. There is evidence of interaction in a number of posters and announcements, and the occasional plant. There is also a carpet with a pattern, and this differentiates it (as well as its age) from the carpet on the green mile.

'The green mile', zone three

Zone three has not always been referred to as the green mile. Its present function came into being with the advent of a new organizational structure some three years ago. Prior to this it formed part of a psychiatric ward for older people and was by all accounts in poor condition. The new organization had come together through sequential mergers of geographically disparate mental health services. There was thus a sensitivity as to where any headquarters might be based, and an apprehension that it would be located within the county's city and therefore at Buncross House. It might then be seen as confirming concerns that the city service would be a dominant partner in the merger process and asset-strip its rural partners. Initially there had been much talk about having a virtual headquarters and about board meetings revolving around the county. There would not be 'a centre' although there would need to be offices.

In its early days, zone three was more generally known as 'the golden mile', an ironic reference to the supposed qualities of its occupants, who were seen as the 'chosen', an elite group elevated from the common mass of staff. Over time, the term was replaced in popular usage by that of 'the green mile'. This development accompanied the evolution of power relations in the organization, and in particular seemed to become more popular after the professional demise of a director who had had to leave and who was seen as the victim of a scapegoating process.

I learned in my interviews with participants that many of them associated the phrase 'the green mile' with Stephen King's book and a consequent film about death row starring the actor Tom Hanks. In the story, the green mile is the walk to the electric chair. The condemned men wait their time in cells on either side of this forbidding passage. In the tale, there are powerful themes of resurrection and sacrifice and, paradoxically, hopelessness and despair. The hero is one of the condemned men who is executed for the crimes of others and able to exercise miracles. He is able to cure the sick and bring the dead to life (an interesting analogy for mental health professionals). One of the guards is a brutal sadist who delights in the pain of the prisoners. This story clearly held a resonance for many of those involved with this study. Working within senior management was perceived as a high-risk occupation in which emotional pain, self-sacrifice and feelings of humiliation were to be expected. The terminology may also reflect the ironic use of humour both as a means of catharsis and as a way of coping with perceived power relations through the use of mockery. Bakhtin makes this point when discussing the use of parody among writers during the Middle Ages, but the same could be held true for many organizational conversations:

> Is the author quoting with reverence or on the contrary with irony, with a smirk? Double entendre as regards the other's word was often deliberate . . . there were quotations that were openly and reverently emphasized as such, or that were half hidden, completely hidden, half conscious, unconscious, correct, intentionally distorted, unintentionally distorted, deliberately reinterpreted and so forth. The boundary lines between someone else's speech and one's own speech were flexible, ambiguous, often deliberately distorted and confused.
>
> (Bakhtin, 2002, p. 69)

One of the participants reported as follows: 'When I go and see Vera [the chief executive] I feel as if I'm sitting on the electric chair and I never know whether she's going to turn it on or not.' This sense of apprehension in which one's survival might be at stake was common among the participants.

> 'I don't want to be seen, you might have your head blown off although it might eventually grow back. I don't mind being a twinkling star. If you're too bright, you're either imploding or exploding.'

However, these responses located with the CEO would also be familiar to her, with very similar anxieties of being removed from office and held accountable for events beyond her control.

Such responses indicate a heightened sensitivity to power relations in the immediate environment, a feeling of being trapped and an apparent danger in standing out. Making another direct allusion to the film, one participant described the green mile as 'locked cells full of condemned people'. There was a strong sense of people serving out a sentence which involved a great deal of self-sacrifice, including potentially the ultimate one of their own careers. At the same time, self-esteem was garnered through being involved at the apex of organizational hierarchy: 'I feel like I'm one of the gang.' Discrepancies with private feelings of discomfort were often dealt with by explanatory platitudes such as: 'At this level that's what's expected of you.' There was therefore a sense that a cohesive identity was being formed whose tenuous gratification rested upon being involved with an elite group, martyrs to the noble cause of public service, even though this might result in their own demise.

There is a further link with the death penalty and a culture of individual accountability in which context is negated and individuals are expected to fall upon their swords (accept professional execution) in the event of organizational crisis. I suggest that there is a patterning of power relations particularly apparent in the USA and UK which reiterates the accountability and expendability of the individual at moments of social crisis, accompanied by the displacement of feelings of humiliation and shame. This is exemplified in issues around the death penalty, both in the criminal sense in terms of execution, and symbolically in the corporate sense in terms of scapegoating. Sarat, in a recent article (2000, p. 1), comments:

> Newt Gingrich once said that the key to building a new conservative majority in the United States rests with 'low taxes and the death penalty.' At least insofar as the death penalty is concerned, a generation of politicians has cultivated exactly the public sentiment Gingrich was counting on. From Richard Nixon's 'law and order' rhetoric to Bill Clinton's pledge to represent people who 'work hard and play by Ye rules,' they have insisted on individual responsibility and harsh punishment and a direct link between the two that excludes consideration of other social causes of crime, much less social responses to it.

This dynamic, the location of accountability at an individual level without reference to the individual's context, operates powerfully in public sector life, where individuals are made accountable for events beyond their control and may be sacrificed for corporate ends. Thus the metaphor of 'the green mile' suggests a quality of evil or of processes experienced as inherently destructive as opposed to life affirming.

However, not everyone I spoke to felt the same. Some participants chose to distance themselves from the green mile analogy. For example, this is Jim speaking:

Jim: 'Some people call it the green mile but it doesn't feel like that to me.'

NS: 'What does that phrase mean to you?'

Jim: 'Well I suppose they mean that film about the electric chair but I don't see us as prisoners or anything like that.'

The corridor in context: effects of national policy on feelings of security and issues of identity

My role in the organization is twofold: partly clinical but mostly organizational. Initially, my organizational consultancy role was defined with a great deal of autonomy. I was expected to support managers through a post-merger process, to help out in difficult organizational situations, and to design and convene processes which aided organizational development. Having been in the above role for about nine months, I had started to notice the thematic content of the material presented to me by managers and especially directors. This tended to revolve around private feelings of being overwhelmed which could not be displayed to others. There was a further theme in my sessions with managers on the green mile and this revolved around a preoccupation with their relationship with Vera, the CEO. Specifically, this referred to situations in which they had been insiders in what was perceived as Vera's inner circle and then suddenly found themselves repositioned and apparently rejected. These stories were frequent and persistent, and central to the departure of three directors through resignation and suspension. I did not know, at this point, that I was about to experience a similar dilemma, profoundly affecting my sense of what Laing (1990) refers to as ontological security. Laing uses this concept as a way of describing the roots of psychopathology in early experience. He describes how, if things go well in infancy and childhood:

> The individual . . . may experience his own being as real, alive, whole; as differentiated from the rest of the world in ordinary circumstances so clearly that his identity and autonomy are never in question . . . as having an inner consistency, substantiality, genuineness, and worth. . . . He thus has a firm core of ontological security.
>
> (Laing, 1990, pp. 41–42)

However, if the nurturing environment fails, then the individual may 'feel more unreal than real . . . so that his identity and autonomy are always in question . . . and unable to assume that the stuff he is made of is genuine, good, valuable' (ibid., p. 42).

I am suggesting here that this sense of ontological security is also helpful in understanding experiences of organizational life. Senses of meaning and identity inextricably permeate roles and organizational positioning. At work, as elsewhere, this sense of who one is, is gained through the continuity and reiteration of patterns of relationship. If these patterns change suddenly, violently or unexpectedly then disturbances of identity may ensue, sometimes accompanied by accentuated attempts to understand and construct meaning. These reactions in organizations are often evidenced when people leave, are made redundant or otherwise repositioned, and during times of organizational restructuring when all of the above may occur.

In my own experience I suddenly found myself moved to an office off the green mile, deprived of access to the CEO and repositioned with a new line manager who had been unsympathetic to my work. I was disturbed by the experience and this disturbance informs the personal context of my inquiry into the corridor. However – and perhaps this is also an attempt to deal with fluctuations in ontological security – there is a tendency to over-determine meaning in organizational life. As Wilensky (1967, p. 3) puts it:

> Too many critics of the organizational and political sources of our troubles see diabolical plots where there is only drift, a taste for reckless adventure where there is only ignorance of risks, the machinations of a power elite where there is, in William James' phrase, only a 'bloomin' buzzin confusion'.

This is not to say that we can or should avoid the construction of meanings in our work lives but rather that we should therefore carefully explore the contextual issues from which events arise. Vaughan (1998, p. 22) summarizes it thus:

> A fundamental sociological understanding is that interaction takes place in socially organized settings. Rather than isolating action from its circumstances, the task of the scholar is to uncover the relationship between the individual act and the social context.

Vera would be able to rationalize all the decisions which led to my repositioning. For example, the development of organizational structures necessitated the appointment of new managers who had to be found offices. It also did not make sense for me to be line-managed by her when there was a head of organizational development. However, my felt experience of exclusion and anxiety echoed too closely with the material which others had repeatedly presented to me to allow for a completely individual interpretation. There was a patterning of affectual responses here in which we were all perhaps caught up and which I needed to make sense of.

This was a climate in which targets, and perceived performance to attain those targets were the only legitimate discourse. As one participant put it, 'the organizational plan is the only game in town and if it's not in it it's out'. Through this process, managers were held individually accountable for a linear progression in organizational outcomes which they often struggled with, or found impossible or pointless to achieve. This quest for targets and outcomes was centrally driven and managed top down from the Department of Health via the Strategic Health Authority and local NHS Trust boards. At a local level, it translated into tensions in working relationships where centrally driven strategy met the reality of local conditions. Vera's position was extremely difficult and sometimes vulnerable in this regard. Her role was to steer and oversee the translation of national strategy into organizational performance, for which she was accountable. The cultural climate tended to predicate feelings of exclusion, isolation and dissonance in sense making as organizational realities became unduly weighted and constructed in top-down ways. I believe Vera found herself bridging numerous conflicts around her direction from the Strategic Health Authority, and conflicting pressures and paradigms from within her own Trust.

National policy with its emphasis on the top-down modernization of the health service was therefore inevitably leading to a pressure for correct appearances in line with that policy. This pressure created a split between the required external appearances and the complex experiences of day-to-day service provision. Thus a dissonance between private experience and corporate appearance arose which increasingly threatened to undermine the ontological security of health service workers.

There is only one game in town, and if you're not playing then you are off the board. Such dynamics threaten to alienate health service workers. They give rise to metaphors such as 'the green mile' whereby people express, in sardonic form, feelings of acute insecurity, powerlessness and alienation from the given organizational norms. Let us now explore further how these dynamics are expressed on the corridor.

Walking the mile: presentation of self as an embodied experience

Both in interviewing participants and in my own observations and experience, the act of walking in the senior management corridor is a complex one requiring particular presentations of self that will vary and fluctuate according to precise location and encounter with others. I experienced different areas of the corridor as evoking shifts in emotional nuance and anxiety, and these tended to relate to perceived power relations. For example, I have had, on occasions, distinct physiological reactions such as an increased heart rate and adrenal flow when walking past the offices of my line manager and the CEO. However, the environment of the green mile was in itself a sufficient trigger to induce a physiological response so that, by just walking through its door of entry, I felt a non-specific sense of apprehension. As Damasio (2000, p. 58) puts it:

> The pervasiveness of emotion in our development and subsequently in our everyday experience, connects virtually every object or situation in our experience, by virtue of conditioning, to the fundamental values of homeostatic regulation: reward or punishment; pleasure or pain; approach or withdrawal; personal advantage or disadvantage; and, inevitably, good (in the sense of survival) or evil (in the sense of death). Whether we like it or not, this is the *natural* human condition.

As previously stated, there is some evidence that body language may change for some on transition between zones, and this is especially justified if we accept that our bodies' performances are regulated through emotion. Appearance and self-presentation are also picked up on and rectified if too dissonant. Thus one participant informed me that 'I was told to look confident, like "I'm getting on with it, I'm on top of it"'. Another was 'told to smile' when walking along the corridor. This suggests that people are seeking to form each other's styles of presentation and, by implication, reading the body as a vehicle of communication. I had some evidence of this in my preliminary attempts at observation when I was seen to express dissonant social cues. People stepped in rapidly to try to modify my physical communication to within familiar patterns. I will call this style of intervention a *forming intervention* to draw attention to the quality of influencing another's physical gesturing. Whether such acts are conscious intentions, as such, seems to vary, and may be in relation to perceived power chances.

The experience of having one's identity overtly managed can be profoundly disturbing and wounding, and may leave recipients feeling powerless and humiliated. The following story illustrates this but I emphasize that the protagonist's point of view is one narrative among the multiple narratives that it might be possible to elicit from others in this situation. Lisa, training to be an executive, related the following experience:

> 'I was approached by Julie [a senior manager], who asked how I was feeling and I was honest but Julie pulled me up on it and told me how to present myself, saying "This is what I want to see from you, this is what I expect." She called it "reputation management" and then the next day we had a meeting with the CEO who asks me why I'm always so negative and they both started telling me how to present myself. I started sobbing and left the meeting in tears. Next day I came to work and put my mask on. I even found myself buying a beige shirt to match the corridor. Neither of them came anywhere near me and then after a few days Julie says to me: "You must have been feeling like shit, but you came back to work and no one would know." A few weeks later Julie rings my training programme and says "I think we've turned the corner". Actually the whole thing was just external compliance and as a result I've been fighting off a major depression. I felt really alienated. I wanted to give them feedback but feared for my future.'

The above relates overt tactics to establish a corporate presentation of self within the domain of the corridor. Julie's behaviour implies a perception of the corridor as a public space in which outsiders will view the 'face' of the organization. From Julie's point of view, she is fulfilling her responsibilities in training Lisa for her future role as a CEO, and understandably sees Lisa's appearance and perceived attitude as legitimate territory to explore. This might help Lisa in her future role. However, Julie is unaware of the impact of her intervention in terms of its reinforcing patterns of relating in public sector work life which lead to feelings of alienation, mechanization and despair. These patterns of relating tend to only validate the appearance of functional, competent, professional performance by people who are in control of the situations which they manage.

Forming interventions are frequently more subtle and possibly not consciously intended as such. However, they may be just as disturbing, and those in positions of hierarchy can be as much on the receiving end. This is Derek's story. He is one of the most senior managers.

> 'At lunchtime I go to the kitchen. It's very interesting, an opportunity for a bit of social chit-chat. You get to see who looks after themselves; who eats and who doesn't. I cook my Uncle Ben savoury rice in the microwave and then walk back along the corridor to my office. When

I do this people often smile at me as I pass. What are they thinking as they smile? It could be they're thinking "Look at that twat Derek with his food" or they might be pleased. Sometimes people say "You've got your lunch there Derek". If you eat at your desk, people react and say things like "That smells lovely" or "I don't like that". I was walking down the corridor thinking and someone said "Cheer up Derek". After that I keep my head up and smile if I see someone. When they said "Cheer up", I actually experienced embarrassment, shock and worry. Will this person think I'm not coping? Will this person say "Derek's struggling"? I thought "Ooh dear, does it look to them like I'm struggling?" Somebody else I know, and I can't say who, was told to smile.'

I suggest that the above narratives reveal a self-organizing process of interactional patterning in which participants seek both consciously and unconsciously to form the identities of those around them. At the same time, those seeking to form are themselves being formed in terms of identity in the daily process of social encounter. Furthermore, it would seem that Julie's intervention had a wider impact than Lisa and began by proxy to form the behaviours of a number of managers, as in Derek's 'Somebody else I know and I can't say who . . .' comment. There is also a theme that it is not all right to be seen to be struggling in public ('. . . and I can't say who . . .'). Feelings of pressure and stress must be kept as a private experience, walled off as it were from recognition by others and sometimes even from oneself.

This is John, a service director, talking:

'I was driving in to work and I felt nothing but then I noticed that there were tears rolling down my face and I was shaking. But I felt nothing. It was like another person, crying and shaking. I guess it's stress at work.'

John is describing an experience of dissociation, normally seen in acute stress reactions. The symptoms he describes are usually associated with post-traumatic situations but here are linked with the stresses of managing a mental health service. John's experience of his own body, and his emotional dissociation, reflects the taboos being formed within his work matrix around keeping 'negativity' as a private and individualized experience.

What is being revealed as thematic in these stories is wider organizational patterns of relating in which there is an accentuation of dissonance between public display and private experience. Although this dissonance may be found as a feature of all working life, there is an amplification of that feature which I suggest is related to the emphasis on target setting and performance prevalent within the public sector. This emphasis is experienced at all managerial levels as an individual accountability for achieving organizational targets, failure of which may lead to humiliation, shame and potential loss of role. In my experience, these anxieties are experienced at all levels of management but are usually hidden. They frequently arise from the unpredictable nature of organizational process, which inevitably means that people find themselves in uncertain and frustrating places which belie the paradigm of linear control dictated by action planning and the performance agenda. Managers may then feel that they are failing and inadequate in their roles because the only legitimate discourse available may be one predicated upon controlling the achievement of specified targets. As the organization shifts continually and unpredictably through the complexity of its interaction, opportunities and events arise which at a local level may render particular targets impossible and even senseless, but which none the less must be implemented.

The above stories also show how power relations are lived affectually as whole body experiences. The participants talk about these experiences in a very physical way through the panoply of their senses, referring as they do so to the ways in which they feel their identities being formed through the medium of their bodies. Although we may not necessarily acknowledge it as such, the experience of being in relationship with others is always an emotional and physical one. As Damasio (2000, p. 17) puts it:

> Emotions are complicated collections of chemical and neural responses, forming a pattern. . . . All emotions use the body as their theater (internal milieu, visceral, vestibular and musculoskeletal systems), but emotions also affect the mode of operation of numerous brain circuits: the variety of emotional responses is responsible for profound changes in both the body landscape and the brain landscape.

Patients on the green mile

The situation on the green mile is further complicated by the occasional presence of patients occasionally walking to and from one of the wards, no other access being available than via the senior management corridor.

There is thus to be sometimes witnessed a strange juxtaposition of people intent on being perceived as highly performing and competent professionals with people in a variety of disturbed mental states. On occasion I have experienced this situation as something akin to the patient expressing a disturbance that might also resonate with the private experience behind the polished 'impression management' of the senior manager.

I find that in walking along this corridor, I am often acutely aware of others who are around and of others who may be around at any moment. I am also aware of how I speculate upon the ways these others may be positioning themselves towards me and whether they are seeking contact or not. In this activity, I endeavour to manage the impression I create so that my visible appearance to others may at times be at odds with feelings of confusion, anxiety and apprehension. The presence of patients on the corridor does not arouse in me feelings of discomfort but I am aware of a heightened state of vigilance should I encounter them. However, in my conversations with others, it became apparent that managers from a non-clinical background were nervous in the presence of patients and regard them in their own minds as alien and unpredictable beings. Here are some typical responses:

> 'They make me nervous. One of them came into my room to ask for something and I was worried, I didn't know what to do. It's difficult to know what to do when there are patients about. I hang around to see if I'm needed.'

However, sometimes there are disturbances, as Cora, a cleaner, graphically describes:

> 'Nobody speaks to the patients. They act like they're not there. Milly put some window boxes full of plastic plants on the corridor and twice some patients pulled them down on the floor. One patient screamed at me, "DON'T SAY GOOD MORNING TO ME!" and "I WILL KILL YOU!" There was a large plastic palm outside Sally's office and a patient came along and started beating the walls with it. One day someone came up to me and said "Have you got a pair of scissors? There's a 15-year-old girl hanging from a tree and I want to cut her down." Later I was on the same bus as that patient and she suddenly started loudly accusing me of stealing money from her. It was very embarrassing and I was worried people would think I was a thief.'

There is, for me, a quality of anger in the events described above which leads me to wonder whether the environment of the corridor, and the perceived behaviours on it, might call forth, from some patients, enraged responses. Kay, a manager, remarks:

> 'It must be very difficult for some of those patients, walking down that corridor especially when they've just been admitted. They're very vulnerable and I think it raises questions of confidentiality about who sees them in that state. They must wonder where the hell they've ended up when they see all those people in suits. It's a very strange first impression for them. If I was them I would feel quite angry.'

In my observations of behaviour on the corridor, there would seem to be some evidence to confirm Cora's observation that 'nobody speaks to the patients'. Most people walk along the sides of the corridor and this is particularly apparent when there are patients about. Exceptions to this are the patients themselves, who invariably walk down the middle, as do the directors of the Trust. Walking along the sides may have something to do with avoiding the tensions which walking along the middle might evoke in a direct encounter with patient or director. Both may be perceived as power holders in their own right: the former because their behaviour may be unpredictable and unresponsive to social cuing; the latter because of dependencies in the line management relationship. Members of staff also need to differentiate themselves from patients and are therefore dependent upon them in terms of social and economic identity. Without the patient there would be no staff.

In order to explore further the nature of how meanings are constructed around interaction and what the corridor represents, I want to examine G. H. Mead's concept of the social object.

The corridor as a social object

> The earliest objects are social objects, and all objects are at first social objects. Later experience differentiates the social from the physical objects, but the mechanism of the experience of things over against a self as an object is the social mechanism.
>
> (Mead, 1938, p. 429)

What I understand by Mead's use of the term 'social objects' are those features of experience which call out from us a correspondence of attitude, an approach which we can recognize in our own and others' responses. In effect this means a tendency to act in particular ways. Mead cites property as an example of a social object since we must find within ourselves a complexity of attitudes towards exchange, buying and selling which will make relational acts around property feasible. We find in our own responses to property an attitude which Mead refers to as the generalized other, essentially a condensation of social experience, of social attitudes which we can call forth in the private role play of the mind.

> We can talk to ourselves, and this we do in the inner forum of what we call thought. We are in possession of selves just in so far as we can and do take the attitudes of others towards ourselves and respond to those attitudes. We approve of ourselves and condemn ourselves. We pat ourselves upon the back and in blind fury attack ourselves, but usually it is with what I have termed the 'generalized other' that we converse, and so obtain to the levels of abstract thinking, and that impersonality, that so called objectivity that we cherish. In this fashion, I conceive, have selves arisen in human behavior and with the selves their minds.
>
> (Mead, 1925, p. 272)

To Mead, the self is a social object and so also are institutions. As individuals, we call forth attitudes both from within ourselves and from others which have distinctive patterns and in which the total complexity of the social act may be discovered. In this way Mead suggests that human beings are unique in their capacity to create social objects and societies. Human beings have a unique capacity to call forth in themselves an experience of how others may gesture and respond in relation to social objects. Mead links the notion of social objects with the issue of social control. In Mead's terms, self-organization occurs in human society because of the constraints and attitudes called forth by social objects. Social objects organize our acts.

> In so far as there are social acts, there are social objects, and I take it that social control is bringing the act of the individual into relation with this social object. With the control of the object over the act, we are abundantly familiar. Just because the object is the form of the act, in character it controls the expression of the act.
>
> (ibid., pp. 273–274)

How, then, in the light of the above, does the corridor function as a social object? The nature of the social object which is being created, and which in some way is reified in the architecture of the corridor and its accoutrements, may be explored through the responses it calls forth among the organizational participants. Thus if we take the different zones of the corridor in this study, we can see that the responses which they call forth from people illuminate the qualities of the institution as a social object and the way in which government policy influences such responses. In Mead's terms this means that people's actions are formed by their attitudes towards the institution as a social object: 'the object is the form of the act, in character it controls the expression of the act' (ibid., p. 274).

The corridor as a social object is a public space. It constrains, through the attitudes towards it, the types of acts which are possible. Thematically, most participants remarked upon the difference between zone three (the green mile) with its carpet, soft lighting and lowered ceilings to the dark areas of lino in zones one and two. The responses called forth from the incumbents of the green mile were often guilt, embarrassment, feelings of insecurity and exclusion, and sometimes of rage from those positioned elsewhere. This is a locum consultant talking (his office is located in zone 4):

> 'I know it's irrational but I feel this absolute rage whenever I walk
> down that corridor! [the green mile]. All those people with their shiny
> computers and cushy jobs! They're completely out of touch with all
> the shit!'

Such themes in the emotional responsiveness of the participants are of particular interest in the way they reiterate the frequent feeling states of those who find themselves involved as patients with psychiatric services.

What I am suggesting here is that the institution as a social object is formed by those involved with it, both staff and patients, but that this object thus created also simultaneously forms and organizes the ongoing identities of participants. Without the social object there would be no means of people bringing off the complex social act of institutional life. They can do this because they can call out both from within themselves and from each other a generalized attitude towards the institution which then serves to organize their interaction. This attitude, which is experienced by selves in their private mental role play as a conversation with a generalized other, is the ability to find in oneself the complexity of the social act, to be able to call up in oneself the responses which will be evoked in others in the course of interaction. I emphasize here that this generalized attitude does not mean that everyone has the same attitude; rather that there are patterns of response to the social object which allow for the construction of meaning and purpose and which constrain people to iterative patterns of interaction.

People's ideas about an institution are not only predicated upon espoused values such as 'we are all here to deliver the best possible health and social care to people with mental health difficulties', but also formed from the ongoing matrix of interaction which constitutes that institution. This ongoing matrix of interaction is experienced physiologically through emotion. The institution as a social object is experienced as affectual responses by its participants, which are to be found in the felt experience of the patterning of their power relations. Thus there may be a tendency for the power relations which may occur between patients and clinicians to be reiterated between managers and clinicians, with the latter feeling an erosion of their autonomy and a monitoring of role and resource, a dictation and control of work task (which to a patient would be control of life tasks), and all underpinned by the sense that the other just does not understand what it's like. This dynamic may occur because it is present as a quality of the generalized other which is continually formed by and forming the process of interaction. It is therefore tempting to see in the physical characteristics of the corridor zones, and their furniture, an architectural reification of the patterns of interaction which serve to imbue the qualities of the institution as a social object.

As I have said previously, there is a prevalent discourse in public sector work life in which performance is evaluated primarily in terms of the achievement of centrally planned targets. The normative task of the organization may then be experienced as shifting from the provision of health care (developing and supporting the quality of interaction at a local and clinical level) to one of justifying the organization's performance to inspectorate agencies whose tools of coercion include, via the publication of league tables and star ratings, the power to shame and humiliate, and again imbue the institution as a social object with those qualities.

Performance and impression management

Goffman, in his expositions of social behaviour, emphasizes the notion of performance and what he terms 'impression management'. Unlike Mead, who suggests that it is the development of social objects which forms people's behaviours in institutional settings, Goffman adroitly uses theatrical analogies to explain his perceptions:

> Within the walls of a social establishment we find a team of
> performers who cooperate to present to an audience a given
> definition of the situation. This will include the conception of own
> team and of audience and assumptions concerning the ethos that is
> to be maintained by rules of politeness and decorum. We often find
> a division into back region, where the performance of a routine
> is prepared, and front region, where the performance is presented.
>
> (Goffman, 1990, p. 231)

In terms of what we can see expressed in the corridor zones, there is a
disconcerting split between the appearance of, and performance on, the
green mile, identified and homogenized by a management discourse,
and the appearance of, and performance on, its neighbouring zones, with
their shabby paintwork and exposed wiring, identified and homogenized
as a clinical discourse. The headquarters area must be seen as performing.

One day, I noticed a secretary walking along the corridor in a very
purposeful way; her body language could be described as being clipped
and precise with a sharp, staccato style of walking. She held a file tucked
tightly under one arm. I was fascinated to see that as she left the corridor
and entered another zone, her posture and way of walking changed
significantly and became much more relaxed. This occurrence brought
to mind Goffman's (1990, p. 231) observation that:

> A social establishment is any place surrounded by fixed barriers to
> perception in which a particular kind of activity takes place. I have
> suggested that any social establishment may be studied profitably from
> the point of view of impression management.

The corridor as a social establishment may therefore be explored in terms
of the responses called out through the body language of the secretary
whose behaviour changed so dramatically when exiting the green mile
for the dark region of the 'gulag'. Performance is paramount; one must
be seen as getting on with it. In Mead's terms the difference in physical
behaviour in one zone from another would suggest that, in her own
experience, she is calling up a different sense of social object. As she
goes through a door to another zone, particular tendencies to act are
called forth and expressed physiologically while other responses cease
to be stimulated.

In terms of performance, the contrast of the green mile with the other
zones brings to mind the dissonance between public display and private
experience. This is a feature of all social life, but in this context is

amplified by the notion of the institution as a social object in which a particular style of performance is called forth to bring off the social act. Private experience, if dissonant to the NHS plan, is rendered invisible or inadmissible. Presentation of self becomes synonymous with corporate presentation.

For example, on the green mile there is a theme which concerns the accentuation of self-presentation as a high-performing individual in control. However, this seems frequently to mask a dissonant private experience, which has been remarked upon elsewhere in this chapter. In the corridors this dissonance is played out not only in the attention given to some areas and not to others but also in the unstated but self-organizing dress code of the green mile, where suits and jackets tend to predominate. The sartorial expressions of professional performance, status and control also provide a type of professional protection of anonymity in which signs of private experience and thus exposure can be reduced to a minimum. According to one participant: 'When I've got an important meeting, I say to my wife, "I'm putting on my armour today". Sharp suit – tie – the works. It says "I mean business!"'

The implication here is that the clothing has both a defensive function – it is seen as armour – and an offensive function which helps to mobilize aggression and feelings of being in control. The suit is sharp. Business is 'meant'.

Exceptions

This study has focused upon the senior management corridor and its contextual surroundings. Of the twenty participants interviewed, most focused spontaneously on the green mile and had their most intense emotional experiences within that area or in reaction to it. However, the following conversation with Carla, an executive director, illustrates the importance of history in participants' reactions. She is one of the longest-serving members of the organization.

NS: Tell me something about how you see the corridor.
Carla: Well, they're like different countries, the different parts. They represent different cultures and speak different languages. Both when you get on to the carpet and when you get on to the lino, there are people sitting like border guards watching who's crossing. The lino bit is very loud. You can hear your footsteps and of course so can other people.

NS: How do you see the different cultures?

Carla: One's like the 1980s (zones one and two) and the other's the twenty-first century (the green mile). Generally speaking the new culture is much better.

NS: Why's that?

Carla: Well, there are good things about targets and it's a lot better than the old days when there was a hatred of any innovation. I couldn't stand it back then [pre-merger].

Carla's response is unusual among the participants in that her most heightened responses are not directed towards the perceived hierarchy on the green mile. She suffered under the old regime and associates it with an organization run in shadowy and unaccountable ways. For her the green mile (and noticeably she never used that phrase) represents some relief and a progression from the oppression she experienced in the previous organization. History is clearly important here, since most of the participants are new to the organization and would not be able to locate themselves in relation to the corridor's past in the way in which she is able to do.

Further exceptions in this study are found in attitudes towards the study itself by participants. Of the twenty or so people involved, the majority responded in an interested and supportive way, seeing it as a positively beneficial project in organizational terms. An invitation to talk about the corridor was experienced by many as directly cathartic, allowing for the expression and making sense of feelings and preoccupations which had hitherto found no forum for communication. In this way the study may have helped in bringing lonely and split-off aspects of work experience into relationship with others, and thus provided a useful opportunity for making sense of confusing and sometimes difficult feelings in relation to the corridor.

However, one consultant psychiatrist and the chief executive had different responses. The former responded with sarcasm and hostility. The conversation with her about the corridor seemed to evoke a great deal of anger about how poorly she and her colleagues were treated as doctors. Having identified me as a manager, she then associated me with her plight and became very critical and personal towards me about 'your office, your curtains, your pictures'. She precipitately left the room, saying as she went that she was going to get on with some 'real work'.

Vera, the CEO, adopted a formal and, to my mind, defensive tone. She declined to see me to have a conversation about the corridor. She e-mailed me asking if I had informed my line manager (I had) and that 'I must make it quite clear that you are not to proceed with this piece of work any further until it has been approved by the organizational development steering group'. I was disappointed at this. The organizational development steering group, which comprises Vera, Anne my line manager and two other managers, meets very infrequently and it could be months before I might hear anything. I brought it up with Anne, who chairs that group, and she said, leaning forward slightly and with a look of smiling confidentiality, 'You will understand that I will have to choose the right moment with Vera. Can you leave that with me, is that all right?' She sat back in her chair with a look of what I felt to be self-satisfaction while I nodded in dumb and helpless acquiescence. I had deliberately worked up the hierarchy in my conversations, leaving Vera until last lest the rug be pulled from beneath my feet. In this I have not been mistaken.

My hypothesis about Vera's reluctance is that such a project may have aroused anxieties about exposing the underbelly of the carefully managed corporate performance presentation. This would be understandable at a time when the organization was under review by various inspectorates such as the Commission for Health Improvement. However, it would also be symptomatic of the tendency to alienate and silence anything that could be construed as dissonant with the impression management of public sector services.

Conclusion

This study about a corridor explores some of the ways in which we form each other's identities in an institutional context. We are iteratively engaged in a process of constituting and reconstituting the conditions and actions of each other but we are not merely doing this. In our interaction we introduce idiosyncratic differences based upon our unique differentiation as individuals in terms of time and space, and the constructions of meaning which we help to form from those positions. The group and the individual may be aspects of the same human phenomena but we are, perforce, located uniquely as individuals in terms of time and space.

For obvious physical reasons, we cannot occupy the same space at the same time as another and therefore we each have a unique life experience of the world about us. Nobody can live exactly the same life as another and herein lies our individuality. At the same time we are group- and sense-making animals, and our selves arise inextricably from our social experience, without which we would cease to meaningfully exist. It is, however, in the inevitable, and sometimes very small, differences which arise between us that we find the movement which means that we cannot merely reiterate past patterns. What is unpredictable is how such differences in the iterative patterning of social relations might be amplified and thus reconfigure those patterns of interaction.

In this study, I have drawn attention to how the senior management corridor is formed in an ongoing way as a social object by those involved with it. This object, a cumulative process of generalized attitudes towards the institution, also forms, at the same time, the interaction and emotional responses of participants. This process can be meaningfully thought about as occurring through the continuing power relations of participants. In other words, the generalized attitudes which constitute ourselves are formed through the interplay of power relations between organizational subgroups. This occurs as well within those subgroups and through the organization and indeed society as large groups.

It would not be correct to think of these organizational subgroups as having clear boundaries, since participants can claim multiple group memberships, many of which permeate through apparent boundaries. None the less, group identities are recognizable as generalized attitudes towards home, work and society. The social objects thus formed are permeated with the attitudes towards the power relations involved. Attitudes towards the senior management corridor reflect a preoccupation with the perceived power relations both on and in relation to the corridor, with positions taken up accordingly. Gossip, innuendo and subtle and not so subtle rhetorical devices are employed in which denigration of perceived power holders is used to establish 'us and them' group identities. These identities are required in order to preserve senses of autonomy, self-esteem and power, but none the less are also imbued with the 'generalized attitudes towards' other groups.

The experience of the corridor is first and foremost an embodied experience. People respond to the corridor with the full panoply of their senses. The sounds and smells of the place, its tactile qualities, as well as its visual impact all play their part in forming the responses of participants, and affect them physiologically both through stimulating the senses and by evoking emotion. The corridor is experienced in terms of emotional zones in that different areas stimulate different states of emotional arousal which again correspond to the perceived power relations. This accordingly affects the behaviours of participants, who often find that they present themselves differently in different zones. These zones are not fixed in that they can change with the time of day and the people who may be around. Distance regulation between bodies and the ways in which encounters are negotiated on the corridor evoke continuing dilemmas for participants. Encounters on the corridor oblige people to do something. They may adjust their positioning, their self-presentation, avert their gaze or greet, negotiate a conversation, or negotiate an extrication from a conversation, but they must do something. This having to do something obliges people to enter an interaction of gestures and responses in which people construct the meaning of what it is that is occurring. Those meanings are often then further elaborated within subgroups of perceived alliances.

The construction of meaning outside of those subgroupings represents the mature work of organizational reflection, and this is more difficult and anxiety provoking and likely to arouse resistance, anger and strategies of avoidance since it may expose the rhetoric of gossip and the extant power relations. Despite all of the above, participants are likely to behave as if much of this is invisible. They do not necessarily notice, in a consciously reflective way, the corridor and its complex responsive processes. In one sense they walk past their experiences without noticing them. As Bauman (2003, p. 147) has remarked,

> One does not see what is all too visible, one does not note what is 'always there', things are noticed when they disappear or go bust, they must first fall out from the routinely 'given' for the search after their essences to start and the questions about their origin, whereabouts, use or value to be asked.

My experience of talking to participants about the corridor was frequently of a paradoxical situation in which people generally seemed familiar with feelings in that context but at the same unfamiliar, as if they were becoming aware of them through the course of a conversation. I suggest that this is due to the opportunity of the conversation about the corridor in providing a language for making sense of their experience which was hitherto unavailable. Thus people need to construct discourses between themselves in order to articulate and make sense of consciousness, in effect to make consciousness available for reflection.

Many participants saw the corridor as functional in oiling the wheels of organizational life. People used the corridor to make appointments, 'to find out what's going on', to 'catch up' with others, to offer and receive impromptu support and to make visible displays of relations with significant others. This 'informal' contact was highly valued by many who spoke of encounters in the corridor being less constrained than those behind closed doors. Several attributed this to the availability of exit strategies such as being able to precipitately terminate a conversation through claiming lateness for a prior appointment. One participant, based in another location, confessed that he came occasionally to the corridor in the hope that he might bump into people who would be useful to him. This was the only way in which he could secure contact with senior managers who were constantly cancelling and 'reprioritizing' their appointments.

Some – and this was particularly true of those at director level – found the corridor something of a double-edged sword. To enter the corridor was to immediately face the potential prospect of being lobbied opportunistically by several people with urgent and complex requests. Therefore the 'back door' was often used to escape from unwanted approaches. The corridor also served a clear 'social' function for some, who complained that if they did not venture out into the corridor for contact, they would spend their working days in complete isolation. Many lamented the lack of any communal space where people could relax together. The kitchen was seen as too small, and too close for comfort to the chief executive's office. There was an overarching theme of comparing the senior management corridor with its adjacent corridors and the stark contrast between them, experienced by many upon the green mile with feelings of guilt and by those outside as 'managers making it all right for themselves'. This latter observation is a good illustration of the point made by Elias as to how those being gossiped about may identify with the gossip through their group identity: 'Merely by living in a specific neighbourhood individuals were judged and treated, and to some extent judged themselves, in accordance with the image which others had of their neighbourhood' (Elias 1998, p. 251).

The contrast of the corridors, the appellation of 'the green mile' to the senior management section and other descriptive euphemisms serve to illuminate the qualities imbued in the institution and wider NHS as social objects. The responses called forth from participants illuminate issues around divisions between clinicians and managers and the personal consequences of the performance and target culture. This chapter therefore highlights the way in which government policy in public sector services affects interaction at a local level. I suggest that there is a tendency to devalue anything which lies beyond the parameters of centrally driven policy and strategies of impression management. The façade of modernization must be preserved. This leads to feelings of alienation and anomie, with consequent problems for the workforce. None the less, and inevitably, differences and deviance from the proscribed norms find expression and have to be engaged with.

Finally, since the commencement of this project, there has been an escalating series of interventions upon the fabric of the corridor itself. Doors have been changed and moved about, cracks sealed over and paint applied. Signs have gone up and even two pictureless frames have appeared. Ostensibly this is in response to an impending CHI [Commission for Health Improvement, which ceased operating in March 2004] inspection, but I cannot help wondering whether conversing about the corridor may be producing some unintended consequences.

References

Bakhtin, M. (2002) *The Dialogic Imagination*, Austin, TX: University of Texas Press.

Bauman, Z. (1999) *Culture as Praxis*, London, Thousand Oaks, New Delhi: Sage.

Bauman, Z. (2003) *The Individualized Society*, Cambridge: Polity Press.

Bourdieu, P. (1998) *Acts of Resistance: Against the New Myths of our Time*, Cambridge: Polity Press.

Cassell, P. (ed.) (1993) *The Giddens Reader*, New York: Macmillan.

Castells, M. (2004) *The Information Age: Economy, Society and Culture*, Oxford: Blackwell.

Damasio, A. (2000) *The Feeling of What Happens*, San Diego, New York, London: Harcourt.

Dandeker, C. (2003) *Surveillance, Power and Modernity*, Cambridge: Polity Press.

Diski, J. (2004) 'Think of Mrs. Darling', *London Review of Books*, 26, 5 (4 March): 13–17.

Elias, N. (1998) *On Civilization, Power, and Knowledge*, ed. S. Mennell and J. Gouldsblom, Chicago, IL: University of Chicago Press.

Giddens, A. (1987) *Social Theory and Modern Sociology*, Cambridge: Polity Press.

Goffman, E. (1966) *Behavior in Public Places*, New York: The Free Press.

Goffman, E. (1981) *Forms of Talk*, Oxford: Blackwell.

Goffman, E. (1990) *The Presentation of Self in Everyday Life*, London: Penguin Books.

Hillier, B. and Hanson, J. (1984) *The Social Logic of Space*, Cambridge: Cambridge University Press.

Laing, R. D. (1990) *The Divided Self*, New York: Penguin Books.

Mead, G. H. (1925) 'The genesis of the self and social control', *International Journal of Ethics*, 35: 251–277.

Mead, G. H. (1938) *The Philosophy of the Act*, Chicago, IL: University of Chicago Press.

Mehan, H. (1979) *Learning Lessons: Social Organization in the Classroom*, Cambridge, MA: Harvard University Press.

Menzies Lyth, I. (1988) *Containing Anxiety in Institutions*, London: Free Association Books.

Powell, A. (1971) *A Dance to the Music of Time. A Question of Upbringing*, London: Collins.

Ryave, A. and Schenkein, J. (1974) 'Notes on the art of walking', in R. Turner (ed.) *Ethnomethodology*, Harmondsworth: Penguin Education.

Samson, R. (1990) *The Social Archaeology of Houses*, Edinburgh: Edinburgh University Press.

Sarat, A. (2000) *'DEATH ROW, AISLE SEAT'*, *The American Prospect* (14 February): 5–9.

Silverman, D. (1985) *Qualitative Methodology and Sociology*, Aldershot: Gower.

Vaughan, D. (1998) 'Rational choice, situated action, and the social control of organizations: the Challenger launch decision', *Law and Society Review*, 32, 1: 23–61.

Wilensky, H. (1967) *Organizational Intelligence: Knowledge and Policy in Government and Industry*, New York: Basic Books.

Editors' introduction to Chapter 5

A critical aspect of improved quality of health care is obviously the prevention of medical errors, and this gives rise to the call for clinical risk assessment in the health sector. In this chapter, Karen Norman, formerly Nurse Director of a National Health Service Trust, explores the thinking underlying the approach to clinical risk assessment in the UK, pointing to how it reflects the same kind of systems thinking that underlies the current mode of public sector governance in general. Every health trust is required to have a risk assessment strategy and system, which is periodically inspected so that lessons may be learned from serous clinical incidents. The chapter identifies the retrospective and pro-active approaches to clinical risk assessment mandated by government bodies such as the National Patient Safety Agency. The pro-active approach, known as clinical risk profiling, requires the identifying of potential risk issues and their ranking according to a measure of seriousness so that the most serious may be targeted for preventive action. This retrospective approach involves the investigation of serious clinical incidents. The investigation, to be conducted by an objective and independent observer, follows linear step-by-step procedures meant to identify the facts about what actually happened and so uncover the root cause of the incident. This is then supposed to lead to action ensuring that it can never happen again. Norman shows how this approach leads to the apportionment of blame. A particular individual clinician may be blamed, or the blame may be ascribed to the 'system', or both may be blamed. This then means that all the other individuals who may have been involved in some way do not need to take personal responsibility for what has happened.

In this chapter, Norman reports the reflective conversations she and a colleague had about the preparation of a report on one serious clinical incident at her hospital. Her colleague expresses his frustration as he attempts to objectively follow the procedure and so uncover the factual root cause. His frustration arises from the different, and conflicting, stories that different people involved in the clinical incident tell him about what happened. In their discussion, they realize that this experience challenges taken-for-granted notions in the mandated approach to reporting on serious clinical incidents. They begin to question whether it is possible to be objective in any simple way. For example, during discussions with the manager supposedly to blame for this incident, the investigator inevitably comes to know the manager as a person and may begin to interpret events in such a way as to protect that manager. In other words, we do not normally treat each other simply as objects – emotion inevitably colours what we do in relation to each other. Even more problematic is the notion that an investigator can uncover the facts about what actually happened and so identify a root cause. Norman draws on the perspective of complex responsive processes to argue that different people will inevitably make different meaning of the same events. Furthermore, as we tell our story about what 'actually' happened, each of us is reconstructing the story anew in the light of what we now know and what we anticipate for the future. The mandated approach to reporting on serious critical incidents implicitly assumes a linear view of time in which the past is over with and the meaning of an incident lies in the past. By going back to the past we can discover what the meaning is. The perspective of complex responsive processes focuses attention on the present, arguing that we are always making new meaning in the present – in effect we rewrite history, affected by what has happened and also by what we now expect will happen. If one takes this view of time, it becomes quite understandable that an investigator's attempts to uncover what really happened will be frustrating.

As Norman and her colleague continue their discussion about accountability for the clinical incident, they question the apportionment of blame to a particular individual and to the system. They begin to see that many people were involved in some way, including both of them. This conclusion does not lead them to argue against preparing the report. Instead they now approach its preparation in an involved way by circulating drafts of the report to others involved and arranging for them to meet for a discussion which is then reflected in the next draft. They notice that in this conversational process, those involved begin to change their practice in ways they probably would not do if they simply read the completed report. We think that what this chapter does is problematize the easy assumption that simply following mandated procedures will bring about desired change. In addition, the chapter points to how change emerges in local interaction in which the discussions around preparation of the report effect change.

5 The experience of clinical risk assessment in the health sector

Karen Norman

- Mainstream ways of thinking about clinical risk management in the NHS
- Investigations into serious clinical incidents
- Exploring retrospective and prospective approaches to risk management
- Undertaking SCI investigations in order to learn from the past
- Introducing a perspective informed by complex responsive processes
- Implications for practice when locating causality for incidents in the individual, the system or both
- Objectivity and the scientific method
- Challenging the notion of an 'independent observer'
- Accountability and learning lessons
- Conclusion

I am with a group of colleagues who have been nominated as the '*Clinical Risk Pillar Leads*' for their clinical directorates. The purpose of the day is to introduce them to the concepts of clinical risk management and explore how they might want to develop these ideas within their directorates. We are about halfway through the morning and the presentations thus far have generated some lively debate and interest. Stephen, the Associate Medical Director for Clinical Risk, has caught people's attention by some staggering statistics regarding the level of harm caused to patients as a consequence of errors in health care. Stephen's slides summarize some of the key findings from the 1999 National Academy of Science's Institute of Medicine report *To Err is Human* (1999). This found that medical errors in hospitals in the USA killed between approximately 44,000 and 98,000 people a year – which he notes is the equivalent of three 747 jumbo jets filled with patients crashing every two days. He states that medical errors kill more people than AIDS, breast cancer or road accidents. The report also revealed that medication errors affect more than one out of every 100 hospital patients, and 7 per cent of inpatients contract a hospital-acquired infection. Although I have seen these figures a number of times, I am still shocked by them. I also enjoy watching colleagues' responses to this. There is often a tendency to think of clinical risk management as somewhat boring, but these figures inevitably assist in challenging some of these assumptions.

Alan switches on a television documentary I have not seen for some time. This tells the story, through dramatic reconstruction, of a young boy, Ritchie, who was admitted to Great Ormond Street Hospital and who died in agony after Vincristine was mistakenly injected into his spine. The initial thrust of the documentary appears to be one of seeking the individual who was responsible for the mistake. At the time, allegations of manslaughter were made against the doctor concerned and this raised significant consternation in the medical and national press. Halfway through the documentary, we are introduced to the professor who has been asked to lead an enquiry into the death. He takes over as the main protagonist of the story. Dramatic camera angles accompanied by suspense-generating music show the professor sweeping majestically down the corridor armed with piles of notes that will enable him to reach his 'verdict'. He describes how initially he was totally convinced that it was gross negligence on the part of the individual doctor. However, after the arrival of two new piles of evidence, he had begun to piece together a catalogue of errors which had led him to conclude that it was '*the system*', rather than the individual doctor, which was at fault.

The programme reconstructs these events in a compelling and emotive way that leaves me feeling extremely distressed. Ritchie's mother describes the terrible suffering he went through before he died and describes some of the events leading up to this. These events are tracked backwards to reconstruct a linear pattern consisting of a chain in which one action led inevitably to another. We learn that vincristine is normally never stored in the area where the procedure is carried out because of the known risk of mistakenly administering it. However, on this occasion, the staff were unfamiliar with the procedure and not aware of the rule about storing the drugs. The documentary takes us back to the beginning and describes how Ritchie was mistakenly fed a digestive biscuit and as a consequence (since food should be withheld for several hours prior to an anaesthetic) his treatment was delayed. At this point, the camera zooms in on a hand holding a biscuit and a voice-over cuts in to inform us: 'What emerged was a much more complex picture of small mistakes all the way down the line leading slowly but directly to Ritchie's tragic death. When Ritchie arrived at Great Ormond Street in the early hours of July 25th 1997, doctors discovered that he had recently eaten a biscuit. This one digestive biscuit turned out to be the bizarre catalyst that defied the hospital's safety procedures and led to Ritchie's tragic death.'

I am surprised to find myself extremely irritated at the way the film unfolds. The last time I watched it, I recall thinking it was a useful means of moving away from a more traditional approach, initially advocated in risk management where the blame for mistakes is located with the individual practitioner, to one which takes account of problems in a wider 'system'. This is now being increasingly promulgated as a useful framework in clinical risk management. I try to identify for myself what it is in the film that now irritates me so intensely. I conclude it is because:

- The inference that a biscuit can in some way be responsible for the death of a child seems ludicrous to me.
- The latter point seems to me to be a misrepresentation of some of the useful elements of systems theory.
- The documentary postulates a position where the 'cause' of Ritchie's death lies *either* with the individual *or* with 'the system'. This is a position I find myself disagreeing with – for reasons I shall explore further in this chapter.

Mainstream ways of thinking about clinical risk management in the NHS

The way of thinking I have described above is reinforced by the frameworks that practitioners like myself are being taught to use. One such framework has recently been issued to NHS trusts by the National Patient Safety Agency (NPSA) regarding the suspension of medical staff who are involved in clinical incidents. A flow chart is presented which guides the reader from one question to another, leading to the appropriate decision regarding suspension. When I use this flow chart, I notice how I am led to conclude that culpability for the errors lies *either* with the individual *or* with the system. I now recognize this way of thinking as a dualism which is a feature of systems theory. Here, humans are thought of as rational, autonomous individuals who observe systems objectively and ascribe purposive behaviour to them. Causality here is rationalist, and a rational human being is free to choose. On the other hand, humans are also thought of as parts or members of the system being observed and so are subject to formative causality, where they are formed by the system. This implies that humans are not free to choose but are subject to the purpose and formative process of the system. Systems thinkers themselves have identified problems with this analysis, and the evolution of soft and critical systems thinking towards the end of the twentieth century has attempted to address them (Checkland, 1983; Jackson, 2000; Midgley, 2000).

A systematic approach to clinical risk management is being mandated in all trusts as part of an inspection process (Health Care Commission, 2004). This requires us to have a strategy and system in place for investigating, reporting and learning lessons from serious clinical incidents (SCIs). I think it is important to make a distinction between the systematic frameworks we design and use in organizations, which we often call systems, such as clinical risk management systems, and speaking about the organization 'as if' it were a system. The former understanding of 'system' is a necessary and desirable tool to be used in my work, but the latter, namely thinking of the whole organization as a 'system', is far less helpful. In order to explore this more carefully, the following section develops the key features I now recognize in aspects of risk management that appear to treat the organization as if it really were a system.

Investigations into serious clinical incidents

The way in which we investigate clinical incidents within my own organization has the following characteristics:

- The purpose of such investigations/enquiries is to uncover some kind of 'objective truth' which is believed to be enfolded in the set of circumstances leading to the incident.
- Emphasis is placed on the importance of '*objectivity*' in order to uncover this 'truth'. Hence investigators are selected on the basis of some kind of impartiality in order to avoid biasing the findings due to emotional connection to the incident or personal prejudices. Personal credibility, expertise and integrity are also selection criteria for investigators.

- Such investigations are grounded in the paradigm of a scientific research method, where an independent objective observer constructs a hypothesis through scoping the investigation or agreeing terms of reference to identify the questions that need answering. The investigator then seeks evidence in a rational and logical manner in order to generate conclusions.

- In order to do this, different tools and techniques are used to extrapolate, collate, analyse and synthesize data in a way that enables robust conclusions to be drawn about the 'cause'. Such techniques include (Dineen, 2002) root cause analysis; barrier analysis; informal interviews; written statements; time lines/chronology of events.

- At the conclusion of the enquiry, the panel presents its findings on 'what really happened' and identifies where accountability for this lies.

- The panel makes recommendations for improvement which typically stress the importance of 'learning lessons' from this incident and of disseminating these more widely in order to reduce the likelihood of recurrence. It is commonly said that this is to ensure that *this can never happen again*.

For example, one SCI I was involved in had to do with the admission of an unconscious patient known to be on continuous ambulatory peritoneal dialysis (CAPD). The patient's husband, a doctor, accompanied her to hospital, having diagnosed his wife as hypoglycaemic, that is, suffering from low blood sugar. The patient's blood sugar levels were checked by the nurse on the ward on our portable machine and her blood sugar readings were within normal limits. However, the patient remained unwell and her husband insisted that she be given a bolus of dextrose, after which she subsequently improved. The husband contacted the chief executive's office to complain when he was later made aware of a Medical Devices Alert (MDA/2003/01) which had been issued three months previously by the Medicines and Healthcare Products Regulatory Agency (MHRA). This alert highlighted the risk of a potentially fatal overestimation of blood glucose levels when Brand A test strips are used for patients who are on treatments containing maltose, as was the patient in this case. In conversations with the nursing staff on the renal ward, the patient's husband confirmed that the unit was using the 'Brand A' monitor and that the nurses were aware that there was a potential problem with this. The husband was understandably concerned that nursing staff were openly prepared to use equipment which they knew to be potentially dangerous and requested that the event should be investigated as an SCI. The investigation, which I will call the Clayton

Unit Investigation, identified a range of complex issues which I shall now explore further.

Reflections on the causes of the Clayton Unit SCI

It is late one afternoon and I am on the phone to Mike. Mike is an Assistant Director of Clinical Governance, with responsibility for clinical risk. We have worked together in different capacities over the past ten years. I have just been reading an early draft of the report he has produced on the Clayton Unit investigation. Mike is expressing his frustration with writing this report. He is finding it difficult to come to any conclusion about '*what really happened*'. He is describing how he had *thought* he had grasped some conclusions but then he would interview someone else who would completely turn all these ideas upside down again. He explains that it was like turning over lots of different stones and then finding a whole new can of worms that needed '*sorting out*'. As I listen to him I find a lot of what he is saying resonates strongly with me with respect to my experience of being involved in similar investigations. I recall my own annoyance with my inability to get the facts to fit together neatly to form a clear picture so I can write a report. Mark describes very vividly how everyone seems to have a 'different take' on what happened – even those closely involved in the same incident.

As we talk about the inevitability of people having different perceptions, Mike comes up with the idea of holding a seminar as part of the training programme for dealing with SCIs. He decides to use a critical incident in a football match as an analogy for an SCI. At this seminar, Mike shows some film clips he has selected from *Match of the Day*. The commentators, players and fans all express very different perceptions, both about what they think they are seeing and about who they believe is responsible for the incident on the pitch. Through working in this way, we start noticing how past experience, biases and prejudices affect perceptions of what has happened. Mike shows clips of footballers recalling 'a long history' of rivalry between the clubs and 'history repeating itself'. This always seems to generate lively conversation with our seminar participants, who also have 'different takes' on what they think they have seen. Mike shows clips against a time line and we find ourselves making one judgement when we look at a snapshot of the incident itself but our perspective seems to change when we look later at clips taken before and after the incident.

We have run this seminar several times now. The last time, Mike mentioned that he had changed his mind yet again about what had happened after seeing the clips again and discussing interpretations with participants. These reflections question the validity of the linear way in which we have been making connections when investigating SCIs and our assumption that objective facts lie in the past in a way that views the past as unchanging. It seems to me that we are struggling with the first assumption listed above with respect to our taken-for-granted method of investigation, namely that there is an objective truth which is 'there', waiting to be discovered.

Garfinkel (1967) studied how juries make decisions, finding that jurors did not first decide the harm and its extent, then allocate blame and finally choose the remedy. Instead, they first decided a remedy and then decided the 'facts', from among alternative claims, that justified the remedy. Jurors essentially created a sequence that was meaningfully consistent and then treated it 'as if' it was a thing that actually occurred. 'If the interpretation makes good sense, then that is what happened' (Garfinkel, 1967, p. 106). Hence facts were made sensible *retrospectively* to support the jurors' choice of verdict. Garfinkel summarized decision making in commonsense situations of choice in this way:

> In place of the view that decisions are made as the occasions require, an alternative formulation needs to be entertained. It consists of the possibility that the person defines retrospectively the decisions that have been made. The outcome comes before the decision.
>
> (ibid.)

What I find intriguing about the above is its implication for our whole approach to investigating clinical incidents. This is a radical challenge to explanations of decision making which posit that we think first and then act.

Exploring retrospective and prospective approaches to risk management

On discovering new information and discussing this with people through our SCI interviews, we constantly make new sense of what happened during the incident. As we do this, we reinterpret other information we had gleaned previously. I see that the theoretical approaches outlined above seldom make reference to these kinds of activities. In particular,

I am struggling with the proposition which leads us to believe that we are establishing the 'facts' from the past which in some way are fixed. I now understand that the meaning we place on events leading up to the incident will inevitably change *after* the incident as we make a new kind of sense of it. In doing this I am drawing on a different notion of causality to that evidenced in much of the risk management literature – namely rational (cause/effect) and formative (systems theories). I have gained these insights through exploring the theoretical perspective of complex responsive processes of relating (Stacey *et al.*, 2000). Stacey and his colleagues describe the phenomenon I am experiencing in the following way:

> micro-temporal structure is the gesture and the response the gesture calls forth, taken together. The here-and-now, then, has a circular temporal structure because the gesture takes its meaning from the response (micro future) which only has meaning in relation to the gesture (the micro past), and the response in turn acts back to potentially change the gesture (micro past). The experience of meaning is occurring in a micro present and it accounts for the fact that we can experience presentness. What is happening here is truly paradoxical, for the future is changing the past just as the past is changing the future. In terms of meaning the future changes the past and the past changes the future and meaning lies not at a single point in the present but in the circular process of the present in which there is the potential for transformation as well as repetition.
>
> (Stacey *et al.*, 2000, p. 35)

As I reflect on these views, I come to realize that they have the potential to orientate our approach to SCIs in very different ways. Traditionally, one focuses on attempts to design the future in a way that reduces risk, which we refer to in risk management as a pro-active approach. To summarize, this includes an attempt (known as 'clinical risk profiling') to predict key areas of concern in order for preventive action to be taken to reduce the risk of things going wrong. Hence we identify a 'gap' between where we are now and where we need to be, and through action planning we identify how to 'close' that gap. For example, one approach currently being promulgated involves identifying potential risk issues and calculating an overall risk rating for each issue by multiplying the '*probability*' of something happening by the '*severity*' that would arise as a consequence. A list is then drawn up, ranking issues in order of severity, and colour-coding them using a traffic-light system in which the red-rated issues are to receive urgent and immediate attention (Ireland *et al.*, 2002).

While this approach can be useful, it has limitations if used in a way that abstracts from meaning in people's everyday practice. Conversely, we sometimes focus on learning from the past, referred to most commonly in the risk management literature as a 'reactive' strategy, which is what we are doing when we investigate SCIs to discover what went wrong. In order to explore this latter approach in more depth, I return to my conversation with Mike, before developing some of my own ideas about an alternative approach to clinical risk management which focuses on the present, rather than past- or future-orientated approaches.

Undertaking SCI investigations in order to learn from the past

As we continue with our telephone conversation, Mike and I joke about the fact that when we had undertaken our training on tools and techniques for investigating incidents it seemed as though the process of collating the incident report should be very straightforward (see Dineen, 2002). It was presented to us as a matter of collecting all the different pieces of the jigsaw and putting them together in a way that gave a very clear picture. From this '*evidence*' it should have been easy for the lead investigator to unveil some kind of denouement and present the real truth about what had really happened. Dineen's investigation training was informed by the work of influential writers on clinical risk management (CRM) within the NHS, namely Reason and Heron (1997) and Vincent (2003).

These writers call for a review of the case records to scope or frame issues to be investigated; undertaking interviews and receiving statements; undertaking an analysis; and preparation of the final report. Once the interviews and analysis are completed, the author of the report should make a composite of all of them, detailing the whole incident from start to finish. If the protocol is followed systematically and the interview and analysis are conducted thoroughly, the report and implications of the incident should emerge from the analysis in '*a relatively straightforward fashion*' (Vincent, 2003, p. 449). Once this composite is complete, it is stated that there should be a clear view of the problem and the circumstances which led up to it, and the flaws in the care processes should be readily apparent. Vincent recommends that the report consider the implications of the incidents for the department and organization and that this section should summarize the general contributory factors and the implications for action. Lessons learned should be drawn out and action plans developed to deal with the problems should be formulated.

In spite of our understanding of this model, Mike's experience was that the pieces of evidence he was collecting did not seem to be fitting together in this neat way. He said something like: 'Initially it seemed a straightforward case of human error. The MDA alert should have gone to the Unit and the person responsible for sending it did not do this. In spite of this, however, it seems many people were aware of it. Now I am sitting here having interviewed a dozen people who all tell stories that contradict each other and send me off in a completely new direction which unearths a whole new can of worms. This uncovers a whole new set of issues I feel need investigating. It seems to involve everybody in the Trust! I have even discovered something connected with this that came over my desk some months ago – and yours – so we are all implicated! I can't believe how complex it is and how difficult it is to piece together and make any sense of it.'

We have a detailed discussion around our difficulties in trying to piece together, in a coherent way, all the different fragments of information collected during the interviews and to determine the 'root cause' of the factors that had led to the error. What our experience of this investigation seems to be indicating is that it is virtually impossible to identify a linear chain of events from which we could demonstrate a cause and effect to link back to some underlying '*root cause*' as suggested.

In risk management, systems thinking has helped to develop alternative frameworks which make a useful contribution to overcoming the limitations of technically rational approaches. Specifically, they seek to overcome the problem of locating the 'cause' or 'blame' for the mistake with the individual practitioner. A common framework is the *Swiss Cheese* model of accident causation. It is based on the analogy of errors being like the holes in a Swiss cheese. Normally, the holes in the cheese do not go all the way through. By analogy, mistakes in hospitals often get '*blocked*' (as in the cheese) by a barrier (a check in the system). I notice how this way of thinking assumes there is a 'right way' of doing things which, if we can in some way unlock or discover it, we can control through putting in place the necessary barriers. However, on rare occasions the hole goes all the way through, the cheese and our '*barriers*' fail, the holes 'line up' and a catastrophic incident occurs. Authors of such approaches then typically try to identify where the 'holes' may line up in order that preventive action may be taken. A common feature of such systems is to encourage staff to identify 'red flags' in processes in order that feedback may be used to return the system to a safe state. Some approaches seek to build these 'red flags' into 'the system' itself in an attempt to 'human-proof' it. There are other features of this approach which remind me of the useful work done by Senge (1990) in this field in addressing some of the shortcomings of hard systems thinking. What I see in some of the CRM approaches (which are struggling with similar issues) is an attempt to identify what Senge would call 'leverage points', in order that the manager can spot them and in some way intervene to control them. What this kind of thinking does not address is where 'the system' comes from in the first place. I see a tendency for it to describe the professionals within it as passive victims, rather than active participants in its creation. This has a fundamental impact on the concept of accountability – 'the system' is to blame in a way that relieves individuals within it of accountability for their actions.

In a more recent article, Vincent adopts similar reservations to mine and signals a move to a systems-based approach. He notes:

> The purpose of such analysis is often framed as the need to find the root cause of an adverse incident, tracing it back over a series of events to some fundamental problem. However, this perspective is misleading. . . . First, it implies that the incident has a single root cause, or at least a small number of causes, but this is an over-simplification. Usually, a chain of events and a wide variety of contributory factors lead up to the event. . . . For these reasons, we prefer the approach called 'systems analysis' over 'root-cause analysis.'
>
> (Vincent, 2003, p. 1051)

Introducing a perspective informed by complex responsive processes

My study of complex responsive processes has led me to consider a different perspective compared to the pro-active and reactive approaches described above. Complex responsive processes focus on change arising from our interactions with each other in 'the living present' (Stacey *et al.*, 2000). This notion of focusing on the present (as opposed to the past and future) and how this orientation could offer a radically different perspective on risk management has become a key interest for me.

There is a growing interest in complexity sciences in the NHS with respect to what this can teach us about how organizations function. Reference is made in the risk management literature to this branch of science as well. For example, Firth-Cozens (1995) uses an analogy from chaos theory to argue that health care behaviours can be divided into those that are habitual and routine, those which are largely routine and able to adapt to fit changing circumstances, and those which cannot easily be foreseen and so require a different type of learning activity around anticipation. She notes that although many of the routine procedures arise from previous training and are informed by guidelines and protocols, in other areas working practices exist which should be tackled through the establishment of habit. She suggests that a team is an appropriate organizational unit to determine what these habits are and how they should be developed through the use of evidence or guidelines where these exist. She also advocates periodic use of 'horizon gazing' in order to anticipate potential changes and new risks, and to share these within the wider organization. She also notes the importance of diversity in teams (Firth-Cozens, 1998; Ilgen, 1999), pointing to how this broader knowledge base increases the team's ability to address its tasks well, so long as all team members feel able to participate in decision making.

My observation would be that although claiming to draw from branches of chaos theory, interpretations such as those made above still have a number of features of systems thinking and, as a consequence, the limitations which I have already identified. I now see that this kind of interpretation leads to the split I have described above between reactive and pro-active approaches, which are either past- or future-orientated rather than reorganizing the present. I notice how Firth-Cozens assumes we can divide health care behaviours into the '*habitual/routine*' and those which '*cannot be foreseen*', and, depending on which we are dealing with, can prescribe different kinds of learning activity. This way of thinking therefore also has implications for the actions we choose to take when considering how 'organizations' learn – which is a central concern for those of us working in risk management. The difficulty I have with such interpretations is that I am now arguing that we cannot know what the outcome of our action will be until we make sense with others about its meaning (Mead, 1934). Therefore, in the movement of our action, we cannot know, until it is complete, whether the outcome will be the 'habitual, expected, or surprising and unexpected'. We can only judge this in retrospect. For me the use of the word 'habit' in this way is problematic since it implies a 'thing' which is there, rather than something that emerges in our interaction with each other which has the potential for replication or change. I no longer think of habit as something we can decide beforehand through a blueprint which we then enforce or socially re-engineer. This is because my experience of the Clayton Unit investigation is that the guidelines that are in place are often not routinely followed. In the past, my response would have been that we therefore need to re-enforce the content of such guidelines. Many of our action plans post-SCIs include a requirement that all unit staff attend training on them, or confirm they have read and understood them. Yet it strikes me now that such strategies do not seem to eradicate a common root cause in many of our SCIs, namely staff failure to follow procedures. The question as to why we are unable to follow guidelines (or 'simple' rules) in human organizations becomes central.

I also have difficulty with respect to tools such as 'horizon gazing'. This is because I have learned that one of the features of complexity theory is the nature of unpredictability in complex systems. Therefore, if we take some of these ideas seriously, the notion of trying to predict the unpredictable would seem to be inconsistent with the insights from complexity science. We cannot therefore appeal to it as a source of validation for such approaches. Another fundamental insight from the complexity sciences is that genuinely new emergent patterns arise from *within* the organization itself and this occurs as a consequence of the resonance and interaction of the agents within it. Hence no one single component can effect change on its own; all play a part. In this sense, organizational change is genuinely self-organizing and emergent.

My argument would be that these two insights offer a radically different understanding of what is going on in critical incidents. The first of these is that patterns of activity we experience in organizations emerge not from some blueprint or plan, or because someone at the top of the organization has set the mission and values, but in a self-organizing manner. The daily micro interactions, which are expressed through our everyday conversations and the patterns that emerge in them, are both predictable and unpredictable, stable and unstable, *at the same time*. Hence what I experience has an element of familiarity about it and this is grounded in my past experience. It is very rare in my daily life that things occur which are so unfamiliar I can make no sense of them at all. Yet at the same time small and unexpected differences can occur and become amplified, which then surprise me.

I see this expressed when people remark '*this was an accident waiting to happen*', which reflects the recognition that what has occurred was in some ways anticipated, and conversely expressions of complete surprise such as '*I never expected this to happen to me*', indicating an encounter with the unexpected. I also note that the explanation of causality here is very different from that expressed in systems thinking as evidenced in the risk management literature. Unlike a linear process of cause and effect which is tracked back to an underlying root cause, or a formative framework informed by systems thinking (*Swiss Cheese*), causality in complex systems emerges from *within* the interaction itself. All actions and inactions by the agents contribute to the next iteration or pattern of the organization and each gives rise either to a new iteration or to a replication of previous activities. This is very different from systems thinking and its notion of cybernetic feedback which works to maintain a system in a state of equilibrium, thereby dampening down any unexpected amplifications in order to keep a system within pre-existing parameters. In the latter, genuine novelty cannot arise, whereas in complex response processes of relating, which draw on analogies from the studies of complex adaptive systems, it can and does. This radically different notion of causality offers a better explanation of the phenomenon Mike and I are discussing with respect to his frustration at his inability to identify clear root causes in the renal incident. What he seems to be describing to me feels more analogous to complex interactions which give rise to patterns which are both predictable and unpredictable at the same time.

This way of understanding has had a fundamental impact on my practice for the following reasons. First, it presents a radical challenge to one of the underpinning assumptions in risk management, namely that we can fix or solve the root cause of mistakes to prevent the same thing from ever happening again. If patterns of human interaction are iterated from moment to moment as, at the same time, replication and potential transformation through the amplification of tiny events, then there will always be the potential for mistakes to be repeated or for patterns to radically improve. In this way of thinking the root of all change lies in the action we take as the living present. Therefore, what has become a major issue for me is focusing on my contribution to what is happening 'here and now', because I am accountable for the outcomes. I now understand these outcomes as paradoxically controllable and uncontrollable at the same time in that I can influence them by my acts and omissions but my control of them is constrained by the actions of others.

This raises very serious questions with respect to the notion of accountability because I have to accept responsibility for the outcomes that arise from my action or inaction with respect to the things I pay attention to in my everyday working life, even though I cannot control these outcomes. What therefore becomes important is how I improvise within the situations that present themselves to me, which have both an air of familiarity about them and sometimes an element of surprise. Second, what takes on an increasing significance in this way of thinking is recognizing patterns and themes in conversations which have the potential for replication and transformation at the same time – themes such as how we can effectively distribute MDA notices, how the actions people take on receipt of these notices are recognized as patterns we need to continually revisit and pay attention to. Stacey elaborates on the importance of patterns through analogies with complex systems, and notes:

> When it operates in the paradoxical dynamic of stability and instability, the behavior of the system unfolds in so complex a manner so dependent upon the detail of what happens that the links between cause and effect are lost. One can no longer count on a certain input leading to a certain given output. The laws themselves operate to escalate small chance disturbances along the way, breaking the link between an input and a subsequent output. The long term future of a system operating in the dynamic of stability and instability at the same time is not simply difficult to see: it is, for all practical purposes, un-knowable.
>
> If this is applied to organizations, one would raise questions about decision making techniques that involve step by step reasoning from assumptions about the future. One would have to rely instead on using qualitative patterns to reason by analogy and intuition. Those who succeeded would be those who saw patterns where others search for specific links between causes and events.
>
> (Stacey, 2003, p. 229)

These insights offer an alternative way of understanding and dealing with some of the issues Mike and I have been tackling.

Implications for practice when locating causality for incidents in the individual, the system or both

As I am talking to Mike, he describes how after interviewing the staff, he changes his mind about sole responsibility being with the risk manager and instead is beginning to think that this is a 'systems error'. He starts to explain to me how our internal system for cascading MDA alerts is a systems problem. His investigation has shown that over the past year this topic has been discussed at three formal Trust committees and numerous informal meetings between staff across our Trust. It seemed clear at the time that the MDA system was set up with the risk manager having responsibility for cascading alerts through an agreed route, which would then be actioned locally by relevant staff. Although the alert stated it needed to go to the Clayton Unit, because he was new in post and in the absence of any comprehensive Trust directory of services, it seems that this was overlooked. Mike is identifying that in spite of this oversight, numerous people were none the less aware of it through other means. The question we keep returning to throughout our investigation is why none of them had taken any decisive action about the alert or the problematic machines. However, as the investigation continued, it became clear that there *were* things which some people had done. In operating theatres, some managers had decided to purchase a different machine, which we later discovered was in breach of our Trust policy. Ironically, there was a meeting planned in the Clayton Unit on the day of the incident where this issue was on the agenda. However, for me, a fundamental issue remains regarding responsibility and accountability in this incident, and how we deal with and speak about accountability implications if we think a 'system' can make mistakes or take decisions.

Our SCI report concluded that '*both staff and systems failed to mitigate the error*'. I note in our report how we also make assumptions about 'levels'. We quote from a nurse who said: 'As I understood it, it would be the Trust's decision on what blood sugar monitoring equipment we used.' It is also noted in the report that if this is the case, 'it appears unclear about where corporate responsibility lies'. Reading this now, I am troubled by the lack of clarity about what we mean when we talk about 'corporate responsibility'. This is because the corporation is not something or someone I can point to in our structural chart or have a conversation with about my concerns. I have come to notice, through this investigation, how common it is for us to talk about our Trust as an '*it*' to which is attributed the capacity to act with intention; hence the above quote from a nurse who believes that 'the Trust' will make the decision about the equipment.

This brings me back to the point made earlier about the important distinction I see between talking about the systematic tools that humans develop in the course of their everyday work and talking about the organization 'as if' it really were a system, as the nurse (and those of us who wrote and endorsed the report without questioning this) was doing. I am reminded of Griffin's (2002) work on this. He describes how in today's society we speak about large organizations, consisting of thousands of employees, as acting with culpable intention and being ethically responsible. He notes: 'When we talk in this way, we are talking "as if" an inanimate, nebulous entity called a corporation, or a "system", can have intention but in doing this we tend to forget the "as if"' (2002, p. 2).

This resonates significantly for me with respect to the quote from the nurse, which typifies the approach to clinical risk management in the NHS, as identified in the television documentary, where culpability was initially placed with the doctor and later with 'the system', within which the biscuit was identified as the catalyst. This way of thinking is well developed in the literature on clinical risk management. For example, as well as identifying the human causes, either individually or in teams, the literature makes the distinction between active failures, consisting of mistakes made by practitioners in the provision of care, and latent failures which represent flaws in the administrative and productive systems (Eagle *et al.*, 1992).

Management decisions and organizational processes are then seen as being at a different '*level*' to that of the individual practitioner. The defence barriers at a different level 'fail' and the holes for the Swiss cheese line up and 'cause' an incident. This way of thinking has clearly powerfully influenced our conclusions in our report. This conceptualization regarding different levels is reinforced in our everyday conversation at work, where I often hear people talking about the importance of the need to take patient safety more seriously 'at Board level' or 'Trust level'. Yet in rereading the Clayton Unit report, I can see the limitations and indeed the dangers of this way of thinking. This seems to me to abrogate individuals from any personal responsibility for their participation in the circumstances which contributed to the clinical incident. What happens when we think in this way is that we locate ethical responsibility in both '*the system*', simply taking it for granted that a '*system*' can be ethically responsible, and in a few individuals, for example, the Chief Executive of the Board. Griffin (2002) points to how, in doing this, we adopt a particular view of leadership in which it is the individual leaders who are blamed or punished when things go wrong or praised and rewarded when things go right. The rest of us are allocated passive roles as victims of '*the system*' and of manipulative leaders, and our salvation lies in the actions of heroic leaders. He concludes that in thinking in this way, we are obscuring how we are all together involved in the dangerous situations which arise.

It seems to me that what Mike and I are struggling with is the limitations of our frameworks to adequately explain the phenomena we are experiencing in our practice when trying to investigate clinical incidents. Specifically, we seem to have moved from one unsatisfactory way of working (in which clinicians were blamed, shamed and punished for making mistakes) to another which seems to locate the cause for the mistake at some higher 'level' by defining it as a systems error for which 'the Trust' has responsibility and accountability. This also seems to be unsatisfactory, both in terms of its theoretical basis and in practical terms with respect to co-creating a situation where it is possible for professionals to believe they are passive victims of some higher system that takes responsibility for their practice.

Further developments in systems theory have recognized these limitations and problems, and have attempted to deal with them. For example, some do focus on social relationships in the notion of communities of practice (Wenger, 1998). However, Stacey (2003), while noting that these developments have introduced very important social, ethical, ideological and political aspects of the decision-making processes encountered in organizational life, also notes that they do not depart from the key aspects of systems thinking. Hence they continue to be based on the spatial metaphor of an '*inside*' or '*outside*', which introduces a dualist way of thinking in which one causality applies to the inside, and another to an outside. The '*inside*' moves according to formative causality, and the outside, ultimately in the form of autonomous individuals who draw the boundaries, is still subject to rationalist causality as seen in the television documentary.

To summarize, I have argued thus far for the important distinction between designing and using systems as tools in our work (which I believe is useful) and the problems inherent when thinking of the organization as if it really is a system. I have begun to explore the distinctions between risk management approaches that look either to the past (through learning lessons from mistakes) or are future oriented (through risk assessment and horizon scanning). I have also introduced the theory of complex responsive processes of relating, in which there is a different explanation of causality in organizations. This focuses on the root of all change arising from our interactions with each other in 'the living present'. What I have found in recognizing these distinctions is that these insights have started to influence me with respect to my actions when investigating SCIs. I will explore this in more detail below.

Objectivity and the scientific method

I return to my conversation with Mike about his draft report on the Clayton Unit incident. We turn to a slightly different topic which had been of concern to me. A number of sections in his report contain a lot of detail and some attempt to draw conclusions. Yet the section Mike had written about the MDA notice and why this had not been distributed seemed to make virtually no mention of the responsibilities of the named individual who was supposed to trigger the process. I noticed that it seemed to go into quite a lot of detail about a range of (seemingly justifiable) mitigating circumstances as to why this had not happened. While talking through my observations about this on the telephone with Mike, there was an uncharacteristic silence at the other end of the line for a short while. His reply was something like: 'Yes – I know. To be absolutely honest, when I interviewed him he seemed like a nice bloke. I felt really sorry for him because he was obviously upset about what had happened and worried about the consequences. I've also heard that his boss has got a reputation for being a bit tough about things like this and I was concerned that if I did not focus on the wider issues there could be a danger that he might lose his job.'

Some time later, Mike and I discuss this conversation. We reflect on how, in spite of what the theory on our incident training had taught us, it is virtually impossible to remain 'truly objective'. We note how we all bring our own biases, prejudices and previous experience to each new situation. Thus even though we may know very little about a specific situation if we are brought in as an 'outsider', we quickly form relationships with, and opinions about, the individuals whom we are investigating. Inevitably this affects the conclusions we draw. We talk about the sense of accountability and responsibility we both felt when leading such investigations and drawing such conclusions. If we 'get it wrong' we could either unfairly jeopardize someone's professional reputation or, conversely, fail to take action that could lead to another incident which causes harm to other patients.

I see how such approaches are grounded in the scientific method, in which an independent observer uncovers some kind of universal 'truth'. What Mike and I seem to be discovering is that the 'truth' (or people's perceptions of it) is different and shifts constantly, and that there are limitations and flaws in an investigation framework promulgating an 'independent' investigator.

Challenging the notion of an 'independent observer'

These insights provoked further discussions with the rest of the CRM team which led us to change a number of features in our investigation process including:

- Convening a small, diverse team to scope and oversee investigations.
- Peer reviewing of progress of each ongoing investigation at our weekly meetings.
- Ongoing discussions on the balance between 'insider' investigators and 'outsider' support for our team.

These changes were influenced by our growing recognition of:

- The importance of diversity in changing patterns of behaviour.
- The importance of reflection with others as a means of generating new knowledge and sense-making processes.

To summarize, Mike and I were becoming increasingly sceptical about the validity of the notion of the objective investigator. I became curious about how this had been developed, and revisited the literature to explore this further.

Stacey (2003, p. 413) notes:

> Neither researcher nor manager can step outside the conversational processes that are the organization simply because their work requires them to talk to others. What they say affects what they hear and what they hear affects what they say. From this perspective, then, a manager cannot stand outside organizational processes and control them, direct them or even perturb them in an intentional direction. All such intentions are gestures made to others in an organization and what happens unfolds from the ongoing responses. One might call this a methodology of emergent enquiry.

Complex responsive processes theory therefore moves away from the notion of the manager as objective observer. Instead, we are understood to be participants in complex responsive processes, engaged in emergent enquiry into what they are doing and what steps we should take next. We may also be enquiring into the nature of our own complex responsive processes of relating. This is what it means to be reflective. This theory provides an explanation of what managers are doing, rather than of what they should be doing (Stacey, 2003, p. 414). This is why, in my narrative, I increasingly focus on the detail of my everyday practice and how I make sense of it. I now find myself doing this with my work colleagues with increasing frequency, whereas in the past we spent more time speaking of what we 'should' be doing rather than what we '*are*' doing.

As Stacey observes, it would be methodologically inconsistent of such a theory to attempt to yield general prescriptions on how self-organization should proceed and what should emerge from it. Such an interpretation would be the direct opposite of what it is explaining. Instead, the theory of complex responsive processes invites recognition of the uniqueness and non-repeatability of experience.

> Organizations characterized by the dynamics of bounded instability
> will therefore all be unique in some important way. The experience of
> one cannot be repeated, at important levels of detail, by another.
> Giving examples of success in one organization to managers in
> another is likely to be spurious.
>
> (Stacey, 2003, p. 415)

This causes Stacey to postulate that this is probably why the track record of identifying attributes of successful organizations is so poor. He suggests that instead of looking for understanding in other people's experience one might look for it in one's own experience (ibid.). In this way of thinking, intention and design are understood as emergent and problematic processes. These insights are significant for me with respect to my work on CRM. Mike and I are constantly 'tweaking' our investigation process through negotiation with the team as a consequence of our discussions about what we are doing and what seems to work and what needs to change. It also helps explain why our attempts at following frameworks to disseminate best practice are only partially successful.

I now understand that organizations change when the themes that organize conversation and power relations change. Learning is change in these themes. Knowledge is language, and meaning emerges as themes interact in conversations (Stacey, 2003, p. 417). From a complex responsive processes perspective, surprise becomes part of the internal dynamic of the processes themselves. This approach offers a different interpretation of the notion of accountability from those offered earlier, which locate accountability for error with either individual clinicians, the system or both. As Stacey notes:

> The systemic theories . . . implicitly assume that the criterion for
> choosing a quality action is its outcome. Quality actions are those that
> produce desired outcomes. However, in an unpredictable world, the

outcomes of an action cannot be known in advance. It is necessary to
act and then deal with the consequences. . . . One is not absolved of
responsibility simply because one does not know the outcome. Even if
I do not know how my action will turn out, I am still responsible and
will have to deal with the outcome as best I can.

(Stacey, 2003, pp. 420–421)

I also now recognize that this perspective does not mean there is no
control; simply that it is understood in a different way. Stacey frequently
points out that all acts of relating impose constraints on all. Control
takes the form of relating itself; that is, it is a mutual constraint.
Self-organization involves a process of mutual constraining and hence
a paradox of enabling and constraining. I have come to recognize that
rather than being an independent investigator whose responsibility it is
to discover 'The Truth' about what has happened, I now see myself as
an active participant in the ongoing enquiry into how we can make
our hospitals safer for our patients. The focus of my work is therefore
different. I find myself having a greater sense of responsibility for trying
to focus on what I can do 'here and now' to improve things. I place a
greater emphasis on conversations with staff to encourage sense making
about what has happened, sharing drafts of reports in order to explore
together what went wrong and encouraging them to think about what we
are learning and what is changing. We have started a new section in our
reports which attempts to capture these changes as they are emerging.
Although uncomfortable, there is also a richness to this way of working
which I enjoy. I used to become frustrated with our old reports, the
findings of which were often contradicted by staff, who also often failed
to complete the agreed action plans. I had wondered what needed to be
changed to engender a sense of ownership or accountability for change.
I came to understand this differently through another conversation about
the renal incident.

Accountability and learning lessons

Mike and I are discussing his progress with the interviews as part of the
renal investigation. He is relating the story of one of the nurses whom he
has interviewed. At the beginning of the interview he had a sense that in
some way the nurse felt that what had happened was peripheral to any
of her own actions and it did not really have much to do with her in
practice. He said that what was interesting was that as they had begun
exploring the issues more deeply he had sensed a sudden change in the

conversation. He said something like 'it was as though she suddenly recognized that in some way she was implicated in all of this'.

He went on to say that she had made a comment like '*goodness – this seems to come back to me!*' This resonated with both of us. As noted earlier, we had already acknowledged that this particular investigation seemed to trace its links back to ourselves and this had evoked a sense of anxiety for both of us. Was it our fault? Would someone blame us for this? This 'felt' experience of accountability is expanded in the risk management literature:

> I felt a sense of shame like a burning ulcer. This was not guilt: guilt is what you feel when you have done something wrong. What I felt was shame: I was what was wrong. And yet I also knew that a surgeon can take such feelings too far. It is one thing to be aware of one's limitations. It is another to be plagued by self-doubt. One surgeon with a national reputation told me about an abdominal operation in which he lost control of bleeding while he was removing what turned out to be a benign tumor and the patient died. 'It was a clean kill', he said. Afterward, he could barely bring himself to operate. When he did operate, he became tentative and indecisive. The case affected his performance for months.
>
> (Gawande, 2002, p. 61)

And the implications of the absence of this feeling:

> Even worse than losing self-confidence, though, is reacting defensively. There are surgeons who will see faults everywhere except in themselves. They have no questions and no fears about their ability. As a result, they learn nothing from their mistakes and know nothing of their limitations. As one surgeon told me, it is a rare but alarming thing to meet a surgeon without fear. 'If you're not a little afraid when you operate', he said, 'You're bound to do the patient a grave disservice.'
>
> (ibid.)

For me, what is important about these stories is the shift in awareness and attention which enables us to see ourselves as active participants who contribute to what is going on. I believe this insight is fundamental to the notion of accountability. Once this insight is gained, I think we account to ourselves in the silent conversations we have with ourselves in a different way, about who we are and what we think we are doing. This 'conversation' with ourselves occurs at the same time as we are accounting to others for our ongoing contribution to the process. I think this is a very different notion to a perception of being some kind of objective observer or alternatively a passive victim within a 'system' which is somehow believed to cause all these incidents to happen.

I ask myself if learning occurred for the nurse quoted above and, if so, how I would explain how this occurred. I would argue that she had undoubtedly learned, as evidenced by the following sequence of events that happened a few weeks after Mike relayed this conversation to me. Another MDA was issued concerning a particular piece of equipment used by diabetic patients. The first thing I noticed was how my own response to this alert differed from my response to the one that had arrived before the Clayton Unit incident. Although I am copied in on these notices 'for information only', I now find myself scanning the distribution list to check that everyone I think should have been copied in has in fact been copied. I forwarded it to a few additional people and recall thinking that they would probably get it through one of the other distribution routes but it was better to be safe. I then noticed another interesting shift. In a very short space of time I had received a plethora of e-mails from a number of nurses who had been involved in the Clayton Unit incident. They were asking questions about this latest alert, double-checking that we had done everything we should have done. Some had suggestions for things they thought we ought to be following up on. This was a marked difference from an observation in the Clayton Unit investigation, where everybody thought everybody else must have been taking some action. What I noticed here was a shift where people had recognized personal responsibility in ensuring that things had happened.

Similarly, Mike had also sent some e-mails with advice on how to act. He also dropped me a note commenting that it seemed that 'lessons had been learned' as a consequence of the renal incident. So what had been learned and how? To me, the process was much more complex than the 'sender–receiver' model of communication would indicate (Fraser, 2002). This would account for the change through our 'sending' the messages which were 'received' and enabled the recipient to change their 'mental model'. One could perhaps argue in this way if the new system for distributing MDAs, which was one of the recommendations arising from the Clayton Unit report, had been implemented. However, it had not, and the nurses who contacted me were not aware of any changes. Therefore, they were not simply following some newly imposed rules. I account for the changed responses of Mike, myself and the nurses through the theory of complex responsive processes. I am arguing that what we experienced was the transformation of familiar patterns of working because of the shift in our attention that arose from our direct personal experience in the serious clinical incident in the Clayton Unit. This was also, I believe, more profound because of the intense emotions that arose as a consequence of potential serious harm to a patient. I think the feelings that arise at such times with respect to the emotions of anxiety, shame and fear are a fundamental part of the learning process (Aram, 2002).

If I am honest, however, I have to admit that I am now probably not paying as much attention to MDAs. On returning from a week's leave, I had over 300 e-mails and I had forwarded the MDA for my PA to print out so I could read them later. Yet interestingly, feeling guilty and raising my anxiety through re-reflecting on this, I know I will go back to this on Monday and double-check them all. This highlights an important issue with respect to sustaining changes in practice. The emotional engagement is a strong motivator, and we need to find ways of keeping alive the themes and replicating and amplifying them. This is not something that can be done via a one-off campaign and we cannot assume that changes in the short term are always sustainable. This is reinforced as I reflect on a number of patterns that seem to repeat themselves every few years with respect to patient safety. We seem to get a cluster of patients falling out of bed followed by a flurry of activity and then audits which show significant improvement. Yet some time later the cycle is repeated. I recall my Chief Executive getting very cross with me because he '*thought we had fixed that*'. I have noticed similar patterns with respect to certain medication errors, elements of documentation, and compliance with health and safety regulations.

Conclusion

In this chapter, I have been arguing that the split between past- and future-orientated approaches to risk management covers over the way in which our perceptions of the past change as we make judgements about the future in making sense of our experience. In paying attention to this, I have stressed the need to explore in conversations with others their perspectives of what has happened in the past, identifying with groups how and where these perspectives differ and noticing how this can lead either to a recognition of difficulties in a way that leads to transformation, or to repetition of a 'stuck' pattern as people's perspectives remain unchanged. I have been shifting my understanding of the processes of 'investigating' clinical incidents and this has led to changing practice as follows:

- Moving away from an approach where an objective 'observer' seeks to uncover an absolute truth, to a team-based approach where diversity is provided by a member of the CRM team and local knowledge by an 'internal' investigator.
- Seeking to discover different perspectives on 'what happened' and bringing together practitioners to make sense and learn from their experience.
- Exploring ideas around storytelling in organizations as a way of sharing lessons that describe the emotional content of such experiences rather than our formal reports, which seem to ignore this dimension.
- Expecting and seeking differing perspectives rather than trying to force a consensus on what happened where this does not seem to exist.
- Placing much greater emphasis on 'the present' when incidents are first reported in order to explore with staff the learning and actions that are happening now rather than a focus/belief that learning/action happens at a distant point *after* the incident.
- Avoiding locating blame/cause for accidents and mistakes in a higher 'system' or solely with an individual and working with others to explore their responsibility and accountability in forming and shaping the events while also recognizing the external influences which impact upon such situations.
- Recognizing the importance of the quality of relationships within teams and the correlation between poor team working and clinical errors, and paying more attention to these factors when exploring what went wrong as part of our 'investigation'.
- Using our CRM meeting to explore and critique what we think we are doing, recognizing the small changes that emerge each time we do this and capturing this learning in a written form.

References

Aram, E. (2002) 'The experience of complexity: learning as the potential transformation of identity', unpublished thesis, University of Hertfordshire.

Checkland, P. B. (1983) 'OR and the systems movement: mapping and conflict', *Journal of the Operational Research Society*, 34: 661.

Dineen, M. (2002) *Six Steps to Root Cause Analysis*, Oxford: Consequence Consulting.

Eagle, C. J., Davies, J. M. and Reason, J. (1992) 'Accident analysis of large-scale technological disasters applied to an anaesthetic complication', *Canadian Journal of Anaesthesia*, 39, 2: 118–122.

Firth-Cozens, J. (1995) 'Tackling risk by changing behaviour', *Quality in Healthcare*, 4: 97–101.

Firth-Cozens, J. (1998) 'Celebrating teamwork', *Quality in Healthcare*, 7: 53–57.

Fraser, S. W. (2002) *Accelerating the Spread of Good Practice: A Workbook for Healthcare*, Chichester: Kingshaw Press.

Garfinkel, H. (1967) *Studies in Ethnomethodology*, Englewood Cliffs, NJ: Prentice Hall.

Gawande, A. (2002) *Complications: A Surgeon's Notes on an Imperfect Science*, London: Profile Books.

Griffin, D. (2002) *The Emergence of Leadership: Linking self-organization and ethics*, London: Routledge.

Health Care Commission (2004) *Framework for Risk Management*, London: Commission for Health Improvement.

Ilgen, D. R. (1999) 'Teams embedded in organizations: some implications', *American Psychologist*, 54, 2: 129–139.

Institute of Medicine (2001) *Crossing the Quality Chasm: A New Health System for the 21st Century*, Washington, DC: National Academies Press.

Ireland, A., Tomalin, D. A., Renshaw, M. and Rayment, K. A. (2002) 'Clinical risk profiling tool for trusts', *International Journal of Health Quality Assurance*, 2: 15, 94–98.

Jackson, M. C. (2000) *Systems Approach to Management*, New York: Kluwer.

Mead, G. H. (1934) *Mind, Self and Society*, Chicago, IL: University of Chicago Press.

Midgley, G. (2000) *Systemic Intervention: Philosophy, Methodology, and Practice*, New York: Kluwer.

Reason, P. and Heron, J. (1997) 'A participating inquiry paradigm', *Qualitative Inquiry*, 3, 3: 274–294.

Reason, J. T., Carthey, J. and de Leval, M. R. (2001) 'Diagnosing "vulnerable system syndrome": an essential prerequisite to effective risk management', *Quality in Health Care*, 10 (suppl. II): 21–25.

Senge, P. (1990) *The Fifth Discipline: The Art and Practice of the Learning Organization*, New York: Doubleday.

Stacey, R. (2003) *Strategic Management and Organisational Dynamics: The Challenge of Complexity* (4th edn), London: Pearson Education.

Stacey, R.., Griffin, D. and Shaw, P. (2000) *Complexity and Management: Fad or radical challenge to systems thinking?*, London: Routledge.

Vincent, C. (2003) 'Understanding and responding to adverse events', *New England Journal of Medicine*, 348: 1051–1060.

Wenger, E. (1998) *Communities of Practice: Learning, Meaning, and Identity*, Cambridge: Cambridge University Press.

Editors' introduction
to Chapter 6

An important element of governance in the public sector relates to complaints procedures. All organizations in the National Health Service in the UK are required to have a clearly specified set of procedures for dealing with complaints from service users. Such complaints are officially welcomed as a way of obtaining feedback from patients and as a means of learning lessons from poor practice. In this chapter, Penelope Lacey, a manager in the podiatry service of an NHS Trust, describes the complaints procedures in her organization and gives an account of her experience of operating them.

In her organization, a distinction is made between formal and informal complaints. Verbal complaints are dealt with informally unless they are made to the senior management, in which case they are considered to be formal. All written complaints are taken to be formal. Informal complaints are dealt with directly and do not have to be reported and recorded in the complaints system. All formal complaints are recorded and one of the measures of improved service is a reduction in numbers of complaints, or, more accurately, formal complaints. Lacey describes the detailed, time-prescribed, step-by-step procedure which must be followed in the case of formal complaints. The official position of both government agencies and Lacey's own organization is that complaints are to be dealt with in a 'no-blame' culture. In Lacey's experience, the major issue giving rise to complaints has to do with having to wait a long time for an appointment for treatment, or even being denied one. This situation arises due to limited health care resources in the face of an almost unlimited demand. Heath care services therefore have to be rationed and patients experiencing this rationing naturally complain – they have the expectation that they will be attended to in a nationally provided 'free' service. Lacey says that the resource constraints on the podiatry service are particularly acute. For this reason, palliative care, such as cutting toenails, receives low priority. Thus while the number of elderly people demanding this kind of attention is rising rapidly, the resources for providing it are being reallocated to other podiatry services. It is not surprising then that the podiatry services feature rather badly in the quarterly Board reports on complaints, provoking senior management irritation.

Against this background, Lacey tells the story of a particular complaint. An elderly gentleman under the care of one of the podiatrists complains verbally to the senior management when he is denied an appointment for his toenails to be cut. He is told by a receptionist that he must wait three months for his next appointment because this is the official procedure. However, his podiatrist, ignoring the procedure, has told him he could return after six weeks. It is Lacey's job to deal with what has now become an official complaint. She describes the experience using the metaphor of pinballs. The pinball effect, as she calls it, takes the form of the complaint being knocked from one person to another. Lacey describes how complex this seemingly simple formal complaint becomes. Had it been informal, Lacey argues that she could have dealt with it directly within a day or two. Instead, the formal complaint involved fourteen people, four policies, many hours' work and many days of waiting before the complainant received his appointment. The pinball effect arises because, despite the rhetoric of 'no blame', an individual, and once again, as in the risk assessment procedures described in Chapter 5, the system are in fact usually blamed. Everyone is therefore trying to pass the source of the complaint on to someone else. Lacey talks about a generalized culture of paranoia among the staff and describes the complaints procedure as an elaborate system for shifting blame. She also talks about the fear and shame aroused by being identified as the source of a complaint and the complaints system as an elaborate procedure to avoid feeling shame. In the story about the toenail complaint, Lacey also brings out how clinicians find subtle ways of sabotaging the rationing process with which they disagree.

In this chapter, Lacey argues for a shift in thinking about responsibility when things 'go wrong'. Instead of automatically ascribing responsibility to an individual and/or to a system, she calls for a more relational view of responsibility. This chapter is an interesting example of how much of what is generally important across an organization – indeed, across an entire sector – can be revealed in one simple story.

6 The experience of power, blame and responsibility in the health sector

Penelope Lacey

In the United Kingdom, the task of providing primary care for acute and chronic deteriorative pedal (foot) conditions in the public sector falls to the podiatry services of the National Health Service. The aim of this service is to keep people mobile and independent so that they can carry out normal daily living. There are two core strands to the way in which the service is provided, which are generally known as routine/'palliative care' and specialist care. Due to the wear and tear of a lifetime, often extracting a heavy toll on the human foot, the podiatry service has always delivered routine care to elderly patients. Since the proportion of the elderly in the population has grown, the demand for these services has vastly increased. In the past thirty years, advances in modern podiatric practice have simultaneously increased the scope of practice, where it now incorporates specialist care for patients in areas including biomechanics, podiatric surgery, diabetology and rheumatology. Given resource constraints, the podiatry service has met increased demands for specialist care by slowly moving away from routine, palliative care.

The result has been the development of a mismatch between patients' expectations and the ability of the podiatry service to meet the increased demand. Furthermore, there has been little or no new investment in podiatric services to cope with this expanding gap. Consequently, the issue of who is responsible for the care of 'low or basic podiatric needs' such as toenail cutting is an area of dispute between the general public and the NHS. This issue creates a great deal of tension in the organization where I work. In this chapter, I explore how I have come to experience these tensions and to think about the ethics of responsibility in the NHS. I want to highlight the way in which responsibility is 'knocked' about in the organization. I describe the complaint procedures through which patients can express their dissatisfaction. These procedures generate unintended tensions, such as an endless search for who is responsible for any unsatisfactory service. The search is for something or someone to blame, to be responsible for what appears to have 'gone wrong'. I have come to think about this as the pinball effect. As the complaint enters the organization it gets knocked from one person to another, leaving individuals reeling from the impact as they try to protect themselves from attributions of blame.

The fungal nail infection complaint

I had spent a few days away from my office and returned to discover one of those heart-sinking moments when I saw that the e-mail 'in box' had expanded out of all proportion. I noticed that three of the messages referred to the same patient: one from my personal assistant, one from the clerical staff on the front reception, and one copied to me from the senior management team. The message from the senior management team had bounced between three of the directors, with the final note addressed from the new Chief Executive Officer (CEO) to my direct boss, stating: 'We seem to be getting too many of these podiatry complaints.' This comment riled me because the new CEO had clearly not been fully briefed on the historical pattern of complaints. The game of pinball and the search for who was responsible had begun and had already knocked against five individuals. They had swiftly and correctly knocked the pinball in my direction. Thus the decision as to whether I should accept responsibility did not take much deliberation, since dealing with complaints is part of my managerial remit. I would be to blame if I did not respond and take some sort of action. However, I felt that the CEO's message already seemed to imply an element of blame. Why was this?

In order to answer this question I intend to set the scene and digress from the narrative for a short time. This backdrop includes a description of the organizational 'blame culture' and an introduction to alternative ways of thinking about blame. The background also includes a detailed description of the complaints procedure I refer to throughout this narrative. I will show that blame is intrinsic to the complaints procedure and, although this process is supposed to support a neutral investigation process, in fact it acts as a mechanism of blame attribution.

Responsibility and blame

The podiatry service receives a large proportion of the complaints made to my organization. Consequently, a great deal of my workload involves managing and dealing with complaints. The organization nurtures a 'no-blame culture', which suggests exoneration for anyone who might be involved. This philosophy is referred to in two major documents from the Department of Health: *An Organization with a Memory* (2000) and *Building a Safer NHS for Patients* (2001). According to this philosophy, complaints are 'welcomed' as a way of registering feedback from direct patient–service contact and as a means of 'learning lessons' from poor practice. However, the Board of the Trust takes a fairly punitive stance if a particular service receives too many complaints. The quarterly Board reports showed a consistently high number of complaints received by the podiatry service. The Board took the view that something had to be done to resolve this; someone must be to blame for these complaints. So, despite the no-blame rhetoric, it seems that a powerful blame culture does exist. The belief seems to be that once the offending person or thing has been located, further mishaps will not occur.

'No-blame' culture was developed in the early 1990s following investigations into major incidents or serious near misses in the nuclear and aviation industries. The underlying concept was that if blame was removed, employees would not cover up small accidental errors. This, in the long term, should lead to a reduction in the risk of major catastrophes. However, 'no blame', as a conceptual label, did not translate well into practice in the NHS due to the procedural frameworks, which focused on 'locating' blame as a way of explaining what had gone wrong. Because of this, the recent trend has been in the direction of an 'open and fair' culture. Lord Hunt, the former Parliamentary Under-Secretary of State for Health, has said that we should not rush to find culprits or point the finger of blame. He argued that the fault lies in the systems supporting the delivery of safe, good-quality health care rather than with health care professionals. He said that in an organization as complex as the NHS, things will go wrong and patients will suffer unintended harm. When this happens, the response should not be one of blame but one of learning, a drive to reduce the risk of harm to future patients, and a concern for staff who may suffer as a consequence (Hunt, 2002). What Hunt does, rather bravely, is to acknowledge that harm does occur to patients and that things inevitably do go wrong. Although he challenges the attribution of blame to the individual, he then blames the system.

James Reason, Professor of Psychology, speaks to these two models of human error, namely the 'person approach' and the 'systems approach'. The person approach focuses on attributing blame to the individual for human fallibilities such as forgetfulness, carelessness, negligence, moral weakness, recklessness, and poor attention and motivation. He says:

> Blaming individuals is emotionally more satisfying than targeting institutions. People are viewed as free agents capable of choosing between safe and unsafe modes of behaviour. If something goes wrong, it seems obvious that an individual (or group of individuals) must have been responsible. Seeking as far as possible to uncouple a person's unsafe acts from any institutional responsibility is clearly in the interests of managers. It is legally more convenient, at least in Britain.
>
> (Reason, 2000, p. 2)

I would suggest that blaming individuals is the dominant way of thinking within the organization I work in. Reason says that this approach has 'serious shortcomings and is ill suited to the medical domain' (Reason, 2002, p. 2). This is due to the complexities of modern health care, which make it difficult to attach blame to a single individual. He suggests that by attributing blame to individuals, two features of human error are not taken into account. First, 'it is often the best people who make the worst mistakes – error is not the monopoly of an unfortunate few' (ibid.) Second, mishaps are not random but 'fall into recurrent patterns. The same set of circumstances can provoke similar errors, regardless of the people involved' (ibid., p. 3). It follows that rather than blame individuals, one should examine the 'system'; that is, the organizational context consisting of the standards, protocols, guidelines and procedures in which the errors occur. Effective organizational systems offer a framework by which people follow a linear, step-by-step approach to performing particular tasks. The reason for introducing such systems is to offer countermeasures:

> based on the assumption that though we cannot change the human condition, we can change the conditions under which humans work. ... When an adverse event occurs, the important issue is not who blundered, but how and why the defences failed.
>
> (Reason, 2000, p. 2)

It seems to me that this either/or way of thinking leads to a systemic focus being used as a means of avoiding confronting the individual and the individual focus being used as a means of avoiding confronting the weaknesses in the system. It strikes me that these approaches, namely individual and systems, pay little attention to the interactions between individuals; that is, the way in which individuals relate to one another or to the organizational systems in place. We all know that things go wrong, but it is difficult to accept that mishaps are an intrinsic part of human interaction. The complaints procedure may be thought of as a way of avoiding facing up to the fact that mishaps do inevitably occur as a part of human interaction.

Within the organizational context, thinking about complaints in a linear fragmented manner is problematic because each person is thought to be solely responsible for a delineated portion of action as opposed to thinking about the interconnectedness of responsibility. Sheila McNamee and Kenneth Gergen, in their book *Relational Responsibility – Resources for a Sustainable Dialogue*, offer an alternative to the system and individual approaches. They agree that individuals are responsible for things going wrong, but say that we should not limit our thinking to this. They take a relational perspective 'in which relatedness (as opposed to individuality) holds a central place' (McNamee and Gergen, 1999, p. 11). They propose four different ways of thinking about relatedness:

- *Internal others* (Cooley, [1902] 1964); Mead, 1934; Vygotsky, 1978; Bakhtin, 1986). This is the notion that we are socially constructed beings and not independent selves. The self comes into being by social imitation (Cooley, [1902] 1964) and role play (Mead, 1934), a process by which we develop the capacity to take on the attitudes of others, through our own silent conversations. Thus when we speak we may be using our own voice, but it is also constructed from myriad other voices.
- *Conjoint relations* (Shotter, 1993; Gergen, 1999), in which meaning arises through the patterned interaction of individuals.

- *Relations among groups*, which attends to the relationships between groups as opposed to relationships between individuals.
- *Systemic processes* (von Bertalanffy, 1968), in which there are no independent units. The focus here is on relationality.

Gergen and McNamee argue that contemporary Western thought has its origins in the idea of the individual as a 'subjective agent'. Thus we understand our world in terms of individual identities, with each of us possessing the reflective capacity to plan and solve problems. As a consequence, we are in complete control of our actions. It is because of this that we 'honor the state of the individual' (McNamee and Gergen, 1999, p. 6) and reject any thought that might jeopardize our sense of independence. In this model, our language, and the way in which we conduct ourselves, is based on this isolated state of the individual. Therefore, responsibility cannot be located anywhere else but with the individual.

The alternative view is one where we exist only in relation to others. 'It is out of relationships that we develop meaning, rationalities, the sense of value, moral interest, and so on. From such arguments, we succeed in developing discursive resources that shift attention away from individual sources of action to the sphere of the relationship' (McNamee and Gergen, 1999, pp. 10–11). By this means, responsibility is made relational. These views have affinities with the ideas in group-analytic discourse (Foulkes, 1948; Dalal, 1998), as well as the ideas of Stacey and colleagues (2000) in their descriptions of complex responsive processes (see chapters 1 and 2 in this volume).

Formal or informal

In my work context, I am responsible for logging all the complaints relating to the podiatry service. Complaints are received from patients, relatives, neighbours and fellow health care workers in person and through e-mail, letters or phone calls via reception, the main office and senior management offices. Written complaints are responded to in writing and are considered 'formal', to be dealt with following a precise procedure, while verbal complaints are generally considered 'informal' and more often than not I am able to offer an immediate response if they come to my direct attention. The formal procedure involves the following steps: acknowledgement of the complaint within two working days; investigation and report of findings in ten working days to establish who was responsible for the issues raised; and a draft response to be sent to the CEO for a full response within a further ten working days. There are often delays in this procedure due to the complexity of incoming routes. The complaints typically relate to a number of different issues and it is not always clear which manager should be responsible for responding. Complaints often get passed around a number of service managers, who might comment on the complaint in order to absolve themselves of the responsibility for investigating it and then forward it to the next manager. Frequently, complaints end up at my door a week or so after they were initially received elsewhere in the organization. This reduces the time available to investigate, report and respond. The result is a desperate rush to get something out to the complainant within the procedural deadlines. Complaints are not popular with managers because dealing with them is often complex and difficult. The formal process does not necessarily end with the response from the CEO. If the complainant is not satisfied with the initial response there is a procedure for appealing to an appeals panel. There are also other appeal mechanisms, which eventually lead to the Ombudsman.

In the particular case I describe above, the complaint entered the organization via the CEO's office and, because of this, even though it was a verbal message, it was considered to be a 'formal' complaint. The route by which the complaint enters the organization therefore dictates how seriously it is taken and how it is handled. I have often questioned why the point of entry into the organization should indicate the way in which the complaint should be treated. I keep a log of all the informal complaints, which are never reported to the Board. Keeping the informal complaints 'a secret' means that the true picture is never seen. I have questioned this categorization, suggesting that all the complaints could be reported; after all, a complaint is a complaint. The senior management team informed me that revealing the true picture would reflect poorly on my own ability to manage the service effectively and it would not be sensible for the organization to report a large number of complaints. The response from colleagues was, 'Don't expose yourself as incompetent, best to keep the informal complaints quiet.' I found this quite shocking. What it demonstrates to me is the powerful sense of fear permeating the organization because the blaming process itself shames the one who is designated responsible. I have been very aware of this fear and in turn felt ashamed on the occasions when blame has landed at my feet as the designated person responsible for the podiatry service. The consequence of this is destructive to my own sense of self, since I am the manager of a labelled 'problem' service. This leads to a sense of exclusion from the group of peers to which I belong.

Perhaps this categorization is necessary, for if we were to use the formal mechanism for every complaint, the NHS would grind to a standstill due to the time and energy required. The informal process can often sort things out quickly and efficiently, while the formal procedure is cumbersome and unwieldy, and the response is delayed due to the need to thoroughly investigate the issues. The intention of providing a detailed investigation in order to find a resolution and learn from the events is a good one but the complexity of connections revealed by these investigations can lead to incredibly complicated responses to a simple request.

To return to the story, I could not work out exactly what the complaint was about from the e-mails. One message referred to a difficult interaction with the reception staff, another simply said that the podiatry service was terrible, and the messages from my personal assistant asked me to contact the patient urgently as there was a clinical problem. 'It must be serious,' I thought to myself. The patient was obviously upset and this, together with the fact that half the senior management team now knew about the complaint, led me to panic and think I would be blamed if I was not able to resolve this complaint quickly. It seemed that several pinballs of responsibility had been set in motion and had all knocked against me simultaneously.

How the complaints procedure generates tensions

In the main, complaints consistently refer to the lack of service provision. Patients complain that they are unable to obtain appointments and have to endure long waiting periods. The tension generated by the lack of service capacity appears to be located in three sets of relationships: between patients and reception staff, reception staff and clinicians, and clinicians and patients. Patients complain primarily about the 'rude attitudes of the reception staff'. Reception staff members are experienced as the main barrier to obtaining appointments and so patients vent their frustrations on them. Frequently the complainants refer to heated debates patients have entered into with reception staff. These attacks from patients, in turn, have a knock-on effect upon reception staff. They dislike dealing with podiatry patients because they consider them to be demanding, rude and aggressive. The issue of limited service capacity is then located in the relationship between front-line reception staff and podiatry patients. A level of mutual contempt is generated by the situation and both parties end up feeling that they are being treated unfairly.

There are frequent ructions between clinicians and reception staff generally due to differing views about how appointments should be organized. From the clinical perspective the podiatrist may recommend a particular treatment regime requiring a number of appointments or longer treatment times. This is generally considered highly inconvenient by the reception staff since it limits the number of appointments they can offer 'walk-in' patients, which in turn means they get the flak. The receptionists have fairly sophisticated booking procedures which they rigidly follow and clinicians often subvert them, sometimes intentionally, because they need to see patients for repeat appointments sooner than the procedures allow, and sometimes unintentionally by booking out annual leave or time to attend meetings. The receptionists experience the cancelling of the clinics as an attack on them. This sort of exchange tends to generate a mutual sense of contempt between clinical and reception staff. On the whole, patients think that basic treatment should be offered on a more regular basis, something that the service is unable to sustain. As a result, clinicians often feel 'attacked' and blamed by patients for not meeting their expectations. Clinicians become frustrated through their attempts to fulfil the responsibilities allocated to them by the organization. There appears to be mutual projection of resentment and anger in these relationships as each of the three parties – patients, reception staff and clinical staff – see each other as the enemy. Consequently they bounce the pinballs of responsibility between them in search of something to blame for the limited capacity of the service. From a managerial perspective, depending on the nature of the story, I take up the position of judging whether to attribute the blame to the peeved patient, unhelpful receptionist or unprofessional clinician.

My first and only contact with Mr X

Although Mr X is the key character in my story I had only one contact with him directly, and that was a fifteen-minute conversation on the telephone. I rang Mr X, introduced myself, apologized for not responding sooner and asked how I could help. He replied, 'I want to complain, I've had a terrible time and I think it is disgraceful!' I said, 'OK, before we go into what has gone on, can I just take a few details?' I asked for his full name and title, address, date of birth, phone number and the clinic the patient had attended. Then I asked, 'Can you tell me which ethnic group you belong to?' 'What do you want to know that for?' he asked. 'It's part of the organization's monitoring procedure to ensure that we are providing appropriate services to reflect the ethnic mix of the whole community,' I replied. 'Don't see why you need that, for this, what's that got to do with my feet?' was his answer.

I could sense that Mr X was beginning to get a little irritable, so I left the question to one side. The formality in the procedure infuriates patients because all they want to do is to tell you their story. However, the procedure must be followed precisely; otherwise there would be a complaint about the investigation of the first complaint. One could think about the formal questioning as an attempt to knock the pinball of responsibility back to the patient before we, the organization, contemplate taking on the responsibility of setting the actual complaint procedure in motion. If the patient is not willing to proffer responses in order to complete the tick boxes in the paper exercise, the formal mechanism cannot be activated. In a way, it is tantamount to blackmail: 'If you don't play by the rules of the game, then we don't play this particular game.' Often, when patients complain, they are reluctant to give any personal details for fear of retribution. The ethnicity question is often treated with suspicion. Patients are reluctant to disclose their ethnicity or they question why the information is required. Patients fear that this kind of categorization may lead to their being treated differently or excluded. However, the organization has a statutory obligation to collect 95 per cent of the ethnicity data. Thus the blame here could be attributed to the 'system' in that the procedure itself uses a number of set questions which are seemingly irrelevant to the complaint and lead to unexpected tensions between the helper and the helped. I did not press the ethnicity question with Mr X since I actually agreed with his point. Until I had actually heard what his concerns were, I would not know whether his ethnic background bore any relevance to the complaint. Thus already I was deviating from the formal procedure in response to Mr X's observation.

I asked Mr X if he could tell me what had happened. He rattled out his story hurriedly in more or less one breath: 'I am a very ill man, you know. I have a heart condition and I'm diabetic. I phoned to make an appointment to have my feet done and just kept getting the answerphone. The message said to leave my details but I don't talk to those things and nothing ever happens if you do leave a message. So I came down to the clinic in person. It's not easy for me to get out, you know. When I got there a rude young man looked me up on the computer and told me that I couldn't have an appointment until the end of July. He told me that the computer said that I only needed an appointment in three months' time but that's too long to have my nails done. The podiatrist, a nice young man, told me to come back in six to eight weeks' time, which means I should have an appointment this week. I need to have my toenail checked. The doctor gave me tablets for my toenail, you know, and they have side effects. I feel sick all the time, which is no good for my diabetes, and the doctor told me I should have my foot checked before I stop taking them. I have been taking them for four months and want to know if they have worked. I can't wait until the end of July. You must get me an appointment.' It was hard to scribble notes fast enough to keep up with the pace of the story. I said that I was sorry to hear what had happened to him and asked a few more questions. It is often the case that the stories are so densely woven that it is difficult to make sense of what the patient's concerns actually are.

The organization places great emphasis on taking responsibility and being seen to take action in order to resolve complaints. However, when I ask the patients what they would like to happen, there is frequently a silence. It seems that once the complainant's story has been heard and acknowledged, the 'wind is taken out of their sails'. The consequence of this is that there is less concern about subsequent actions, and all they often seem to want are apologies from the organization for the distress caused. If the organization apologizes, then in effect it has accepted responsibility for what has occurred. Clearly, in the case of Mr X, he wanted not only an apology but also the appointment he had been instructed to obtain by the clinician. A simple request, one might think, but not always within the context of the National Health Service. I informed Mr X that I would have to investigate his complaint and I would get back to him later that day.

If I were handling the complaint informally, I would have been able to offer Mr X the appointment he wanted. However, since I was investigating the complaint under the formal procedure I had to make enquiries into other people's actions. For example, Mr X had perceived the receptionist's action as a barrier to getting the appointment he wanted. However, the receptionist had in fact followed the correct procedure in relation to the organizational systems. He had checked the patient's return time on the computer entered by the clinician following the previous treatment, and informed him that he was not yet due for an appointment. The system was introduced to cope with the overwhelming demand for the service in an attempt to offer a fair allocation of resources. In this case, if I offered an appointment to Mr X, I would undermine the receptionist's action and be subverting the system. Mr X was unaware of the system and therefore from his perspective it would be easy to locate the blame with the receptionist since he was the one who declined to give the patient the appointment. It was this difference that led to the heated exchange between them and to the accusation that the receptionist was 'a rude young man'.

Complaints are corrosive of my sense of well-being since they often feel like personal attacks on myself. The letters are personally addressed and written in a confrontational tone and phone calls are often abusive. My normal response to a critical attack would be a 'fight-or-flight' response, neither of which is appropriate in the work context. To exercise responsibility as a manager during these conversations requires me to suppress my underlying emotional responses to the attacks. The true feelings, such as anger and fear, which are evoked become muted by the 'appropriate organizational speak'. The organization's procedure works in the direction of inhibiting not only my emotional responses but also my ability to respond directly to the patient's needs. The pattern set up through the formal routine means that what I am able to do is severely constrained. Therefore, over the years I have become exhausted with the repetitive complaint stories, as a consequence of which I have become less sympathetic to the patients' tales.

The investigation procedures require communicating with all the parties mentioned in the actual complaint. These are traced through the patient's notes, diary records, computer records and so on. This in itself can become a very complex task as one connection leads to another. Often, each party will give very different versions of events. As the investigating officer, I am responsible for interpreting the stories and comparing what actually happened to what should have happened. This can be a complicated process because one often needs to oversimplify complex narratives in order to construct a coherent response. In turn, this can lead to a black-and-white picture rather than something dappled, which in practice is more often the case.

Following the telephone conversation with Mr X, I rang the appointment line. The answerphone clicked in, stating that appointments could be booked between 10 a.m. and 12 noon. I was angered by this arrangement, having previously negotiated with the centre manager that the phone line would be open from 9 a.m. to 5 p.m. Formerly, the service had a dedicated staff member to book appointments but this staff member had recently been seconded to another role and we had to resort to the use of temporary staff. There was a high turnover of temporary staff because of the demanding role, the confrontational interactions with patients, and the intricacies of the service and the complex booking system. This, in turn, led to an increased number of complaints. To counteract this situation, the centre manager and I reached an agreement that booking appointments would be the responsibility of the front-of-house reception staff. Three receptionists should, in theory, be able to field all the calls. However, the front desk became inundated with calls from podiatry patients. In order to cope with their other duties, they took it upon themselves to divert the podiatry calls from the switchboard to another line and an answerphone. This was a sensible solution for their problem but it worked against the initial purpose of improving patient access to the appointments. The receptionists' 'solution' ended up restricting access even more.

This restriction again led to a further influx of complaints from frustrated patients. From the 'person approach' this now meant that at least two of the pinballs needed to bump against the reception staff and the centre manager since they had not kept to their end of the bargain. What was actually going on here was that the receptionists had taken responsibility and used their initiative to find a local solution to cope with their impossible task. The responsibility they had chosen had not taken into account the needs of other professionals or patients. They were unable to see the potential consequences of their actions and in actual fact their solution made the situation worse.

Power, responsibility and influence

Over the years it became evident that the patterns of the complaints often reveal organizational issues which go beyond the scope of what I am able to influence directly. For example, I feel unable to change policies that are somehow 'above' me, like the national complaints procedure. As a result, I have to work 'in the moment' within the structures and conditions I am presented with. For instance, according to my own job description I am not responsible for managing reception staff and the aggressive exchanges between them and podiatry patients. Yet at the same time I have indirect responsibility to ensure that patients are able to book appointments. Therefore, the centre manager and I have a joint responsibility to ensure that patients are able to book appointments. Within the organizational framework, I do not 'possess' the power to instruct reception staff in what to do (neither would I want to), so I compensate by 'making friends' with the reception staff as a means of getting things done and influencing in regions where I have no formal power. However, in this instance, due to the recent high turnover of staff the conditions were so unstable that I had not had time to re-establish influential relationships with the receptionists.

Generally I would have delegated the investigation into Mr X's complaint to the podiatry team leader. However, the fear invoked in me by three of the directors knowing about the complaint prompted me to take responsibility for this particular complaint and hold on to this particular ball. Because I already felt blamed in the e-mail from the CEO, I wanted to avoid any further blame. This motivation led me to take action by physically presenting myself to a number of people in order to obtain a direct response.

In the clinic I met one of the podiatrists, who helped me locate the patient's notes. 'Is it another complaint? Hope it's not about me?' She was anxious that she was the source of the complaint. I had inadvertently set off a 'rogue' ball in her direction, so I set her mind at rest and reassured her that the complaint was not related to her practice. What I think this demonstrates is the generalized culture of paranoia among staff in relation to the investigation process. I visited the centre co-coordinator on the way back to my office. Since she is responsible for managing the reception staff, I needed to inform her of the patient's reference to the 'rude young man' and the reported difficulties of patients booking appointments. I was knocking one of the pinballs of responsibility in her direction. Back in my office, the clinical notes revealed that the patient had been visiting the clinic every three months for a number of years to receive palliative care for his feet. Latterly he had also been attending every three months to have his nails cut. One of the large toenails had a fungal infection and the podiatrist had recommended a course of drug therapy. The patient had been advised to go to his doctor and request a prescription. At this point, I sifted through the notes in search of a microbiology report. It is good clinical practice to take a sample of the nail in order to identify the infecting organism before requesting drug therapy from the doctor. There are alternative drug groups that are indicated for specific infecting organisms. Without the microbiological evidence there is a danger that the patient may be prescribed the less effective drug. I could not find a microbiology report or any reference to a request.

So who or what was to blame for this situation? It would appear that the podiatrist had failed to fulfil his responsibility by not taking a sample to identify the infecting organism. It also seemed that the doctor was neglecting his responsibility. The patient had reported side effects from a prescribed drug but the doctor had simply advised the patient to return to the podiatrist. It appeared that the patient had just been the messenger relaying details from one health care professional to another.

I want to return now to the three models referred to at the beginning of the chapter as a way of thinking about this problem, from the individual, systems and relational approaches.

Individual approach

Taking the person approach, one could attribute the blame to any of the three individuals involved. The podiatrist could be blamed for not taking a sample. The doctor could be blamed because he had prescribed a drug based on the verbal request of the podiatrist via the patient, without taking into account the infecting organism and possibly the systemic health of the patient. Neither the podiatrist nor the doctor had warned the patient of possible side effects. One could also argue that the patient had not taken responsibility by neglecting to report feeling unwell earlier and continuing to self-administer a drug. If the blame did land at the feet of any of these individuals one might wonder what purpose this would actually serve. It appears that the individual approach is a way of avoiding the complexities of a given situation and reveals only a partial truth. By locating the blame with a particular individual it closes down the question as to what else may be going on. For instance, the problem may have arisen due to increasing demands on health professionals, which meant that they were obliged to cut corners to get things done.

Systems approach

From the systems approach the situation looks like this. There are guidelines in the podiatry service which set out a procedure according to which the podiatrist should take a nail sample, wait for the results from the microbiology lab and then write to the doctor to request a particular drug. Although the podiatrist did not follow the guidelines, it could be argued that the system was to blame because it was not wholly inclusive. By this I mean that the doctor works as an autonomous clinician, often on a satellite site, and is therefore ignorant of systems put in place by the podiatry service. In other words, the fault lies in the procedures and the way the 'system' was designed. Within the Primary Care Trust many health care teams work from disparate geographical sites. Although they may belong to the same group/organization by name, as the doctor and podiatrist they also belong to localized teams or generic groups of professionals. Local development of systems pertaining to these discrete teams does not take into account others 'outside' the system, as illustrated above. So the solutions at a local level create problems elsewhere. This is not unlike the receptionists' scenario referred to earlier, in which their local solution created problems elsewhere in the network.

Relational approach

From the relational perspective, individual responsibilities would not disappear, but more attention would be drawn to the interactions between the three parties. In this scenario, one could hypothesize that if conversations had taken place between the podiatrist and the doctor they could have discussed and agreed appropriate drug therapy and whether this was the best course of action in relation to Mr X's systemic health, and follow-up care. This might have been followed by a conversation with the patient, warning him of the pros and cons of taking the drug. The patient might well have chosen to take the drug and still experienced adverse reactions but it might have been clearer as to whom he should report these to. In the individualistic model each person sits within his or her own fortress – a fortress surrounding the territory he or she is designated as being responsible for. While sitting in this fortress one is not empathic to the plight of others in similar circumstances. The notion of relational responsibility draws our attention to these others and the fact that we all share the capacity to make errors.

The idea of relational responsibility is complicated because it 'smears' the lines of individual and systems boundaries. As the edges become fuzzier, the notion of relational responsibility becomes more uncomfortable as a concept and there is the temptation to retreat back into the neat lines of individual accountability. From what I have just said, it looks as though relational responsibility could be seen simply as a need to engage in further conversations. But then how does one begin to take into account the attitudes of others during those conversations? McNamee and Gergen refer to another category of relational responsibility, that of 'internal others' whereby 'there are no independent selves; we are each constituted by others. We are always already related by virtue of shared constitution of the self' (McNamee and Gergen, 1999, pp. 11–12). They refer to Mead's (1934) work for developing their concept of the self. Mead's 'self' is formed by three aspects of intersubjective activity, namely language, play and the game. Language is communication through significant symbols by which one can take the attitudes of others towards oneself as an object or self. The development of self-consciousness is in the linguistic activity of playing and gaming through which one can enter into the process of role playing. Mead gives the example of a child at play with him- or herself who is able to take up one role at a time, a 'specific other' such as a doctor or a mother. Among adults, the game is a more sophisticated process in which an individual takes up not only the role of one other but all the other roles, including the rules by which these others play. The individual is able to form a symbolized unity in which he or she is able to bring the attitudes of the 'generalized other' according to which the individual defines his or her own conduct.

So if we return to the scene of sifting through the patient's records, I had a number of questions running through my head. When asking myself 'Where is the microbiology report?', at the same time I would be responding to my own question in a multitude of ways (e.g. 'I would always take a sample before requesting a drug, what was Marvin up to? Maybe he did and for some reason chose not to document the fact. The request/sample could have been lost as there had been reported difficulties at the microbiology lab. Could the organization be liable for side effects? I must ensure that all the staff receive training to avoid a recurrence, there's that nice Italian microbiology consultant who used to work at the hospital, he was always podiatry friendly, maybe I could ask him'). The different sorts of others are one of the reasons why relational responsibility becomes so complicated because it is not a straightforward process of just talking to others who might be involved. The history we carry, status in roles, power relations, all play a part in how we respond to our own internal conversations, and this affects what we feel able to say, or not, in the moment. There are many aspects that influence the way in which responsibility is exercised. Conflict arises as members of one group think that they are accepting responsibility and act in a certain way, which is then perceived to be totally irresponsible by another. Exercising responsibility therefore becomes more problematic.

Due to limited resources, many NHS podiatry services have introduced eligibility criteria. The organization I work with introduced Criteria for Care in 1998. Eligibility is a misnomer because what the criteria actually do is to legitimize the exclusion of large groups of people who do in fact need care. In truth the eligibility criteria should be renamed 'Criteria for not Care'. There are of course various degrees of health, social and podiatric needs and some patients' needs are more visible than others. It is the clinician's task to judge which needs are legitimate and which are not. As a consequence of this process there are of course differences of opinion about the intensity of care the patient expects and what the organization says the clinician should deliver.

Not surprisingly, despite the introduction of the Criteria for Care, we continued to receive a high level of complaints. The essence of the complaints now shifted from complaints of long waiting times to patients' sheer disbelief at being discharged from a service or given restricted access to the service. The clinicians are now perceived to be the 'wicked' ones by withdrawing the service or informing patients they are no longer eligible for the service. Patients react strongly to the exclusion, since their underlying assumption is that once they have reached retirement age they are 'entitled' to see a podiatrist even for simple tasks such as cutting toenails. It is assumed to be our responsibility to offer this service. Consequently there is a gap and ongoing debate about who is responsible for patients with low podiatric needs.

At the end of each clinical visit the podiatrist informs the patient of the expected return period in relation to the Criteria. The podiatrist who had last seen Mr X had documented a return period of three months. I was relieved to note that this at least had been clearly indicated in the notes. This had been entered into the computer following the treatment, and the receptionist had used this information to rebook. However, the patient had been adamant that the clinician had told him to return in six weeks' time. From the handwritten notes I recognized the clinician the patient had seen and things started to make a little more sense. Events fitted the pattern of this particular clinician's behaviour. Marvin has been working for the organization for fifteen years, but despite numerous interviews he has remained on a junior grade and is resentful of any form of management intervention. He tends to set up a very caring yet dependent relationship with all his patients, who adore him. Marvin does not agree with the eligibility criteria the service has introduced and has a subtle way of sabotaging the policy. One of the ongoing debates that the team leader and I enter into with Marvin is the issue of advising patients to return sooner than the policy dictates. In that moment I could just imagine him telling the patient, 'Well, the policy states you should come back in three months, but if you ask to see me I'll see you in six weeks' time.'

So how was I to understand this? Was Marvin lying? Was the patient lying? Were both of them lying? Or was one or both of them mistaken?

Whatever did happen during the consultation, the result was that the patient's expectations were raised, which conflicted with the Criteria and details that had been documented both in the notes and on the computer. This in turn meant that the receptionist got the flak and the patient got fed up and complained.

This pattern of conflict is the essence of most of the complaints I manage. McNamee and Gergen note that human interactions fall into repetitive patterns as a result of conjoint relations. 'These seemingly inescapable patterns of interchange are the result of the conjoint actions of the participants' (McNamee and Gergen, 1999, p. 37). In their concept of conjoint relations they move away from individualism and draw attention to the patterned interaction process itself. Shotter (1993) refers to this as joint action and Mead (1934) as the social act in which one creates meaning through a conversation of gestures. Meaning arises through a process of gesture of one individual followed by a response to that gesture by another. It is from this adaptive response that meaning arises.

> As it is reasoned, actions in themselves have no meaning; they acquire meaning only as they are supplemented by the actions of others (Gergen, 1994). Thus, meaning is a by-product of relatedness.
>
> (McNamee and Gergen, 1999, p. 14)

If this is the case then it becomes more difficult to attribute blame to the individual because reprehensible actions are then accomplished in relationships. In addition to this, no relationship is self-contained; the meaning that arose from the single interaction between Marvin and Mr X consequently had a considerable impact on subsequent interactions.

Responsibility born out of allegiances

I want to suggest that responsibility is exercised by the pull of invisible and visible allegiances. These allegiances might be to groups or to an individual's personal ethics and they have a profound effect on the way in which we function in organizations. The question of allegiance is the basis of the ongoing debate as to who is responsible for the gap in service provision for patients. Each of us is subject to a number of overlapping and, at times, conflicting allegiances. For example, Marvin has allegiances to his professional community of fellow practitioners, to the organization that employs him, to the multidisciplinary team that he is part of and so on. Each allegiance makes a demand on him as to how he should act, and many of these demands are in conflict with each other; thus one inevitably ends up abdicating one set of responsibilities to fulfil another.

Although Marvin was seen to be doing something on one level by fulfilling his organizational responsibilities by entering the data and writing up the notes, his verbal gesture to the patient was different and leaned towards his personal and professional responsibilities. By selecting elements of conflicting allegiances in different moments, Marvin was finding a way to manage the different sets of responsibilities and reconciling the conflict within himself, but in so doing created havoc for others. As a fellow podiatrist I am likely to ally myself with Marvin and his actions. However, as manager of the service I am paid to follow the organization line so that I too am torn by managing conflicting sets of responsibilities. I contacted the team leader (line manager to Marvin) to inform her about the interaction with Marvin and Mr X, and asked her to find out whether he could recall what might have been said. We agreed that his consistent pattern of generous gestures towards the patients created havoc for the rest of his team members and ourselves. We had given him several warnings on previous occasions, which led us to question whether we needed to enter into the more formal disciplinary procedure. We were using the procedure as a mechanism to force Marvin to take the line of organizational responsibility as opposed to his preferred personal one.

The resolution?

From the evidence I had gathered to date, I took the decision to try to make an appointment for this particular patient sooner rather than later. It was highly likely that the patient had been presented with mixed messages and chose to listen to the one he wanted to hear. I wandered down to the reception area and asked for the appointment diary. 'It's locked away,' she said. 'What do you mean?' I asked. She replied, 'Well, the lady that normally books the appointments is off sick today and we don't know where she keeps the diary.' I asked, 'So what's happening to all the patients who want to book an appointment today?' Her reply was, 'Oh, we just have to tell them to come back or phone tomorrow.' By this time I was getting quite irritated and suggested to the receptionist, 'Well, instead of turning patients away could you make a list of all the patients' details and then when the diary is available you can contact the patients with an appointment.'

'Oh, well we won't have time for that as that's not the normal procedure.'
Here, procedures were being used to legitimize not accepting any sort
of responsibility to book the patients an appointment. I did not 'have' the
power to enforce this action and possibly my irritation got in the way
of influencing a different kind of action. 'Let me talk to the centre
manager to see if she can find someone to help with this today and
tomorrow.' I received a hostile stare, probably because we both knew
that when I highlighted this to their boss she would be instructed to do
it without any further assistance. We were now playing 'ping-pong' with
the pinball and on this occasion I lost the point and carried the ball
with me to the centre manager's office to express my displeasure. She
agreed that this should not be happening and agreed to talk to the staff
to organize something. I left her with the patient's details and was
assured that the patient would receive an appointment the following day.
I specifically asked if the appointment could be telephoned through to the
patient and backed up by the usual letter. I had left a pinball with her, or
so I thought.

I contacted Mr X in the afternoon and, since he was not available, I spoke
to his wife. I informed her of my progress, telling her that the return time
indicated on the record card was three months, and under the Criteria this
was usual for the type of care Mr X required. Clearly there were mixed
messages, which were still under investigation. As I had not been able to
gain access to the diary, the reception would call with an appointment in
due course. I talked her through the clinical picture of the fungal nail
infection and suggested that the side effects be reported to the doctor
as soon as possible. I contacted the doctor's surgery and left a message to
relay the instructions I had left for Mr X.

Mrs X was not particularly happy with this arrangement and challenged
me on the seriousness of her husband's toenail condition. I reassured
her that when Mr X came in to see us we would review the situation and
advise him from that point. The important thing was to address the side
effects Mr X had been experiencing, which were beyond the podiatrist's
remit, and I apologized if the clinician had given that impression. I gave
my direct line and suggested that if there were any further problems Mr X
should contact me personally.

The following week I received an e-mail from my direct boss. He had
been sent a message from the CEO asking, 'Why hasn't this one been
sorted out?' Mr X had telephoned the senior management team to insist
on an appointment. Despite my request, it transpired that Mr X had

actually been sent an appointment by post but had not been notified by phone. I asked the reception why the patient had not been contacted by phone and I was informed that it was not normal procedure. To avoid any further conflict, I took back the pinball of responsibility and called the patient to inform him of the appointment time. In a way I had been acting as a go-between for all of the parties, filling in the gaps for individuals who seemed to be putting a full stop where there should have been a comma.

Marvin, the clinician, could not recall the patient or anything that had been said; therefore no further action could be taken. Thus the team leader simply reinforced the importance of delivering consistent messages to patients and complying with the Criteria. I completed the report and draft response to the patient and this was then sent to the complaints department, who tend to heavily edit the letters. The report and final draft of the letter were then signed off by the CEO and sent to the patient. The patient attended his appointment, received the reassurance he required for the clinical picture, and confirmation of his return time. This particular complaint involved fourteen people, four policies and many hours.

Bizarrely enough, if I had dealt with the complaint informally, I would have negotiated with one of the clinicians directly to see Mr X within a day or two. Meanwhile, following the formal process meant that although Mr X did eventually get the appointment, it was through an extended and convoluted route. Even though I was 'following the formal procedure' I was constantly cutting corners in order to smooth over things in an attempt to resolve the multitude of issues. It would not be possible to live by the official rules, as I constantly needed to improvise outside of the rules to cobble together some sort of solution.

Discussion

Responsibility is not an abstract matter. In order to exercise responsibility it has to be in relation to something or someone. We cannot just 'be responsible'. I want to draw attention to the tussle and muddle we experience in relation to different sets of responsibilities.

The story of the toenail complaint is about a number of individuals acting responsibly in trying to do the 'right thing'. However, despite that fact, things did not work out exactly as intended, even though nobody was actually acting out of malice. At the beginning of this chapter I referred to the relationship of blame to shame, something I would like to return to at this point because I think that shame plays a crucial role in relation to responsibility, especially when things do not work as intended. In the system of rights and wrongs we generally strive to do the 'right thing' to avoid shame. In fact it is a fantasy that we can always get it right, but hope lies in the fact that if we keep tweaking and perpetually correcting, this will eventually happen, and thus we can avoid unpleasant feelings of shame.

There is no escaping the fact that blunders, mishaps and errors are intrinsic to human interaction, and something we experience as shameful. A number of authors say that shame is a social process (Sennett, 1998; Elias, [1939] 2000; Dalal, 2002). Damasio, a neuroscientist who has written extensively about physiological and psychological connections of thinking and feeling, describes shame as a 'social emotion'. He says that these social emotions 'aim directly at life regulation by staving off dangers or helping the organism take advantage of opportunity, or indirectly by facilitating social relations' (Damasio, 2003, p. 39). So shame is not all bad. It is actually a fundamental requirement to enable us to exercise responsibility, calling on something 'deeper' within ourselves to act ethically in relation to others.

In organizations we tend to think of responsibility from an individualistic approach in terms of designated remits and job descriptions. There is the potential for the individual to be shamed for not performing as expected in relation to these documented boundaries. However, if we did just stick to responsibilities outlined in our job descriptions and followed precisely official rules all of the time, many things just would not get done. The paradox is that we need to act to a degree irresponsibly according to at least one set of allegiances in order to exercise responsibility in organizations. Because we are stepping outside of our designated remits, it feels irresponsible in relation to the organization, which in itself is shameful, but at the same time one is acting ethically, responsibly in relation to others, to get work done.

Shame is a social process which is individually felt. Our physiological experience of shame is similar to that of panic. In the short term or 'acute stage', there is a release of hormones, primarily adrenaline, which evokes a low-grade 'fight-or-flight' response: flushed faces, increase in heart rate and so on. This in itself can feel humiliating and isolating, which brings with it the fear of exclusion. To counteract this we ally ourselves with a particular group, in the moment, to diminish the feelings of shame, thus creating a temporary sense of belonging (possibly a sense of false conformity) to relieve the tension of tussling, conflicting allegiances. However, because we have different sets of responsibilities, we are at the same time betraying a multitude of other allegiances, which is also shaming. Thus we get caught up in 'being ashamed, and being ashamed of being ashamed, and being ashamed of causing further shame' (Scheff, 2000, p. 7), by constantly shifting allegiances of responsibility to and from different groupings.

The impact of shame is far more corrosive in an organization such as the NHS, since employees are overexposed to persistent and difficult shaming encounters. Since the NHS promises more than it can deliver, one may say that it is a system which is designed to fail. Since one has to contend with a perpetual sense of failure, one is constantly in a state of shame. However, as one becomes overexposed to this feeling one becomes numb and immune to it. In turn, this leads to a process of shutting down or bypassing 'feeling responses', so we end up being 'dead' bureaucrats. If we look at the way in which the complaint system is set up in the NHS, it is really an elaborate process to avoid shame. The system ensures that blame is located with an individual or place, anywhere else, just so long as it is away from 'me/us'.

In this chapter, I have briefly touched on responsibility and power relations. Power relations affect the way in which we exercise responsibility. Being seen to do the right thing does depend upon who is looking and how others see you. Shame is a public process related to power and status. Having said that, I think it is worth mentioning here that our sense of power in relation to others and the systems affects the way in which we might influence change. The example in the narrative I gave of feeling unable to change procedures that were 'above me' illustrates my point. I was fearful of being seen as an incompetent manager and constantly raising difficulties of working in the present structures. Therefore it was safer to stay silent rather than be publicly shamed.

References

Bakhtin, M. M. (1986) *Speech Genres and Other Esays*, Austin, TX: University of Texas Press.
Building a Safer NHS for Patients (April 2001)
    http://www.doh.gov.uk/buildsafenhs/buildsafenhs.pdf.
Cooley, C. H. ([1902] 1964) *Human Nature and the Social Order*, New York: Schocken Books.

Dalal, F. D. (1998) *Taking the Group Seriously*, London: Jessica Kinglsey.

Dalal, F. D. (2002) *Race, Colour and the Processes of Racialization: New Perspectives from Group Analysis, Psychoanalysis and Sociology*, Hove, Sussex: Brunner-Routledge.

Damasio, A. (2003) *Looking for Spinoza*, London: Vintage.

Elias, N. ([1939] 2000) *The Civilizing Process*, Oxford: Blackwell.

Eshleman, A. (2001) 'Moral responsibility', *Stanford Encyclopedia of Philosophy*, http://plato.stanford.edu/entries/moral-responsibility/.

Foulkes, S. H. (1948) *Introduction to Group Analytic Psychotherapy*, London: William Heinemann Medical Books.

Gergen, K. J. (1999) *An Invitation to Social Construction*, Thousand Oaks, CA: Sage.

Griffin, D. (2002) *The Emergence of Leadership: Linking self-organization and ethics*, London: Routledge.

Hirschhorn, L. (1988) *The Workplace Within*, Cambridge, MA: MIT Press.

Hunt, M. R. (2002) 'Patient safety in the NHS', Speaking notes from National Patients Safety Agency, 20 March, NPSA website: http://www.npsa.nhs.uk/index.asp.

Jarvis, I. and Leon, M. (1979) *Decision Making: A Psychological Analysis of Conflict, Choice and Commitment*, New York: The Free Press.

Lucas, J. R. (1995) *Responsibility*, Oxford: Oxford University Press.

McNamee, S. and Gergen, K. (1999) *Relational Responsibility: Resources for a Sustainable Dialogue*, London: Sage.

Mead, G. H. (1934) *Mind, Self and Society*, Chicago, IL: University of Chicago Press.

Organization with a Memory (2000) http://www.doh.gov.uk/cmo/orgmem.pdf.

Reason, J. (2000) 'Human error: models and management', *BMJ*, 320: 768–770, http://bmj.bmjjournals.com/cgi/content/full/320/7237/768.

Scheff, T. J. (2000) 'Shame and the social bond: applying the part/whole approach to a case study', http://www.soc.ucsb.edu/faculty/scheff/13.html.

Sennett, R. (1998) *The Corrosion of Character*, New York: Norton.

Shotter, J. (1993) *Conversational Realities: Constructing Life through Language*, London: Sage.

Stacey, R. (2001) *Complex Responsive Processes in Organizations: Learning and knowledge creation*, London: Routledge.

Stacey, R. (2003) *Complexity and Group Processes: A radically social understanding of individuals*, Hove and New York: Brunner-Routledge.

Stacey, R., Griffin, D. and Shaw, P. (2000) *Complexity and Management: Fad or radical challenge to systems thinking?*, London: Routledge.

von Bertalanffy, L. (1968) *General Systems Theory: Foundations, Development, Applications*, New York: George Braziller.

Vygotsky, L. S. (1978) *Mind in Society: The Development of Higher Psychological Processes*, Cambridge, MA: Harvard University Press.

Editors' introduction to Chapter 7

A key aspect of the importation of managerialism as *the* mode of public sector government is the requirement that all public sector bodies have mission statements and strategic plans. In this chapter, Séamus Cannon, who is Director of an Education Centre in Ireland, describes his response to this requirement. When inspectors from the Department of Education and Sciences asked for his mission statement and strategic plan, he had to admit that he did not have current examples of these, and this admission was not well received by the inspectors. He found the inspection diminished his confidence in what he had been doing for years and this left him feeling resentful. He was also particularly concerned at the possible responses to the local initiatives which he and his colleagues had been taking for some time. These initiations had led to the operation of a successful publishing business which produces material for teacher training. The profits from this enable his Education Centre to fund other initiatives. His concern was that the government officials would think that these were not 'legitimate'. He feared that the purpose behind the emphasis on plans was really one of securing greater control over educational institutions and that this would lead to the blocking of the successful innovations he and his colleagues had produced. However, he did tell the inspectors about a promising development then under way which was producing an eLearning system. This, however, was emerging without any plan. How is this unplanned emergence of important new activities in the educational sector consistent with the heavy emphasis on predicting and planning?

This experience led Cannon to explore the literature on strategic planning. He argues that it reflects a technical rationality that is inappropriate for thinking about, explaining or taking innovative action. He quotes a paper by Townley, Cooper and Oakes which describes the consequence of applying this kind of technical and instrumental rationality in the public sector of Alberta, Canada. The authors of this paper show how this approach to governance forces people in the public sector to translate their lived experience into standardized managerial language which distorts their practice.

Cannon then goes on to tell the story of how a successful eLearning project, in which the inspectors showed great interest, came about. This is a story of conversations in which surprising transformations emerged which no one intended or expected. The story starts with an invitation to the Centre's publishing division from the Public Relations Department of the Central Fisheries Board (CFB). The invitation is to prepare a poster and classroom learning pack for schoolchildren so that they can learn something about the fishing industry. In the first conversation about this, the nature of the project changes so that it is no longer just an information pack but also an educational activity involving staff from the CFB visiting schools. In another conversation this activity is linked to an eLearning project at another institution. In yet other conversations the work in progress of the project is made available on the internet for teachers to comment upon. Unexpectedly, they involved their pupils, and the project then became a developmental process involving teachers and pupils in a novel way.

What this chapter does is to show clearly the dissonance between the forms of planning supposedly practised in the 'business world' and the practical activities of those actually delivering education. It also shows how innovations and improvements actually emerge in the local interaction, the local initiatives of those actually delivering educational services.

7 The experience of strategic planning and performance management in the education sector

Séamus Cannon

- A painful review: the source of the dilemma
- Strategic planning: the DES approach
- Performance management
- A clash of rationalities
- Technical rationality
- Power and control
- Strategy as an emergent property of relationships: *Something Fishy*
- A new publishing partner
- Fishermen's tales
- From linear to complex thinking
- 'Added value'
- Now it's a classroom resource!
- Emergence and self-organization
- Engaging with 'not knowing'
- How would I answer now?

I am faced with the challenge of knowing what causes my organization to take the form it takes and what causes the pattern of its development into the future. I am, in a sense, required to know the future of my organization and to present it in the form of a strategic plan, when my experience tells me that I cannot know the future with any certainty, that to pretend to set it out in a strategic plan is simply not helpful and could be very misleading. It is this dilemma that I wish to explore in this chapter. I will begin with my recent experience of being asked for a strategic plan, identifying the assumptions about human knowing and relating that underpin it. I will then take a publishing project in which I am currently engaged and explore an alternative understanding of human knowing and relating to see what sense I can make of my experience, particularly with regard to planning. I will contrast the practical utility of these two approaches in my organization, as we try to reconcile local initiative with national policy in teachers' professional development, the core business, as it were, of my organization.

I will argue that mainstream strategic choice theory is rooted in a technical rationality which makes a number of very important, and largely hidden, assumptions about human behaviour, assumptions which profoundly influence the questions we ask and what we learn. This form of rationality is so pervasive in our lives that it has become almost synonymous with rationality itself. It favours a type of technical knowing that excludes a knowing-in-action embedded in practice; it implies particular understandings of causality and of agency which do not correspond to my experience of how my organization is changing. For this reason I will argue that while strategic choice theory provides powerful explanations of the limited, predictable and repetitive aspects of organizational life, it does not afford an explanation for the emergence of the unplanned, or of what is happening when organizational life is disorderly and unstable. It does not acknowledge human freedom of will.

I will argue that making sense of an organization as it forms and is formed requires an understanding of rationality which is congruent with human social interaction and that accords due emphasis to unpredictable human judgement and freedom of choice. Rather than its being determined in advance through the implementation of decontextualized and disembedded intentions, I will argue that the form an organization takes into the future emerges in complex responsive processes of human relating, and in unpredictable ways, in which self-organization through conversation in local interaction is the key element. It is in these local conversations that strategic direction emerges and an unknown future is continually under construction as we learn our way forward. Crucially, strategic direction is apparent in retrospect.

A painful review: the source of the dilemma

I manage an Education Centre whose primary purpose is teachers' professional development. The Education Centre is one of a network of nationally dispersed centres which are managed by local teachers. Some Education Centres, including my own, have parent and school management representatives on their management committees. My organization is largely funded by the Department of Education and Science (DES) but we also generate significant independent income from a successful educational publishing division. The bulk of the courses we run are national programmes prescribed by the DES but we also run local programmes which are responsive to local needs. Over the years, we have taken considerable pride in our innovativeness in the courses and curriculum projects we have developed, some of them originating long before the DES began to invest in teacher professional development on the current large scale. It is from our local innovation, for instance, that our publishing division has emerged.

The DES had been conducting a review of all Education Centres during the previous few months and our turn came up in March. In anticipating the review I regarded it as a fairly low-key event. I was not unduly concerned about it because it had been a good year for the Education Centre and I felt that I was on top of any issues that might arise. When the Education Centre was last reviewed, not that long ago, we were reported on very favourably. The review took the form of an initial questionnaire sent in advance, which gathered some statistical and other data, followed by a day-long interview in the Education Centre with two senior DES officials. At the interview, I was accompanied by my chairperson, himself a local school principal. Because I had held my Annual General Meeting (AGM) a few nights previously, all my reports and statistical material were in place and I was not anxious.

The interview consisted of a conversation around a number of standard questions and, because we were one of the last Centres to be reviewed, the questions had already been well tested with colleagues in other Education Centres, and appeared not to have caused them any alarm. I was, however, surprised at the difficulty and discomfort I experienced in dealing with some of them. One of the officials, in particular, was very persistent. My AGM report, which included a review of the previous year's work and our intentions for the coming year, would be of considerable assistance, I had thought, but as it happened, the report became a real problem. Through it, it was possible to identify very clear patterns in our provision, and gaps were highlighted that might not have come to light if information had not been so clearly presented.

The conversation did not proceed as I had expected. The questions did not elicit from me a way of making sense of my organization that I was comfortable with. There were several occasions on which I felt the need to interrupt the conversation in order to introduce what I thought were important perspectives on our work and initiatives that the questioners would not have known about. As my chairperson put it afterwards, we were telling them things for which they had no questions. On the other hand, they were asking us questions for which we had no answers – either because they had identified real shortcomings or because we actually had never considered these questions ourselves. They showed considerable interest in our publishing division, which had had a very profitable year, and they were concerned as to whether I was devoting too much time to it. I thought they were implying that it was a diversion from core Education Centre work. I showed them how we used our profits to pay for additional staff and resources for the Centre's core work, necessary because of inadequate funding from the DES budget. It was interesting to realize afterwards that, while the great bulk of the work of the Education Centre has to do with national programmes which are rolled out in a standard way throughout the network of Education Centres, the focus of attention for most of the day was on the areas in which we exercised some degree of discretion: DES-funded local courses and the Education Centre's own initiatives.

The questions I had most difficulty with had to do with planning. Did we have a strategic plan? Had we a mission statement? Had we conducted a 'needs analysis'? My response was that we did not have a current strategic plan. We had an old plan and a mission statement, which I rather embarrassingly could not remember. With regard to a 'needs analysis', we had recently attempted to conduct a survey of teachers' needs in the area of information and communications technology, and had such difficulty obtaining the information that we could not be confident of what to make of it, beyond some generalizations. I had to admit that some of our very successful projects had not been evaluated in years but that I had viewed continued voluntary participation by teachers and others as an indication that they were going well. I argued that we did not just respond to what teachers declared as 'needs', but that we also believed in giving a lead, trying things out, some of which seemed to meet 'needs' that emerged only when we offered the service. This had resulted in considerable innovation in the past, of which my interlocutors would have been aware.

I was aware of a degree of resentment on my own part in answering some of these questions. Official funding of our activities was frequently parsimonious and we had to generate independent income to afford the staffing we required. I myself was already overworked, and much more was being demanded of me with little acknowledgement of the value for money we provided. I sensed that much of the thrust of the questioning had to do with establishing more control over the Centre's activities, and initiatives that were not 'legitimate' would not be welcome, even though we were convinced of their value.

When questions were asked about our publishing division, I became a little anxious. Because it is a very successful commercial enterprise it gives us a lot of scope for independent initiative. We hire more staff than DES funding would allow; we fund the local educational initiatives of others as well as our own innovations; and we send delegations to international conferences on a regular basis. More than any other single feature it represents the independence of the organization. For this reason, I tried to avoid discussion of it other than to emphasize how it was contributing to mainstream work of which they would approve. I was conscious that its very existence was a clear statement that we did not share the norms of the DES in all matters. This meant that we were not entirely under their control, and that the power relations between ourselves and the DES were not as they might be if we were not so financially independent.

However, I did mention an unsanctioned initiative, our eLearning initiative in teacher professional development, appropriately named *Something Fishy*, because I knew the Minister for Education and Science would be very interested. From public pronouncements, I knew he was interested in exploring new and possibly more cost-effective ways of providing teacher professional development using modern communications technologies. We were funding *Something Fishy* from our own resources but I was confident that it would evoke a positive response. It was a 'legitimate' activity in the sense that it fitted in with the minister's way of thinking and it also demonstrated the benefit to the DES of our commercial initiative. If it went well, the DES could choose to back it; if it did not, it would not have cost them anything.

In the course of the day, as our conversation went on, I was conscious that I had moved from being confident about our accomplishments to feeling inadequate and defensive. The tone and emphasis of the questioning were not in accord with the way my colleagues and I think of our work. At the end of the review, I felt that I had been exposed as not being aware of what was going on in my organization. I had not been able to present a strategic plan with its targets and performance indicators, and the self-assurance that I had had a few nights previously at my AGM had begun to dissipate. I was in agreement with the officials on the need for accountability, and indeed on the need to plan, but I did not share their understanding of planning, or use their methods of accounting for my practice, and I could not present my own. I was also aware that some of the questioning pointed to real weaknesses in our organization and I was not trying to dismiss the exercise as a waste of time. I agreed with a number of their concerns about how I was spending my own time and how I prioritized work; about the poor balance between post-primary and primary teacher provision in our local courses; and about a failure to get out into schools as much as one would like. There was little sense of affirmation for things that were going well and little acknowledgement of the scale of my workload.

More than anything, though, I was struck by how defenceless I felt in the face of the formidable rationalism of mainstream strategic planning. It is very difficult to argue against. It makes claims for the rigour of its knowledge and for the efficacy of the actions that flow from that knowledge. I had begun the day confident about the way we (by which I mean staff and management) manage our affairs. We do not know where we are going next at all times, but we are confident about our ability to make good choices as opportunities arise in unpredictable ways. By evening I was quite upset, not so much because I had not had a strategic plan, but because I had not been able to account for my practice and for the work of the Centre in any other way either. The Centre does not have a strategic plan in the way it was understood by DES officials, because, intuitively, I do not believe in it, and I am increasingly convinced of the limited utility of systemic planning. But this is not *my* Education Centre, and I was conscious that the organization could be disadvantaged if we did not produce a plan, or find an acceptable alternative way of accounting for our practice. *Why does the kind of strategic planning with which I was confronted on that occasion cause me such difficulty, and how else can I account for my practice? What do I understand planning to be?*

Strategic planning: the DES approach

As I have already indicated, I was surprised by the rigour of our interview and I set out to establish what might be behind it. I started with the Department's own strategic plan – its 'statement of strategy', which contained a section on Education Centres that I had overlooked until now, and I felt a little foolish for having done so.

The Department of Education Strategy Statement (DES, 2003–2005) sets out its mission statement, high-level goals, projected outcomes and performance indicators. The process of creating the strategic plan was designed 'to ensure the maximum level of participation throughout the Department'. Clear linkages were established 'between the DES mission statement, its high level goals and the objectives, strategies, outputs and performance indicators adopted to achieve and measure our success in relation to those goals'. This would result in clarity of purpose, which would allow for greater integration with the processes of business planning and performance management. At all levels, objectives were set and measurements put in place to ensure they would be met (DES Strategy Statement, 2003–2005, pp. 11, 12).

Clearly the senior managers of the DES had devised the mission statement, set the 'high level goals' and prescribed a framework within which staff subsequently drew up more specific objectives and performance indicators. The Strategy Statement uses the language of business, including the creation within the DES of 'Business Units'. Compliance would be monitored:

> The Performance Management and Development System (PMDS) will in turn facilitate the attainment of personal and business unit goals by individual members of staff. In this way, every part of the organization will be working towards the achievement of the Department's mission.
>
> (ibid., p. 12)

While the statement emphasizes that all staff were consulted in developing the objectives and the indicators of performance, Education Centres were not, and this partly explains my own ignorance of it at the time of our review. This lack of consultation also indicates that our role does not include setting our own objectives with regard to implementation of policy.

The Strategy Statement marks a decisive shift for the DES from its previously less centralized and more informal manner, and this was possibly why I was so surprised when faced with the demand for a strategic plan myself. The statement exhibits key characteristics of what Mintzberg called the 'Basic Planning Model' (Mintzberg, 2000, pp. 36ff.) – the separation of conception from execution, the attachment to rational analysis, the commitment to 'value for money' as the public service equivalent of profit maximization, with all of this to be monitored through performance management.

Mintzberg identifies key premises of the 'Design School' approach: the approach should be controlled, conscious and formalized, with each step clearly set out; responsibility for its implementation rests with the chief executive (though this responsibility is typically delegated); fully developed strategies come out of this process and are to be implemented through detailed attention to objectives, budgets and operating plans. Problems are classified in ways which render them susceptible to 'technical solution', and management is seen as the implementation of control-based technical solutions. Igor Ansoff is generally regarded as the originator of strategic planning theory in organizations, and the above extracts resonate closely with his view.

Ansoff observed that in large, purposive organizations (such as the DES), 'change is not welcome; it is to be either controlled, absorbed or minimized' (Ansoff and McDonnell, 1990, p. 239). He defined strategic management as:

> a systematic [attempt] . . . to position and relate the firm to its environment in a way which will assure its continued success and make it secure from surprises . . . [and] the process by which managers jointly formulate strategy has been given the name of strategic planning.
>
> (Ansoff and McDonnell, 1990, p. xv)

This is a remarkable statement of confidence in rational planning and in the ability to control human behaviour. The organization, thought of as something apart from the manager, may be 'positioned' in relation to its 'environment' in a way which 'will assure its continued success and make it secure from surprises' through rational human activity. Elsewhere the authors state that the firm 'chooses the environment' (ibid., p. 127). The underlying rationality implies very forcefully that the future of an organization can be decided in advance, and with certainty, through a process of human reasoning on the part of an individual or group of individuals who place themselves 'outside' the organization. The absence of any consideration of custom and tradition, or even emotion, which might interfere with the free choice of these individuals, and which would be 'not rational', implies an understanding of causality rooted in a mechanical understanding of the social world.

This of course implies a specific understanding of causality: to understand antecedent cause is to understand efficient cause so that if B follows A, then A had caused B. This linearity of thought leads to the view that leadership style affects productivity, for instance, and that change occurs through conscious rational intervention. Agency is understood as the activity of the independent individual who is able to pass judgement on a situation from a detached and impartial point of view. Thinking is split off from action and this 'results in a culture, a concept of agency dominated by the making and unmaking of decisions. It is this that provides the foundation of management as decision-maker and has privileged the logic of calculation over appropriateness' (Townley, 2002, p. 559).

Performance management

Performance management is at the heart of the DES Strategy Statement. The assumption is that successful performance depends upon first defining what successful outcomes would be and then identifying the key actions required to produce those outcomes. The outcomes are then measured and, if necessary, corrective action is taken.

As a practice I find that I intuitively recoil from it, but I do appreciate the rationale for its introduction. Townley *et al.* (2003), writing about the introduction of performance measures in the government of Alberta, Canada, explain it as a response to a perceived lack of accountability in government activities. The rationale for its introduction in Alberta had to do with 'the belief that government should be based *on reasoned justification*' (Townley *et al.*, 2003, p. 9; emphasis added). Similarly, the DES strategic plan had its origins in a very critical report on its operations and on a general government policy to improve efficiency and effectiveness.

The fact that the strategic plan is based on an earnest desire to improve efficiency and to provide better levels of accountability makes it very difficult to argue against. The policy has widespread public support and cannot be readily dismissed as a passing fad. The justification for the introduction of performance measures is that of a better, more reasonable, better planned and more rational public service. What could be wrong with that?

In the Alberta experience, difficulties arose in deciding on performance indicators and on the method of measurement. These caused a distortion in people's practice, since the lived day-to-day experience of interaction had to be translated into a standardized managerial language. Actions and events were reconstituted as policy goals, outcomes and outputs. This language then provided the basis for creating administrative objects and establishing causal relationships. This was then translated into quantified and apparently objectified performance measures within a centralized and hierarchical reporting system that could relate the performance of the individual manager or unit to the whole organization. In Alberta, this new language bore no resemblance to the lived experience of public servants and in itself became an obstacle to the process of introducing performance measures.

Outcome measures were chosen as the main reporting mechanism for stakeholders and the public, and initial enthusiasm for the validity of these measures gave way to disillusionment, as measures were changed, budgets were cut, and there was pressure to protect politicians from poor figures. Under political pressure, public servants feel it necessary to massage the reports to mask a performance that the public may find unacceptable.

A clash of rationalities

What Townley *et al.* conclude is that there is a clash of rationalities inherent in performance management approaches: on the one hand, there is the appeal of *reasoned justification* of one's practice, which encourages reflection on the criteria and grounds for action; on the other, there is the *instrumentalization* of this, accounting for one's practice in a quantitative way. This instrumental rationalization depersonalizes social relationships and extends technically rational control over social processes. In the Alberta experience, 'The operationalization of reasoned justification was undermined by an instrumental rationalization' (Townley *et al.*, 2003, p. 23). There was an underlying belief (among staff being interviewed) in the validity of the appeal to reasoned justification, but also an awareness of the dangers of an instrumental rationality being taken too far in its operationalization. The anticipated opportunity to discuss values, business planning and wider public consultation was a reason why managers in the Albertan public service welcomed the new approach, but this opportunity was lost when attention shifted to technical enquiry. Specific technologies were devised for measuring performance, strategic planning, costing outcomes and outputs, and this exclusive focus caused enthusiasm to dissipate.

Technical rationality

The mode of rationality underpinning the performance management approach, and strategic choice theory generally, is described by Joseph Dunne (Dunne, 1999) as 'technical rationality'. With respect to knowledge it places a premium on objectivity and detachment. The context-dependent experience of the individual is suppressed in favour of a third-person perspective which yields generalized findings in accordance with certain formal procedures. These procedures in turn insist on observation, measurement, replicability and modes of testing. The language adopted is intended to be immune to interpretation 'and all of this ensures predictive value to the findings. Prediction then becomes the basis of control: to explain reality in this mode is to gain power over it' (Dunne, 1999, p. 708).

Technical rationality originated in the reflections of the Greek philosophers on the work of skilled craftsmen. These craftsmen exemplified a kind of expert knowledge, '*techne*', in the application of reason to the materials at their disposal (e.g. wood, clay, leather, stone, metal). They produced artefacts of high quality by working to a preconceived design or form. Form and matter are separate; end is separate from means; and within the productive process, planning and implementation are separate. The planning determines the form and specifies the end as well as calculating the sequence of actions necessary to achieve it in the course of a separate implementation phase. These thinkers, principally Plato and Aristotle, in turn shaped the mould and set the terms within which our notion of rationality is still fixed. It is suited to working to instruction or to a formula already capable of being visualized and does not engage personal judgement and invention.

Dunne observes that in describing the rationalism of the craftsmen in so technicist a fashion, the Greek philosophers were not doing justice to the extraordinary know-how of the skilled craftsman, the knowledge 'in his hands' that was not susceptible to being described in explicit propositions. However, by contrast, he observes that the increasing marginalization of genuine craft skill in modern society allows scientific research to assume and indeed reinforce the instrumental structure of *techne* as the Greeks described it (Dunne, 1999, p. 714). And it is this technical rationalism with its predictive control within limited fields of the material universe that informs strategic choice theory when it is mistakenly introduced to the organization of human action and interaction. Foucault referred to this latter process as 'the emergence of a new technology of the exercise of power . . . which was probably even more important than the constitutional reforms and new forms of government established at the end of the eighteenth century' (Foucault, 1991, p. 66).

Technicizing human practice requires decomposing it into discrete tasks and then analysing systematically the sequence of elements necessary for successful performance of these tasks. Knowledge is disembedded from the immediacy of particular situations in which it is deployed and from the experience and character of its practitioners, making for a 'practitioner-proof mode of practice' (Dunne, 1999, p. 709). Comfortable with certainty and shunning ambiguity, it seeks to reduce the complexity of human interaction to numbers which record performance, the ultimate purpose of which is to exercise control.

The prestige of this form of rationality has grown 'to the point where it is not just viewed as a form of rationality, with its own sphere of validity but as coincident with rationality itself' (Dunne, 1999, p. 708). As a consequence, a form of practice which does not rationalize itself in accordance with the standards of technical rationality, and which gives a strong function to other modes of knowledge, is likely to be regarded as backward, and will be under pressure to conform. This was my experience when I was interviewed: my inability to account for myself and my organization in the required way left me feeling inadequate and vulnerable.

As I was being interviewed that day, I had a sense of things being taken for granted which I felt were indicative of weaknesses in the strategic planning approach being followed. For instance, the DES strategy was purportedly based 'on widespread consultation with all levels of the organization', but we certainly had not been consulted. I also felt that actions taken by us in our organization could possibly change what Ansoff calls 'the environment' at a more global level. I believe that actions we have taken in the past have done so. Initiatives we had taken in the area of environmental education twenty years before had had a significant impact on the revision of that curriculum. Another initiative we took in relation to information and communications technology (ICT) training for teachers has had a demonstrable effect on teacher training nationally. Surely people in other parts of the larger DES organization, many of whom were more influential than ourselves, are working in a similar way. We have established a successful commercial enterprise within the Education Centre which offers a new way of funding public service educational initiatives. Will this not affect 'the environment'? Or, put another way, surely it is the case that 'the environment' does not actually exist other than as webs of relationships that are constantly being formed by, and at the same time are forming, those who are interacting in them? And as for the 'surprises' which Ansoff sought to avoid, I am aware that much of my own learning has taken place in surprises, unexpected encounters that could not have been anticipated, but which have proven crucial in making choices about possible futures for the Education Centre.

Power and control

There is something disingenuous about asking myself and my colleagues in the Education Centre to produce a strategic plan, when one has already been written for us. The DES Strategy Statement deals with the education system as a whole, of which the Education Centre is viewed as but a part. In being asked to produce a strategic plan, what is being asked of us is that we set out how we are going to fit in with the overall plan of the senior officials in the DES, according to their view of 'the environment' and the means by which their desired future state may be attained. Essentially we are being consulted on how we propose to implement an existing plan, and in the only part of our activities that is not already controlled – our local activities, whether funded by the DES or ourselves. A conflict can arise if we disagree on a desired future state, and how we get there. A more fundamental conflict can arise if, as I am arguing, it is mistaken to presume that one can specify the desired future state, and certainly with the degree of specificity that seems to be required. As I have stated earlier, the attraction of technical rationality at the heart of strategic planning is its predictive value, which as Dunne points out is accomplished in part by being 'practitioner proof'. This prediction then becomes the basis of control, which is in my view the real reason I was asked to produce a strategic plan, an expression of a determination to shift the balance of power relations between the DES and the Education Centre.

The focus of the review was on the areas of activity in which we in my organization still exercise some degree of initiative, not on the large national programmes which are provided on a standard basis throughout the Education Centre network and which constitute the bulk of the Centre's work. Over many years the Education Centres were neglected by officials within the DES and this resulted in a considerable degree of freedom in organizing our activities. This discretion has largely vanished in recent years, with dramatic increases in government funding of necessary professional development throughout the education system. In my experience this has been achieved to some degree at the cost of ignoring local initiative in favour of standard provision and increased central control.

I have argued that the technical rationality of mainstream strategic choice theory is not suited to making sense of what causes my organization to take the form it does as we learn our way forward into the future. In the following section I will take a project in which I am currently involved and, looking at it 'from the inside' as it were, will attempt to make sense of an alternative view of how strategy is created and planning takes place. I will argue that an embodied and context-bound understanding of management offers a much richer view of what is actually happening as we act our way forward.

Strategy as an emergent property of relationships: *Something Fishy*

Having considered the discomfort I experienced in the review of the Centre on that day, one thing stands out: the enthusiasm and interest shown in our eLearning project *Something Fishy*. Given the conversation we were having that morning, this might appear surprising, since *Something Fishy* did not form part of any strategic plan and has in fact emerged from a publishing contract that we had negotiated quite independently. We had not in fact set out to develop an eLearning project at all. It continues to be financed by the Education Centre from its own resources.

In the light of the difficulty I had had with the thrust of the interview generally, I propose to trace the process of development of this project as it has emerged in conversation, to try to make sense of strategy and planning as properties of relationships. At the time of writing the project is ongoing.

The story of *Something Fishy* is the story of how the intention to produce a standard learning resource for children has become something much more substantial in the process of production itself. In describing this initiative at this point in time, it is important to emphasize that the process is not complete. In fact, I will argue that looking at the project while it is 'unfinished' will afford a greater understanding of the emergence of strategy in the process. I hope that this will communicate a better sense of the interactions taking place and the opportunities and choices we face continually, and which ultimately are a better indicator of what is going on than any predictive plan or *post-factum* report.

This approach is in conflict with the prevailing mainstream theory of strategic choice as I have described it above, with its emphasis on goal setting in moving towards a knowable future. My contention will be that strategic direction emerges in continuous communicative interaction between people in everyday conversation. It emerges in what John Shotter calls 'a zone of indeterminacy, a zone of uncertainty . . . a zone between *actions* (what I as an individual "do") and *events* (what actually "happens" to, in, or around me, outside of my agency to control' (Shotter, 1993, p. 38). Shotter's approach, which he describes as *'rhetorical-responsive social constructionism'* (ibid., p. 6), is a radical attempt to explore how it is that we come to experience the world, ourselves and our language in the taken-for-granted way that we do, and how we might talk differently about it. He argues for what he calls 'knowing of a third kind', which he describes as follows:

> It is a separate kind of knowledge which is prior to both theoretical and merely technical knowledge. . . . It is an embodied form of practical-moral knowledge in terms of which people are able to influence each other in their being, rather than just in their intellects; that is, to actually 'move' them rather than just 'giving them ideas'.
>
> (Shotter, 1993, p. 40)

Because he is trying to get us to see what we typically don't notice, Shotter introduces a number of linguistic tools to enable him, and us, to open up a participatory, dialogical form of research activity into human practice. These tools include expressions such as 'rationally invisible' (i.e. a phenomenon may not be 'seen' by someone viewing activity from a perspective of technical rationality); and 'joint action', meaning what happens when people coordinate their actions in a responsive way and produce unintended and unpredictable outcomes. While 'joint action' may have outcomes which none of the individuals intended, there is none the less an *intentional* quality to it, apparent to the participants (Shotter, 1993, p. 39). It is through this unsystematic assortment of 'conceptual prosthetics' as he calls them that we can make sense of the background to our lives and in particular to undermine Enlightenment-inspired, systematic, unsituated or decontextualized approaches to the study of mind (Shotter, 1993, pp. 10,11).

In exploring what was going on in the process of creating *Something Fishy*, I intend to use some of Shotter's 'tools' as well as insights from Elias, and from Stacey, Griffin and Shaw on emergence and self-organization.

A new publishing partner

As well as delivering national state-sponsored programmes of professional development, my organization frequently collaborates with other state agencies in producing active learning materials. Some time ago we were approached by an unusual partner, the Central Fisheries Board (CFB), to see whether we would assist it in producing a schools resource pack. The CFB has responsibility for inland fisheries, including immediate coastal areas, and wanted to promote a greater awareness of its role among schools by publishing a curriculum resource pack and poster. We met, typically enough, with their public relations people. I was accompanied by Jennifer, who has been involved in many of our publications over the years. She is a very experienced and able writer of learning materials. In our experience this kind of undertaking is usually viewed by a publishing partner as a public relations exercise. We do not see it like that and part of our work is to help bring about a fuller view of what we can do together.

We spent a long time with them discussing the poster they had designed and which they proposed distributing to schools with the pack. A large number of fish species with names in English and Gaelic were displayed in full colour. We were a little apprehensive of involving ourselves in a project which just fed more information into schools, since they already had a surfeit of posters and packs. We sought to turn the discussion around. We probed them on the work of the Board, what the fisheries officers do from day to day. It became clear that much of their work was concerned with negotiating with local authorities, farmers, construction foremen and industry about the quality of water in their local environment. If the water quality was not of a high standard, fish could not survive and there would be no industry.

It was Jennifer who had the moment of insight: 'Your job is to manage habitat' was her observation. It was a brilliant observation because it shifted the conversation and enabled us to think of the work of the CFB in a way which would allow us to bring it into the classroom as an integral part of the curriculum and not just as a detached body of information. Our marketing friends were bemused at being told their job but they went along with it. It was an exercise in 'joint action', which, to use another Shotter 'tool', revealed something that was there in people's experience but which was 'rationally invisible' to those closest to it. We experienced a sensation of making sense together in a new way, in communicative interaction in conversation. This social process of 'learning our way forward' (Shaw, 2002, p. 46) also helps to form the identity of those of us participating in the conversation, and the identity of our organizations.

Fishermen's tales

However, we were not happy with meeting the public relations department only, and we sought a meeting with the CFB staff who worked in the field. This request caused some surprise, because the intention of the PR staff who met with us was to give us a message which they believed was an accurate representation of the 'reality' of their organization, for us to transform it into a school resource. In previous publishing undertakings I would not have made this request, but it is an indication of how my methodology has changed that it seemed the natural thing to do. I was influenced by my reading of Shotter and others and wanted to make my own sense of the organization. It was necessary, I felt, to participate in conversations with field staff if we were to make sense of their work together.

This meeting was arranged some time later and we spent a very animated Friday afternoon participating in a discussion among a most agreeable and persuasive group of people who were enormously enthusiastic about their work. We had asked that they each describe what they do. In the course of the meeting it occurred to me that they weren't used to meeting like this to converse so freely and that they enjoyed hearing one another's description of their work as much as we did. It wasn't a regular 'business' meeting. We noticed that they paid increasingly less attention to us. Occasionally we interjected but by and large we let them get on with it, animatedly describing 'a world of events and activities, rather than things and substances' (Shotter, 1993, p. 99).

What we were jointly engaged in was trying out new ways of looking at the work of the men and women gathered around the table, helping to create a new identity which would make sense in a classroom as well as among fisheries staff. I was conscious that while the focus of our activities was on the work of the Board, we, as participants in the enquiry, were also changing, forming and being formed in the interaction.

We were challenging a patterned understanding of role that had emerged within the organization over many years. It was evident in the excitement of the conversation that there was much in their experience that had been 'rationally invisible' to them and that could not have been communicated to us by, for instance, the public relations staff. Occasionally, anxieties surfaced about 'the pack' and whether it would represent their work faithfully. In suggesting a new way of looking at the organization were we adding to anxiety that had been hidden from us? Could the idea of producing a schools' pack possibly be a performance indicator in their own strategic plan?

As we conversed, several possibilities began to emerge which we had not anticipated: it became clear that some of these officers were already in the habit of visiting schools and on occasion inviting class groups to lakes or rivers at important times – when fry (young fish) were being released into lakes and streams to restock them, for instance. We wondered whether this could be included in the work of other fisheries officers as part of the development of the pack. It was not possible to develop this idea as much as we would have liked at that time, but we had a tantalizing glimpse of how another resource could be made available in a way which would be very beneficial educationally and would also enable our colleagues in the CFB to get their message across. At the heart of this suggestion was the realization that the formation of real relationships with real people would be more persuasive to children than information, however well presented.

Patricia Shaw writes of the transformative activity of conversation (Shaw, 2002). I felt that in the conversations in which we were engaged with the CFB we were together transforming our way of viewing ourselves and our way of viewing one another. The Education Centre was helping the CFB to create a sense of its changing identity in our conversation while at the same time the Centre was itself being transformed. I was conscious that we could each glimpse possible futures emerging in our conversation.

From linear to complex thinking

Normally I have visualized the production of a publication in three stages: (1) publish the educational materials (write, design, print); (2) train teachers in their use; so that ultimately (3) when they are disseminated to schools children can learn from them. This is a very linear conceptualization and overlooks a much more complex process of development. In the past I would not have been as aware as I am now of interaction between participants in the process, since writers, all teachers themselves, would discuss their work with others, how materials were tested in draft form and how participants in one stage could influence activity in the other. I would have been inclined to overlook the care and thought going into design and presentation. In the case of *Something Fishy* I was much more aware of the intricacy and complexity of what was going on, and I welcomed it. I was also surprised by it, because it was impossible to anticipate it, and the story of *Something Fishy* is also the story of my progression in becoming attentive to what is going on, noticing what I would previously have overlooked.

The process of publication was quite far advanced and I was still thinking in a linear way, step (1), followed by (2), followed by (3). So far our intention was confined to producing a simple publication of a sort we had done before, and the question could be asked: What has all this to do with teachers' professional development, which is our 'core business'? Is it a diversion to have me earning money for the Centre in this way, as I felt was implied during our review? Is it a worthwhile use of my time and Centre resources? This was a preoccupation for me because I had felt vulnerable when gaps were identified in other areas of the Centre's provision during the review. In the course of my involvement with *Something Fishy* my answer to that question was to change, and I became less concerned at devoting time to it. As things were to turn out, the project had a great deal to do with professional development, but not in a way that I could have anticipated. I could not have known in advance of the opportunities that were to emerge as we proceeded, and had I not proceeded I would not have known how to do so. There was not some preordered set of opportunities that we might have known about and which were waiting to be 'discovered'. What I became increasingly conscious of was how participants in the process – teachers, fisheries officials and others – were *creating* opportunities and setting the direction we were going in *as we went along*. The following is an example of what I mean.

'Added value'

Our 'core business' is teacher professional development, and in selling our services as publishers we emphasize the 'added value' of our contribution in this respect. With prospective clients I emphasize that we will provide the necessary teacher training that will ensure the adoption of the publication by significant numbers of teachers. This overcomes the common difficulty of educational packs, many of them very worthy, arriving in schools and being neglected. I had undertaken to put a programme in place in collaboration with colleagues in other Education Centres but had not yet done anything when I met with a friend, Ciara, from a neighbouring Institute of Technology. We began to discuss her institution's interest in eLearning and her recent trip to Canada to visit a college there. She was in charge of the eLearning project in her institution. In the course of the conversation it occurred to us both that *Something Fishy* would be a very good project on which we could collaborate, Ciara to hone her skills, and me to explore eLearning as a medium for the delivery of teacher training. It was no more than that, a conversation around a topic of common interest, but it was quite a significant moment. Once we had agreed to give it a go, we became aware of other possible futures. The Institute of Technology has no formal role in teacher training but it has significant expertise in digital media and, at a time when information and communications technologies (ICTs) are becoming increasingly important in education, new opportunities may occur for them in a new field of teacher training. The Institute has software and technical expertise; we have access to teachers and schools, as well as a considerable record of publishing.

This is a further example of an opportunity that had emerged in conversation. Neither the Institute of Technology nor the Education Centre had been involved previously in eLearning for teachers, and neither of us had set out with the objective of becoming involved. The course content had not cost us anything; in fact we had been paid to produce it, and the Education Centre was in a position to fund the partnership with the Institute of Technology from its own resources. Unexpectedly, we were now talking about possibly the first indigenously designed bilingual eLearning project for Irish teachers.

Over the following month, I liaised with two of our partner Education Centres in our new venture. Using the expertise and facilities of the Institute of Technology, we made available on the web the current version of the text being developed. Our intention had been to use this for teacher training and we asked the participating teachers to give their views on the incomplete material. In fact we did not design the final lessons until we had obtained some advice from teachers on the suitability of the early ones. Viewed from the earlier linear conceptualization of the production, this meant that steps (1) and (2) were now combined. The writing and training process were taking place at the same time. This meant that by now we had an additional seventeen teachers contributing to the shaping of our publication, as they were using it in class. On top of that, and totally unexpectedly, we discovered that the teachers, as well as using the web-based training materials for their own learning, had, in many cases, used the resource directly with their classes. So now steps (1), (2) and (3) were combined in what I would previously have thought of as a state of chaos. And interesting things began to happen.

Now it's a classroom resource!

We now had many children also commenting on the learning materials and we were conscious that the materials, essentially text on screen with limited interactivity, were not designed for children. The encouragement and recommendations we received from teachers and children, however, made us go back to examine the possibility of developing *Something Fishy* as a web-based resource not only for teacher training but also for children's learning. This we had not foreseen, obviously, but it seemed such a good idea when it occurred to us that we felt we had to run with it. When we mentioned it to our clients in the CFB, they too were enthusiastic.

It is important to mention that our relationship with the CFB had by now become much more than a normal commercial relationship. We had contracted to produce a learning pack for students which the CFB was paying for. The creation of eLearning dimensions emerged in the process of development of the learning materials, and the considerable costs involved were being met by the Education Centre out of its own resources. At the same time the Chief Executive of the CFB was kept informed and brought into all the discussions. For both of us the conversations continued to prompt new possibilities and opportunities.

Emergence and self-organization

The original intention in undertaking *Something Fishy* was to produce work cards and teachers' notes, a standard enough production; but what has happened is much more than that: not only have we produced the original educational pack but we have also, with a number of unlikely partners, begun to create an exciting web-based learning resource for students and teachers. In the course of our collaboration, the range of possibility has continually been amplified and outcomes continue to emerge which go far beyond our initial intentions. There has not been a sense of a 'settled' or 'fixed' environment to which my organization would 'relate' in a way which would 'assure its continued success and make it secure from surprises' (Ansoff and McDonnell, 1990, p. xv). Much of the time we did not know what we were doing next and our experience was that the 'surprises' were the best part! It was in the surprises that our learning occurred and guided the next step in developing the project. It is in this sense that learning *is* organization development. We were more conscious of being engaged in making and inventing than in the discovery of something already formed. Throughout the process there has been a sense of continuity and change co-existing in a dynamic way as we judged our next move or 'the *best* next step'.

What I am drawing attention to here is the self-organizing emergence of order in our project. By this I mean that human interaction, when richly enough connected, has the inherent capacity to spontaneously produce coherent pattern in itself without any blueprint or programme. Much more than when working on previous publications, I was attending to the conversations we were having with many diverse participants and noticing the importance of the micro-interactions in our relating. Jennifer's intervention on the occasion of our first meeting with the representatives of the Central Fisheries Board enabled us to interrupt a pattern of thinking and to open up new possibilities. She had not entered the meeting with the idea of describing the work of the CFB as 'habitat management': this knowledge was co-created by those of us participating in the conversation. Similarly, the idea of providing teacher professional development through the medium of eLearning emerged as I have described it in the conversation with Ciara, and the idea of producing a web-based learning resource for children originated in the mistaken (in our view) step taken by teachers who used their own materials with students without our knowledge. Norbert Elias describes the interweaving of intentions and actions of many people as follows:

> *This basic issue resulting from many single plans and actions of*
> *people can give rise to changes and patterns that no individual person*
> *has planned or created. From this interdependence of people arises an*
> *order sui generis, an order more compelling and stronger, than the*
> *will and reason of the individual people composing it.*
>
> (Elias and Scotson, 1994, p. 366; emphasis in original)

Elias challenges the notion of the unilinear sequence of cause and effect in human causality, something which is at the heart of strategic planning theory, and which would have been the way I was originally thinking in producing a text-based classroom resource according to steps (1), (2) and (3). Elias argues that we cannot simplistically ascribe an outcome to a single cause, or indeed to a series of events in a linear development. He uses game models to illustrate the actions and responses of interdependent people as moves in games. He urges us, in anticipating 'what happens next', to attend to how the preceding moves of players have intertwined and to the specific figuration, or network of relationships, which has resulted from this intertwining, and which immediately precedes the move one makes:

> Only the progressive interweaving of moves during the game process
> and its result – the figuration of the game prior to the twelfth move –
> can be of service in explaining the twelfth move. The player uses this
> figuration to orientate himself before making his move. Yet this
> process of interweaving and the current state or figuration of the game,
> by which the individual player orientates himself, exhibit an order of
> their own.
>
> (Elias, 1970, p. 136)

It is in this sense that order is continually emerging in our practice as we carry on, taking account of the changing environment, understood not as something fixed, as mainstream strategic choice theory seems to imply, but as networks of relationships in which we participate as interdependent people. This is a very different understanding of agency and of causality to that which we encounter in strategic choice theory.

Engaging with 'not knowing'

Looking back, it could be construed that we had set out to design an eLearning project and a web-based children's resource, but of course we had not, and given that it has been such a dynamic project to date, we are reluctant to speculate on any final state. It is in engaging with our 'not knowing' that we co-create new knowledge in continuous interaction with our many collaborators, who now include staff in our various institutions, the CFB, Institute of Technology, three Education Centres, seventeen teachers from fifteen schools and their hundreds of children. The children who took part in the pilot project have contributed directly, by way of e-mail and through sharing their experiences with their teachers. The project is being shaped by the users, teachers and students in the very process of using it. Lessons have been revised on the suggestion of users, and the recent announcement of broadband connectivity for all schools encourages us to explore the addition of video and animation to enhance the online resource during the coming months. In this sense, my earlier linear conceptualization of the process has turned out to be quite mistaken. It has been in the apparently chaotic interactions of diverse participants that order has emerged and a much richer process is discernible. Conversations we have had with participating teachers, both online and in person, have been stimulating and informative, and we have learned a great deal about thinking our way forward.

Possibly influenced by my experience of the review of the Education Centre, I was anxious at one point whether we could actually describe what we were doing as teacher professional development. The teacher training materials were being used as class resources and we had, arguably, lost control of the project. One teacher responded, I thought very acutely, that for once professional development was happening *in class*. They were learning how to integrate a new medium into their teaching as they taught; they were learning with their children. In regard to further improvement of the design and content, one of the teachers made the important point that the package should not be too well 'finished': there had to be loose ends, an inconclusiveness that would encourage the children and the teacher to begin their own explorations. This is a suggestion that we have been able to incorporate into a teacher course we have since organized. One class group compiled a quiz on material contained in the lessons and offered it for inclusion. We accepted!

These were very important lessons for us, which guided us in our decision making. The knowledge which we co-created was a 'knowing in action', not a theoretical knowledge, nor simply a technical knowledge. It was what Shotter describes as 'knowing of a third kind'. Interestingly – and Shotter presumably didn't have this in mind when writing in 1993 – these conversations, as well as taking place in bodily interactions, were also being conducted on the internet in the chat rooms we set up.

The process I have described is characterized by high degrees of uncertainty with regard to outcomes, participants and means. What we are learning about developing an eLearning project we are learning from creating one and there is an unavoidable unpredictability about the undertaking, with, on occasion, high levels of anxiety.

This was the project in which the officials who had demanded my strategic plan had shown such an interest. On the one hand, they were adamant that the Centre should plan, set targets, identify needs and evaluate our success in meeting those needs; on the other hand, what they found most interesting in the work of the Centre had not been planned in its final state, did not meet any target or identified need and has not been in the public domain to enable us to evaluate it. It emerged in its current, unfinished form through the process I have described. I think that the enthusiastic response to *Something Fishy* provides a much truer guide as to how things happen in organizations, including within the Department of Education and Science itself, than that afforded by strategic choice theory.

There is evidence that experience in other education systems bears out the importance of attending to emergence and self-organization in educational change. Writing on the need for reform of the English education system, David Hargreaves (Hargreaves, 2002) recommends that what is required is not more improvement of the input–process–output variety, but a transformation of education, drawing on the covert innovation already taking place in many classrooms in the UK, driven underground over years of target setting and surviving despite official disapproval. Encouraging teachers who innovate to share their practice, he uses the metaphor of the spread of infection (hence the title of the Demos pamphlet *Education Epidemic*) to describe how the internet could be used to create innovation networks. Tom Bentley, writing in the same pamphlet, states: 'Government by target is widely accepted to have reached its limits as a strategy . . . setting linear improvement goals and then pushing hard to achieve them can no longer be the dominant principle for reforming large partly autonomous organizations' (Introduction to Hargreaves, 2002, p. 9).

How would I answer now?

Were I now to respond to the request for a strategic plan, I would have to say that I regard it as too confining a way of describing the future of my organization. Yes, of course I would be in a position to supply proposed budgets and indications of staffing requirements with considerable confidence; I would set their minds at ease with regard to financial management. With regard to our local programme of activities, I would reiterate the intentions for the year ahead that I had expressed in my annual report, but I would add that what might transpire at year-end could not at this point be specified with certainty. I would emphasize that in focusing my attention on relating to educational partners in the way I have described it was not possible to predict the outcome. However, I could point to a number of areas of Centre work in which we have recently had very positive outcomes, measured by the level of adoption and teacher responsiveness. I would suggest how they might see for themselves whether they would agree that these were worthwhile activities by speaking with participants in our programmes. I could also point to several other initiatives in various stages of development which hold rich promise, by which I mean that the quality of interaction, and the diversity of participants, is such that I feel confident that something worthwhile is happening.

I would also add that while I shared their concern with the future development of the education system, in my view this would not be achieved by imposing a restrictive conformity on all aspects of our work, that, paradoxical as it may seem, the irritating nonconformity of much of the Education Centre's work was in fact the way the future would emerge. Just as we have in the past influenced the development of policy by exploring new possibilities, so, too, from the messy experimentation that characterizes much of what we do, new opportunities will become apparent, and it is up to us to make the best choice we can, using our judgement to take the next best step, what Elias calls 'the twelfth move'.

References

Ansoff, I. and McDonnell, E. (1990) *Implanting Strategic Management*, Hemel Hempstead: Prentice Hall.

Dalal, F. (1998) *Taking the Group Seriously*, London: Jessica Kingsley.

DES Strategy Statement (2003–2005) www.education.gov.ie.

Dunne, J. (1999) 'Professional judgment and the predicaments of practice', *European Journal of Marketing*, 33, 7/8: 707–719.

Elias, N. ([1939] 2000) *The Civilizing Process*, Oxford: Blackwell.

Elias, N. (1970) *What is Sociology?*, Oxford: Blackwell.

Elias, N. (1998) *On Civilization, Power and Knowledge*, ed. S. Mennell and J. Goudsblom, Chicago, IL: University of Chicago Press.

Elias, N. and Scotson, J. (1994) *The Established and the Outsiders*, London: Sage.

Foucault, M. (1970) *The Order of Things*, London: Tavistock.

Foucault, M. (1991) *The Foucault Reader*, ed. P. Rabinow, London: Penguin.

Griffin, D. (2002) *The Emergence of Leadership: Linking self-organization and ethics*, London: Routledge.

Hargreaves, D. (2002) *Education Epidemic: Transforming Secondary Schools through Innovation Networks*, a Demos publication, www.demos.co.uk.

MacIntyre, A. (1981) *After Virtue*, London: Duckworth.

Mead, G. H. (1934) *Mind, Self and Society*, Chicago, IL: University of Chicago Press.

Mintzberg, H. ([1994] 2000) *The Rise and Fall of Strategic Planning*, London, Harlow: Pearson Education.

Schon, D. A. (1991) *The Reflective Practitioner*, Aldershot: Ashgate.

Shaw, P. (2002) *Changing Conversations in Organizations: A complexity approach to change*, London: Routledge.

Shiel, M. (2003) 'Developing leadership', unpublished D.Man. thesis, University of Hertfordshire.

Shotter, J. (1993) *Conversational Realities*, London: Sage.

Shotter, J. (2003) 'Participatory action research: a finished classical science or a research science?', submitted for publication to *Action Research*.

Stacey, R. (2001) *Complex Responsive Processes in Organizations*, London: Routledge.

Stacey, R. (2003) *Strategic Management and Organisational Dynamics* (4th edn), London: Financial Times/Prentice Hall.

Stacey, R., Griffin, D. and Shaw, P. (2000) *Complexity and Management: Fad or radical challenge to systems thinking?*, London: Routledge.

Townley, B. (2002) 'Managing with modernity', *Organization*, 9, 4: 549–573.

Townley, B., Cooper, J. and Oakes, L. (2003) 'Performance measures and the rationalization of organizations', *Organization Studies*, 24, 7: 1045–1051.

Whittington, R. (2001) *What is Strategy – And Does it Matter?*, London: Thomson.

Index